Real-World Writers

Real-World Writers shows teachers how they can teach their pupils to write well and with pleasure, purpose and power. It demonstrates how classrooms can be transformed into genuine communities of writers where talking, reading, writing and sharing give children confidence, motivation and a sense of the relevance writing has to their own lives and learning.

Based on their practical experience and what research says is the most effective practice, the authors share detailed guidance on how teachers can provide writing study lessons drawing on what real writers do and how to teach grammar effectively. They also share a variety of authentic class writing projects with accompanying teacher notes that will encourage children to use genres appropriately, creatively and flexibly.

The authors' simple yet comprehensive approach includes how to teach the processes and craft knowledge involved in creating successful and meaningful texts. This book is invaluable for all primary practitioners who wish to teach writing for real.

Ross Young was a primary school teacher for 10 years and holds an MA in applied linguistics in education. As a passionate writer-teacher, he now works around the UK and abroad helping teachers and schools develop extraordinary young writers.

Felicity Ferguson was a primary school teacher for 40 years, working as an EAL specialist, SENCO, deputy and head teacher. A writer herself, she has MA degrees in applied linguistics and children's literature and has been involved in a number of literacy-based projects, including children's reading development.

Real-World Writers

A Handbook for Teaching Writing with 7–11 Year Olds

Ross Young and Felicity Ferguson

Routledge
Taylor & Francis Group
LONDON AND NEW YORK

First published 2021
by Routledge
2 Park Square, Milton Park, Abingdon, Oxon OX14 4RN

and by Routledge
52 Vanderbilt Avenue, New York, NY 10017

Routledge is an imprint of the Taylor & Francis Group, an informa business

© 2021 Ross Young and Felicity Ferguson

The right of Ross Young and Felicity Ferguson to be identified as authors of this work has been asserted by them in accordance with sections 77 and 78 of the Copyright, Designs and Patents Act 1988.

All rights reserved. No part of this book may be reprinted or reproduced or utilised in any form or by any electronic, mechanical, or other means, now known or hereafter invented, including photocopying and recording, or in any information storage or retrieval system, without permission in writing from the publishers.

Trademark notice: Product or corporate names may be trademarks or registered trademarks, and are used only for identification and explanation without intent to infringe.

British Library Cataloguing-in-Publication Data
A catalogue record for this book is available from the British Library

Library of Congress Cataloging-in-Publication Data
Names: Young, Ross (Primary teacher) author. | Ferguson, Felicity, author.
Title: Real-world writers : a handbook for teaching writing with 7–11 year olds / Ross Young & Felicity Ferguson.
Description: Abingdon, Oxon ; New York : Routledge, 2020. | Includes bibliographical references and index.
Identifiers: LCCN 2020004627 (print) | LCCN 2020004628 (ebook) | ISBN 9780367219482 (hardback) | ISBN 9780367219499 (paperback) | ISBN 9780429268960 (ebook)
Subjects: LCSH: English language—Composition and exercises—Study and teaching (Elementary)
Classification: LCC LB1576 .Y68 2020 (print) | LCC LB1576 (ebook) | DDC 372.63—dc23
LC record available at https://lccn.loc.gov/2020004627
LC ebook record available at https://lccn.loc.gov/2020004628

ISBN: 978-0-367-21948-2 (hbk)
ISBN: 978-0-367-21949-9 (pbk)
ISBN: 978-0-429-26896-0 (ebk)

Typeset in Optima
by Apex CoVantage, LLC

Contents

Acknowledgements viii
Preface ix

PART A 1

1 Why Real-World Writers? 3
2 How Real-World Writers works 28
3 Welcome Projects: setting up your community of writers for the year 32
4 Will they remember writing it? How to plan a class writing project 39
5 Teaching the writing processes 47
6 How to teach an effective writing lesson: using writing workshop 63
7 Setting up writers' notebooks and personal writing projects 74
8 Meeting children where they are: giving effective pupil conferences 80
9 They do the hard work so you don't have to: marking and target setting 88
10 Oh, for literature's sake! How to build reading–writing connections 91
11 Thinking through writing: writing across the curriculum 104
12 Assessing your writers 111
13 Supporting early, advanced and EAL writers 121
14 Growing a school of extraordinary writers: advice for writing coordinators 130

15	A guide to becoming a writer-teacher	135
16	Frequently asked questions and answers to them	140
17	Terminology	147
18	References and further reading	151

PART B — 157

19	Introduction to Part B	159
20	Poetry	167
	The natural world	*169*
	Animals and pets	*172*
	Sensory poetry	*174*
	Poetry that hides in things	*177*
	'Inspired by . . .' poetry	*179*
	Social and political poetry	*181*
	Anthology of life	*184*
21	Memoir	187
	Autobiography	*195*
22	Narrative	200
	Traditional fables	*200*
	Modern fables	*201*
	Traditional fairy tale	*206*
	Playful fairytales	*207*
	Setting and character-driven short stories	*212*
	Developed short stories	*221*
	Graphic novel	*226*
	Flash fiction	*232*
23	Non-fiction	237
	Information	*237*
	Instructions	*244*
	Explanation	*248*
	Discussion text	*254*
	Science report	*259*
	Match report	*264*
24	Persuading and influencing	268
	Persuasive letters (for personal gain)	*268*
	Advocacy journalism	*272*
	Idea generation techniques	*273*
	Persuasive letter (community activism)	*275*

25	**History**	**279**
	People's history	*279*
	Biography	*284*
	Historical account	*289*
	About the authors	*297*
	Index	*298*

Acknowledgements

Felicity and I would like to thank our friends and families for putting up with us. This book has been five years in the making – their patience, advice and general understanding have been invaluable. Thank you to Dan Stevenson for his lovely illustrations. We would also like to thank our more professional friends and dear colleagues: Nicola Izibili, Pete Barker, Elly Witham, Steve Reed, Marsha Broadbent, Sarah Dale, Sophie Thomson, Liz Cremona-Howard, Murray Gadd, Gill Davies, Jane Skea, Jonny Walker, Tobias Hayden, Ben Harris, Louise Birchall, Sadie Phillips and The Goldsmiths' Company. Also our friends at the UKLA who have always been so supportive, particularly David Reedy, Eve Bearne, Rebecca Austin, Roger McDonald, Kat Vallely, Teresa Cremin, Nikki Gamble, Jo Tregenza, Liz Chamberlain and Tracy Parvin.

Finally, the most thanks go to all the young writers we have been lucky enough to work and write with, particularly Ocean Class, 5RY and 4RY. We hope that you felt there was a fair exchange. We learnt just as much from you as we hope you did from us.

Preface

The teachers we have worked with over the years have convinced us that writing is the greatest subject on Earth. They are right when they say writing is like no other subject. No other subject allows us to give children a voice to tell us who they are, what they know, what they think and what they believe in.

We believe the writing approach explained within these pages is a powerful reminder of why we all became teachers.

There is no greater feeling than having children enter your classroom every day seeing themselves as a close-knit community of apprentice writers. They know that every day, when they enter the writing workshop that is your classroom, it's going to start with you giving them a valuable writing lesson – a writing lesson from their very own writer-teacher.

The children know that the class gets together regularly to take part in whole-class writing projects. This is where you and the children closely examine a type of writing and everyone gives it a go in the spirit of enquiry and creative exploration. During these projects, you have the opportunity to share your own written pieces, explaining how and why you wrote them the way you did. The children will then ask themselves: how can I use this type of writing too? And over the next few weeks, with your help, they make it happen.

The children take their responsibilities for developing their writing community seriously. As the writing progresses, the atmosphere in your workshop is like a publishing house: a mixture of creative excitement and focused professionalism. They want to enjoy their craft but also want their finished products to stand up and be taken seriously by their readers. For example, the children are proud of their class publishing houses, and they work hard together to ensure they represent the very best writing the class can produce – both in terms of composition and technical accuracy.

Writing instruction goes on continuously in your classroom. Children are always in conversation with each other about their developing pieces – giving each other helpful guidance on how to drive their writing forward. It always impresses visitors how the children do this with such maturity. They know how because they have learnt it from you. Every day, you walk around and get into conversations with your fellow writers. Every week, you help dozens of them overcome their writer's block, find the significance in their piece, untie the writing knots they've got themselves into and help them ensure that their writing is accurate and ready for publication.

Preface

You are now good at giving writerly advice because you have started sharing your own writing with your class. By writing yourself, you've become a better teacher of writing. You know what the pitfalls are and how to solve the typical problems all apprentice writers encounter. You've even started sharing what you've learnt about the writer's craft in your mini-lessons. The children really hang on to your every word during those lessons because they respect the fact that they are getting real, practical advice from someone who knows what they are talking about. They trust you.

The children will often groan when you call an end to writing time, but they soon perk up when they realise it's time for author's chair! This is how each day in writing workshop ends – with celebration. Some children will ask to perform the writing they've been working on, sometimes just for fun and other times to seek advice from a room full of knowledgeable and sympathetic writers. Everyone claps at the end.

Over the course of their year with you, they have truly learnt to live the 'writer's life'. Their personal project books spend just as much time at home as they do in the classroom. The children tell you that they have their own writing desks at home now or that they jot down potential 'diamond moments' when they are out and about. Every Monday, they come into class to show you what they've been working on over the weekend. Parents come to tell you that their children's attitudes towards writing have been transformed and that they themselves have been touched by what their children have written.

At the end of the year, their portfolios are overflowing with evidence that they've worked hard to meet and even exceed the expected standards, but more important than that – the portfolios will be treasured items for the children and their families for years to come. They will always remember writing these pieces.

The children have never written so much, they've never enjoyed writing so much and they've never learnt so much as they have with you this year.

PART A

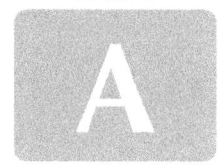

1 Why Real-World Writers?

Real-World Writers is the difference between children writing 'like' a writer and writing 'as' a writer.

Welcome to Real-World Writers. This book has come about because the teaching of writing continues to be a mystery for many teachers. Both of us, as teachers, had very little training or preparation for teaching writing and we as teachers can be inundated by a variety of approaches and training, all promising a lot but often lacking the necessary grounding to be successful in the long term. This is why we have ensured that our book is based on the following:

- Extensive scientific research into the most effective writing instruction.
- Case studies of what the best-performing teachers of writing do that makes the difference.
- Our own research into a *Writing For Pleasure* pedagogy (Young 2019).
- The wisdom of professional writers.

Real-World Writers provides a consistent teaching model which is simple, rigorous and structured. It encourages the whole class to see themselves as apprentice writers who every day write together in what feels like a combination of a creative writers' workshop and a serious, professional publishing house. Teachers who use the Real-World Writers approach recognise that what is offered to children in school must feel real, relevant and meaningful to them if they are to achieve their maximum potential. We believe children don't have to wait until they are older to appreciate the pleasure and satisfaction of being a writer. They can feel it now. Real-World Writers calls attention to the importance of children's lives outside the classroom as valued and legitimate sources of knowledge. As teachers we know that, when children's thoughts, interests and experiences are acknowledged and celebrated as valuable subjects for writing, they are highly motivated to engage at a high level. Children will attend with gusto to every aspect of the writing process and as a result produce truly outstanding pieces.

Real-World Writers ensures that children feel part of an authentic writing community where together they learn about the writer's craft and the processes writing goes through, which genres best serve their purposes, and how grammar works as a tool to enhance what it is they want to say. Children quickly understand that attention to transcription is essential if they are to write well. Much more than this, Real-World Writers allows children to identify themselves as genuine writers, see their writing intentions 'get to work' through publishing and achieve exceptionally well academically.

The power of a reassuringly consistent approach

We know from research that schools do best when they have a reassuringly consistent approach to teaching writing. Real-World Writers can contribute to your school's improvement plans, drive up attainment and help you tick those all-important curriculum boxes. Our consistent approach saves teachers time so they can focus on the things that help children learn. Importantly, once the approach is embedded in your school, you can begin to make it your own. Real-World Writers comes in two parts. **Part A** of this book is about how to teach Real-World Writers, while **Part B** provides teachers with a variety of different class writing projects and accompanying resources.

Why are children *moved* to write?

Writing touches every part of our lives.
Frank Smith

Children write first and foremost for themselves. Like all writers, children share part of themselves in anything that they write. They write because they are *moved* to. They write to find out whether they have something to say or because they most definitely have something to say! They write because they are *moved* to move others. They like the social interaction writing affords them. Children learn that by being a writer, like having a chemistry set, their writing can cause lots of different, amazing, dangerous and significant reactions to occur. Their writing is an artefact that presents their thoughts, feelings, beliefs, values or actions. Their writing says 'this is who I am'. So what moves children to write? It may be to:

Teach others by sharing their experience and knowledge or teach themselves by writing to learn.

Why Real-World Writers?

Persuade or influence others by sharing their thoughts and opinions.

Entertain themselves or others by sharing stories – both real and imagined.

Paint with words to show their artistry, their ability to paint images in their readers' minds, to see things differently, to play around or to simply have fun.

Part A

Reflect in order to better understand themselves, their place in the world or their response to a new subject.

Make a record of something to look back on that they don't want to forget.

These purposes are often interconnected. For example, you can teach whilst also being entertaining. One can often enhance the other. When we paint with words, it can often create a more vivid reflection about an experience. These purposes often rely on each other to be at their most potent and most meaningful. This is always something worth remembering when teaching writing.

Ultimately, writing is a means for children to develop a sense of self, find meaning in the world and impose themselves upon it. Think of the children in your class. What do they want to teach others about? What do they try and convince people of? How do they like to entertain each other and themselves? What do they fantasise about? What sorts of things do they draw or paint when given the opportunity? How do they play and have fun? What do you hear them reflecting on? What stories do they tell? The things children like talking about can often be the same things they are moved to write about.

If children aren't moved to write, you've got a problem. The most important part of teaching apprentice writers is showing them how to find the things they are moved by. Once this happens, they will have the necessary motivation to write to a high standard all the way through to publication. When children have an emotional investment in their writing, they write with more care, passion and attention. They write so that they can say what they really mean, but also who they really are.

What is *writing for pleasure*?

> ***Teachers must help children to perceive themselves as writers before children are able to write for themselves.***
> **Frank Smith**

The notion of writing for pleasure is at the heart of Real-World Writers. We know that children who enjoy writing and are motivated to write are eight times more likely to achieve well academically (Clark 2017). Therefore, *Writing For Pleasure*, as a pedagogy, is a vital consideration when teaching young writers. Our working definition of a *Writing For Pleasure* pedagogy comes from our own research:

> Writing for pleasure is a volitional act of writing undertaken for enjoyment and satisfaction. Therefore, a Writing For Pleasure pedagogy is any research-informed pedagogy which seeks to create the conditions in which writing and being a writer is a pleasurable and satisfying experience. It has as its goal the use of effective writing practices with young apprentice writers and the promotion of the affective aspects of writing and of being a writer.
>
> (Young 2019 p. 13)

The specific sources of enjoyment and satisfaction in and of writing are many and varied and will be different for individual writers in different contexts. However, we argue that there are two types of pleasure in writing, namely, writing *as* pleasure (enjoyment) and writing *for* pleasure (satisfaction).

Writing as *pleasure*

- Feeling a need to write and experiencing the fun and enjoyment in practising the craft of writing.
- Feeling confident and happy when engaging with the different processes of writing.
- Enjoying being part of a writing community, discussing their own writing and how it feels to be a writer.

Writing *as* pleasure is pleasure gained from practising the craft of writing, from engaging in the process or in particular parts of the process, whether it be generating ideas, dabbling, getting the words down on paper or screen for the first time, revising a section till you get it just so, editing to perfection or publishing the final product with care. Joyce Carol Oates and Ernest Hemingway both recorded that, for them, the pleasure was all in the revising. For some, pleasure ends with the completion of the act of writing. The idea that it may be seen by others can fill them with dread!

Writing for *pleasure*

- Having a sense of purpose fulfilled.
- The expectation of a reaction and a response.
- Sharing something to be proud of and feeling you've achieved something significant.
- The discovery of your own writing voice.

Gene Fowler would sarcastically say that writing was easy: all he had to do was stare at his blank piece of paper until drops of blood fell from his forehead. T.S. Eliot claimed that writing is like an intolerable wrestle with words and their meanings. Writing isn't always pleasurable. So why do we put ourselves through it? Perhaps it is sometimes with the view of writing *for the pleasure of a purpose fulfilled* rather than the act itself.

This type of pleasure is the satisfaction that comes *after* the act of writing. It's knowing that you will receive a response from your audience and that your writing will be put to work – sharing your memories, knowledge, ideas, thoughts, artistry or opinions with others. There can also be a pleasure in hearing the meanings other people take from your text. It can also come from listening to your own writing voice, from knowing you said what you meant to say or from achieving what you wanted your reader to feel. Writing *for* pleasure therefore gives children a feeling of empowerment and that their writing has enriched their life and the lives of others.

The affective domains

> *If what we do instructionally achieves the instructional end – A learns X – we have succeeded instructionally, but if A hates X and his teacher as a result, we have failed educationally.*
> **Nel Noddings**

When we teach our young apprentice writers, we must bear the sources of enjoyment and satisfaction in mind and teach with a view to giving them the opportunity to feel pleasure in the craft of writing and in seeing their hard work achieve its intended outcome. If we don't consider these things, our writing teaching suffers and children's writing performance suffers. But how do we encourage such feelings in the classroom? Again, our own research has shown that there are at least six affective domains which contribute to *Writing For Pleasure* (Young 2019). Consider how you can encourage these domains in your classroom.

Part A

Self-efficacy

SELF - EFFICACY
(I CAN!)

'I can do this!'

Self-efficacy is the belief and confidence that you can write well and realise your intentions.

- Writers with high self-efficacy are more likely to succeed academically because they persist at writing even when it's difficult.
- Writers with high levels of self-efficacy are more likely to set themselves challenging learning goals.
- Self-efficacy is increased when young writers know the end goal for their writing.
- Self-efficacy is increased when children can apply in their current writing projects what they've learnt in the past.

Agency

AGENCY
(I HAVE A SAY)

'I have a say!'

Agency is about having control over your choice of writing topic and ownership over how you go about writing it. Agency helps create a culture of writers with self-determination.

- Children like to be able to decide what they'll write about for class writing projects.
- Once experienced enough, children like to choose how they will write, using their own preferred writing processes, and to write at their own pace.
- Children like to have time to pursue personal writing projects.

Part A

Self-regulation

SELF-REGULATION
(I KNOW WHAT TO DO)

'I know what to do and how to do it!'

Self-regulation, the feeling of independence away from continual external intervention, is closely associated with the concept of writing as pleasure.

- A sense of ownership over their own writing craft is immensely important.
- Self-regulating writers have an interest in improving the quality of the texts they create.
- Children need to formulate their own goals for their writing and set their own writing deadlines.
- Children's sense of self-regulation is supported by the explicit teaching of the writing processes, regular strategy instruction and developing their craft knowledge through pupil conferencing.
- They don't feel they need their teacher all the time to be able to write well. They know how to use the writing environment of the classroom and the resources within it to help them succeed as independent writers.

Motivation

MOTIVATION
(I KNOW WHY.)

'I know why!'

The word 'motivation' derives from the Latin *movere* meaning 'to move'. Children are moved to write when they know why they are doing it. They know why they want to move their audience – even if the audience is sometimes only themselves.

- Undertaking the same behaviours as professional writers or those who write for recreation is clearly linked to an increase in children's motivation.
- Motivation is often what gets children through the difficult parts of the writing process because they know why they are staying with it.
- Children's motivation to write is increased when they have ownership over their writing process and publish their finished writing products to a variety of real audiences.
- When children have a personal interest or emotional investment in what they are writing, they have increased levels of concentration and engagement. They can become utterly absorbed in their writing over long periods of time.

Volition

'I want to!'

Volition is the need, urge or internal demand to write.

- Young writers have a sense of volition when writing about experiences they have had or when the subject matter they are writing about is significant or culturally relevant to them personally. This results in the writing itself feeling important, and when things are important to children, they invest more care and effort in them.
- Children want to write because they like the satisfaction that comes from achieving their writing intentions and goals.
- Children who are avid readers are often also avid writers. This is because they are inspired and want to try out the things they are reading for themselves.

Writer-identity

WRITER IDENTITY
(I AM!)

'I am!'

Writer-identity is the feeling of knowing you are a writer and feeling a relatedness to others within a supportive community of writers.

- Children feel like writers when the classroom is a place where authentic writing is being undertaken and discussed and where they are engaged in serious work. Therefore, it should have the atmosphere of a rich creative writing workshop coupled with the seriousness and professionalism of a publishing house.
- Children feel like writers when they are taught how to improve their writing by a knowledgeable and passionate writer-teacher.
- Children feel like writers when they are undertaking projects which match the writing done by fellow writers outside the classroom.
- Children feel like writers when they establish genuine audiences for their writing.
- Children feel like writers when they are given ownership over their writing craft.
- Children feel like writers when they are part of a genuine writing community where they can learn and interact with their fellow apprentice writers.
- Children feel like writers when they don't have the misconception that you can only be a writer if it's your profession or only once you're older. Instead, they identify as writers now. They know writing is a pursuit and a craft and that it can be done for purely recreational purposes.

The most effective practice: what the research says

A teacher's approach to teaching writing is guided by what they think writing, and being a writer, actually is. When subscribing to *Writing For Pleasure* as a pedagogy, you gain an evidence-rich pedagogy which will not only be instrumental in cultivating an enduring love of writing but which also shares the very best principled practices for raising academic achievement. This is because research has long shown that the two are utterly connected. Your ambition must be for children's writing to match (in both composition and transcription) the standards of writing which are achieved out in the world and for children to experience the kinds of pleasure available to writers through personal growth and artistic expression, effective communication of knowledge, and the possibility of making changes for themselves and others. The practices identified here are grounded in the latest educational research into the most effective writing instruction and, importantly, are the ones that are put into practice by some of the most effective *Writing For Pleasure* primary school teachers (Young 2019). To find out more about this research, visit **www.writing4pleasure.com**.

1. Create a community of writers

If we want to create life-long writers, then we need to teach children in an environment which reflects the way writers work. From the first, we need to treat children as genuine writers, albeit apprentice ones. When writers see their teachers as positive, caring and interested in their lives, they are more likely to engage in writing at a high level of achievement. The classroom should feel like a **writer's workshop**. The aim of a writing workshop is to create a community of writers, in which teachers write alongside children and share their own writing practices, and children are shown how to talk and present their writing to others in a positive and constructive way.

Children are also seen as participants in determining writing projects, as opposed to passive recipients of someone else's choice. The community of writers takes part in meaningful practices and writing projects they can identify with. Importantly, in a writing workshop, children are involved in actions, discussions and reflections that make a difference to how they are taught and undertake their writing.

2. Treat every child as a writer

In the writing workshop, effective writing teachers hold high achievement expectations for all writers. They see all children as writers and, from the first, teach strategies that lead to greater independence and ensure all children remain part of the writing community. They make the purposes and audiences for writing clear to children for both their class and personal writing projects. They teach what writing can do. They also model and promote the social aspects of writing and peer support in their classrooms.

3. Read, share, think and talk about writing

In writing workshop, children are given ample opportunities to share and discuss with others (including teachers) their own and others' writing in order to give and receive constructive criticism and celebrate achievement. The writing community begins to build its own ways of talking and thinking as *writers*. This happens best when the writing environment is positive and settled in tone and has a sense of fostering a community of writers.

Part A

4. Pursue purposeful and authentic writing projects

Meaningfulness affects learner engagement and outcomes to a considerable extent. Writing projects are most meaningful to children if they are given the opportunity to generate their own subject and purpose, write at their own pace, in their own way, with agency over how they want to use the genre, and with a clear sense of a real reader. Given these circumstances, writers are likely to remain focused on a task, have self-determination, maintain a strong personal agency over and commitment to their writing, and so produce something significant for themselves and in keeping with teacher expectations. In short, when children care about their writing, they want to do it well.

5. Teach the writing processes

Effective writing teachers give direct instruction in the different components of the writing process (how to generate an idea, plan, draft, revise, edit, publish). They scaffold children's understanding of these processes through demonstration, discussion, modelling and sharing exemplars which they have written themselves. The ultimate aim is for children to relinquish their dependence on this scaffolding and develop their preferred writing process.

6. Set writing goals

To maintain children's self-efficacy, commitment and motivation during a class writing project, teachers should ensure that children know the **distant goal** for the project, that is to say the future audience and purpose for the writing. The class, as a community, should have a say in setting the **product goals** for the project. This is what they will have to do to ensure their writing is successful and meaningful. Setting shorter-term **process goals** (or deadlines) benefits learners in terms of cognitive load, focus, motivation and achievement; for example, 'You have two days left to complete your draft'. However, once experienced enough, children should be able to use their own writing process and only need the final deadline for completing the project; for example, 'You have eight more writing sessions before these need to be ready for publication'.

7. Be reassuringly consistent

Good classroom organisation is absolutely vital as it facilitates learning, ensures focus and builds writing confidence. It also saves time – time that can be used beneficially by the teacher and the children. Resources will be visible and consistent across classes and the whole school and will communicate strategies clearly. Children like the reassurance of knowing how a writing lesson is typically expected to proceed.

Children need three things to happen regularly if they are to develop dramatically and quickly as writers:

1. They need high-quality and informed instruction which helps them know what to do and how to do it.
2. They need a daily opportunity to write and to write about things they care about.
3. They need sympathetic and responsive feedback on how they can make their writing more effective, successful and meaningful.

Therefore, a routine of **mini-lesson**, **writing time** and **class sharing** is the most effective and efficient routine teachers can adopt that attends to these three things. A mini-lesson is a short instruction on an aspect of writing which is likely to be useful to the children during that day's writing. During writing time, teachers conference with groups or individuals. A well-organised classroom ensures children write largely independently. For example, children will know the routines for working on class writing projects and that, once finished for the day, they may concentrate on their personal projects.

8. Pursue personal writing projects

It is essential that children are given time to write for a sustained period every day and to work on both class and personal writing projects. Personal projects should be seen as an important part of the writing curriculum since it is here, through exercising their own choice of subject, purpose, audience and writing process, that they have genuine autonomy and come to understand the true function of writing as an empowering and pleasurable activity which they can use now and in the future. Teachers will hold equally high expectations for personal writing projects as for class projects. Personal projects can provide the teacher with insights into children's personalities and help build relationships and can also provide evidence when assessing children's development as independent writers.

9. Balance composition and transcription

Schools often have their own policies for the teaching of spelling and handwriting. However, studies emphasise that these skills are best learnt in the context of a child's purposeful and reader-focused writing. Mini-lessons on aspects of transcription take place at the beginning of a writing session.

Spelling and punctuation should be largely self-monitored as children write, marking their text for items to be checked and corrected at the editing stage. Invented spellings should be seen as acceptable in the drafting stage, and handwriting skills are best practised when publishing a completed piece with an obvious purpose in mind.

Research shows that there is no evidence to link the formal teaching of grammar with improvements in children's writing (Graham & Perin 2007). Successful writing teachers know that if grammar is to be understood in a meaningful way, it must be taught functionally and applied and examined in the context of real purposeful writing. Grammar teaching should therefore take place within mini-lessons and should, as far as possible, be useful and relevant to the children's writing that day. It's important that children also have mini-lessons in writing study. This is when strategies and craft knowledge for the different writing processes are taught, such as techniques for editing your manuscript, 'dabbling' around a writing idea or how to develop a character.

10. Teach daily mini-lessons

Feeling you can write well on your own is really important to children, and while all children need guidance, advice and individual instruction, they also need to be taught self-regulating strategies through daily mini-lessons. These lessons should focus on how to generate ideas, how to use planners and checklists, or what to look for when improving and revising a draft. They also need ready access to resources for editing and publishing. Self-regulating writers work independently to a large extent, freeing their teacher to conference with individuals or small groups.

11. Be a writer-teacher

Just as it would be difficult to teach children the tuba if you've never played one, so it is difficult to teach children to be writers if you never write. Become a writer-teacher who writes for and with pleasure and use your literate life as a learning tool in the classroom. Children gain from knowing that their teacher faces the same writing challenges that they do. Write and share in class your own pieces in relation to the projects you are asking the children to engage in, but be sure to maintain reciprocal relations when discussing and modelling your own writing processes and the exemplar texts you have written. Sharing the strategies that you really employ in your own writing is highly effective instruction.

12. Pupil conference: meet children where they are

A rich response to children's writing is crucial. Many teachers use both written and verbal feedback. Research particularly emphasises the usefulness of 'live' verbal feedback, which is immediate and relevant and allows children to reflect on and attend to learning points while actually still engaged in their writing. It is seen as superior to 'after-the-event' written feedback. Verbal feedback is given through conferences, which will be short and are most successful in a settled, focused and self-regulating classroom. Teachers give feedback initially on composition and prioritise those who are in most need of assistance. Only later into the child's process do they attend to transcriptional issues. Finally, writer-teachers are better able to advise and give feedback because they understand from personal experience the issues children encounter when writing.

13. Literacy for pleasure: connect reading and writing

Successful writing teachers know that children who read more write more and write better. A reading for pleasure pedagogy (Cremin *et al* 2014; Hansen 1987) assists a writing for pleasure pedagogy since the individual reading of good texts available in school and in class libraries provides children with models and continually suggests and inspires ideas and themes for personal writing projects. Successful writing teachers also know that reading aloud poems and whole texts to the class in an engaged way has a significant effect on children's vocabulary and story comprehension and increases the range of syntactic structures and linguistic features children will use in their writing.

14. Interconnect the principles

Research cannot emphasise strongly enough that all these principles, critical to the effective teaching of writing, are powerfully interconnected and should be considered as such. Think, where do you currently see your practice making links between them, and where is more development going to be required?

Common approaches versus Real-World Writers

Donald Graves (1983 p. 1) says *'all children want to write'*. It is simply a case of allowing them to write about the things they are interested in. If they can speak it, they can write it; if they can talk about it, they can write it down. Most current writing approaches do not seem to realise this. We need to make children aware of how writing can make a rich contribution to their present lives, but unfortunately, writing in classrooms at present is not seen by children as important to them in the here and now. It fails to speak to the real needs and interests pressing on their young minds. It does not currently attend to the burning questions, imaginative ideas or reflective thoughts which their day-to-day experiences conjure up. Children aren't born knowing about the writer's life – we need to teach them about it. We need to teach them about writers' disciplines, their behaviours and their craft. If we don't, children will never develop into life-long writers, and so we are just wasting their time and ours.

An inclusive and well-rounded approach

It should be noted that, rather than ignoring other popular conceptions of teaching writing such as skills, novel-study/book-planning, genre-based teaching or critical literacy, Real-World

Writers, with elbows out, makes itself part of all these approaches and uses them in rich and authentic combination.

- For example, through Real-World Writers, children are given high-quality daily direct instruction and learn the skills vital to writing and being a writer. They apply these skills through pursuing their own writing intentions and through authentic writing projects.
- Children are taught about and discuss genre conventions, but are then invited to use them for their own purposes. They are also encouraged to actively manipulate and subvert these genre conventions.
- Children learn about writing through reading literature. However, they are invited to bring their personal response to literature to their writing and become active participants in reconceptualising what they take from the texts they read, largely through intertextuality. Children also benefit from reading a rich variety of texts written by their peers which are inspired by and produced as a result of differing comprehensions. In this way, they learn from the exploration of their own responses *and* from the responses of others.
- Children learn about critical literacy. They are encouraged to learn from each others' texts, discuss and critique them, and critically reflect on how writing may promote or exclude certain power structures. They are taught how to write to make a positive change and how writing can be used to persuade or to influence. They learn how to live and work within a writing community and how to champion different people's writing voices through the setting up of their own publishing houses. They are invited to consider multimodality through decisions about the publication of their authentic writing pieces.

Final words

Real-World Writers offers a fresh and informed approach. It keeps central the true purposes of writing as a socially significant act, which is undertaken for personal growth, the expression and transmission of ideas, taking action, having fun, reflection and the recording of experiences.

Through Real-World Writers, children make gains from seeing themselves and being seen by their teachers as writers. They are given the agency and the skills to write out their thoughts, desires and intentions into their communities, both in and outside school. You, the teacher, are supported by a research-based, integrated and structured pedagogy which is directed towards helping children to write to a high standard about the things that interest and concern them, with motivation, purpose and pleasure. We believe that you will personally gain from giving more responsibility to the children, from being able to provide high-quality teaching based on what professional or hobbyist writers do, from establishing communities of writers and forming a new, deeper relationship with the children in your class – and from the pleasure of writing yourself. Welcome to Real-World Writers. Enjoy it!

Conclusion

Key points from this chapter:

- Real-World Writers is based on extensive scientific research, case studies of best performing writing teachers, our own *Writing For Pleasure* research and the wisdom of professional writers.
- It's important that classrooms and schools adopt a consistent approach to the teaching of apprentice writers and to writing.
- There are a number of reasons for which children are *moved* to write. These include to teach, persuade or influence, entertain, paint with words, reflect and make a record.
- *Writing For Pleasure* at its most basic involves children *enjoying* the craft of writing and gaining *satisfaction* from their finished writing products.
- Focusing on children's feelings of self-efficacy, agency, volition, motivation, self-regulation and writer-identity will help promote *Writing For Pleasure* and effective teaching.
- The most effective writing practices are those which also promote *Writing For Pleasure*.
- There are 14 principles involved in teaching writing effectively.
- There are significant differences between common approaches to teaching writing and Real-World Writers.
- Real-World Writers is an inclusive approach which involves teaching and learning about skills, genre, literature and critical literacy.
- **www.writing4pleasure.com** is a website that can offer teachers additional support in their writing teaching.

2 | How Real-World Writers works

I feel like if I never wrote – life would be a bit boring wouldn't it – having loads of thoughts but never being able to show it.
Year 4 Child

```
┌─────────────────┐      ┌─────────────────┐
│ Class Writing   │      │   Writing       │
│   Projects      │      │  Study and      │
│  Genre Study    │─────▶│  Functional     │
│                 │      │   Grammar       │
│   A week        │      │  Mini-lessons   │
│ exploring the   │      │                 │
│ project and the │      └─────────────────┘
│ genre together  │               │
└─────────────────┘               ▼
                         ┌─────────────────┐
┌─────────────────┐      │    Writing      │
│    Personal     │      │   Workshop      │
│    Writing      │      │                 │
│    Projects     │      │  Writing time,  │
│                 │      │     pupil       │
└─────────────────┘      │  conferencing   │
                         │   and class     │
                         │    sharing      │
                         └─────────────────┘
```

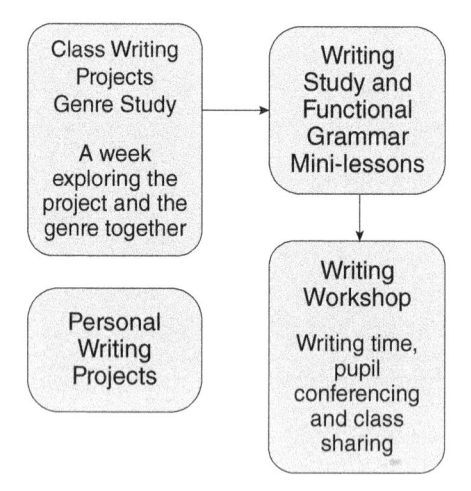

Real-World Writers believes in teaching children as writers. It's based on these four interrelated practices. First, you introduce class writing projects by having a **genre-study week**. These lessons bring the class together to take part in a whole-class writing project. Together, you and the children learn about and discuss the purpose and typical audiences for a particular genre, look at how other writers have crafted it effectively and generate your own ideas for how you want to use the genre for yourselves.

You then move onto the writing weeks. A writing lesson always starts with a mini-lesson. **Functional grammar lessons** give your learners explicit instruction in the various linguistic resources they can use to make their writing successful and meaningful. These lessons show children how and why they use particular grammatical items in the context of their real writing, rather than through the completion of exercises. **Writing study lessons** provide you with the means of engaging children in strategies or techniques for all aspects of the writing process.

The knowledge and skills developed in these learning opportunities form the basis of **the writing workshop**, which is the central part of the curriculum. Writing workshop involves writing every day and encompasses generating ideas, dabbling, planning, drafting, revising, editing, publishing and performing. Children are encouraged to learn valuable writing lessons but also to take the lead in their own writing development. When work on class writing projects is completed for the day, children pursue **personal writing projects**. There are also dedicated personal writing project weeks. It's through personal projects that children use their craft knowledge and understanding of genres and grammar to create accomplished pieces and publish them through their own class publishing houses for others to enjoy. They give children further opportunities to play, be experimental and be spontaneous with their ideas and their writing processes too. Teachers should hold the same high expectations for these personal projects.

The table here shows one way of arranging class and personal writing projects in and across the four year groups of KS2 in England. We have found that teaching around seven **class writing projects** each year works well, with one project normally completed every half term. In part B of the book, we provide different class projects that you can choose from or adapt. However you decide to do it, what's important is that you offer your class a range of fiction, non-fiction, poetry and personal project time. We then suggest there be four occasions in the year when children are given three weeks in which to pursue **personal writing projects**.

	Year 3	Year 4	Year 5	Year 6
Autumn 1	Welcome Project	Welcome Project	Welcome Project	Welcome Project
	Nature Poetry	Sensory Poetry	Poetry That Hides in Things	Social and Political Poetry
Autumn 2	Fairy Tales	Short Stories	Short Stories	Flash Fiction
	Personal Projects	Personal Projects	Personal Projects	Personal Projects
Spring 1	Information	Information	Explanation	Discussion
	Personal Projects	Personal Projects	Personal Projects	Personal Projects
Spring 2	Fables	Short Stories	Graphic Novel	Flash Fiction
	Personal Projects	Personal Projects	Personal Projects	Personal Projects
Summer 1	People's History	Persuasive Letter	Biography	Anthology of Life
	Instructions	Match Report	Advocacy Journalism	Community Activism
Summer 2	Memoir	Memoir	Memoir	Autobiography
	Personal Projects	Personal Projects	Personal Projects	Personal Projects

Yearly Welcome Projects

We believe that every year should begin with a three-week Welcome Project. These projects help settle children into the routines of writing for the year ahead. We know from research that children learn best in reassuringly consistent classrooms and so these yearly Welcome Projects give you time to teach the structures and strategies that will be followed in your writing community throughout the year. This block of time also allows you to get to know your new writers, organise personal writing project books, establish your class publishing houses and choose your class charity focus. For more information about Welcome Projects, go to Chapter 3.

Why repeat some class writing projects?

As you can see, each year children consolidate previously taught genres and are taught new ones. There is a clear rationale for this. We rarely get something right the first time. When children revisit a genre, perhaps in the same year or in subsequent years, they are able to build on their previous experience of writing in it and learn new insights. This means they can play around creatively with its conventions and begin to hybrid it with other learnt genres. As a result, their writing develops in significant ways.

Why poetry at the start of every year?

Poetry is the mother of all genres. It's a versatile medium which informs and aids all other types of writing. Therefore, if we develop children as poets, they will also turn out to be excellent writers. This is why it's a particularly good idea to have a class poetry writing project at the beginning of each year, since, because of the compactness of a poem, children will complete several different pieces early on in the year and will find this an immediate and motivating way into writing. Reading a poem or two aloud to the class every day and inviting personal responses to its sounds and meanings is important in helping children develop a poetic voice of their own. For more information on working with poetry see pages 167–186.

What Would You Like About a Poem?

What would you like about a poem?
What would you say?
What would you love about a poem?
What would be your poem?
What would you write about?
What would you say?
A poem is what you think.
A poem is what you want.
Don't let anyone step in your way.
                              Year 4 Child

Conclusion

Key points from this chapter:

- Real-World Writers involves four interrelated practices: class writing projects and associated genre-study, writing workshop, mini-lessons and personal writing projects.
- Introduce class writing projects though a genre-study week (see page 42).
- It's a good idea to map out which class writing projects will be done when (see page 29).
- It's important that children have an opportunity to repeatedly practise and develop their skills in the most common and personally meaningful genres.
- Ensure you plan in time for children to have 'personal writing project weeks' (see page 75).
- Make sure you do a Welcome Project at the beginning of the year and so introduce your new class to the routines of writing workshop (see page 32).
- After your Welcome Project, begin the year teaching poetry. Poetry is the mother of all genres. The more you develop your children as poets, the better writers they will be. For more information about poetry see pages 167–186.

Welcome Projects

Setting up your community of writers for the year

Children's writing develops most when they are able to work and learn as writers within a genuine writing community that values them and cares about their writing doing well.

Real-World Writers is an affirming pedagogy. A pedagogy with an unwavering conviction that all children can say *what* they mean and *who* they are. It believes that all children deserve to see their worlds and their words make a valuable and satisfying contribution to their community. Each child in your classroom is a working author. They come into class every day knowing that they are going to be working on developing their writing craft. They will learn, through being part of a writing workshop, that writing is rarely a solitary pursuit and in fact can involve many members of their writing community. Excellent examples of this can be seen in *Ralph Tells a Story* by Abby Hanlon and *How a Book Is Made* by Aliki.

We suggest that, before you dive straight into teaching class writing projects, you take some time to set up your writing classroom for the year. By doing this, you give children a real insight into the whole writing process and what it has to offer them as young writers. Every teacher runs their classroom in a slightly different way, so it also gives children the opportunity to know what you expect from them compared to previous years. This is why we recommend every teacher runs a three-week Welcome Project. Later we provide more detailed guidance on what you might do during these first three weeks.

Organising your classroom

Meeting area

You'll probably want a place in your classroom where at the very least you can have an author's chair. This is where you or the children can share writing aloud and the class can give their responses. A document projector is also useful for showcasing writing in progress or for showing examples of different aspects of the writer's craft.

A place for materials

You will want a place where children can access on their own all the equipment and resources they will need when writing. They will require pens, pencils, paper, rulers, dictionaries, common word lists, spell-checkers and thesauruses. You'll also want to include any planning grids, revision checklists, editing checklists or publishing materials. This means you won't need to be interrupted during your daily pupil conferencing.

Class library

To have a successful community of writers you will need help from exceptional authors. A writing classroom is only as good as the class library that supports it. Your class library should be full of high-quality fiction, non-fiction, poetry, picture books, newspapers and magazines. There should also be a place for children's and your own writing to make a contribution too.

Conference table

If possible, you may want to include a space in the classroom where children can quietly discuss their writing together away from others in the class.

Your writing spot

It's important that you have a spot earmarked for where you write amongst the children. This writing spot should change throughout the year.

Rights and responsibilities in the writing workshop

It's a good idea, at the beginning of the year, to establish the rights and responsibilities for your writing workshop. In 2011, The National Writing Project produced its own *'ten rights of the writer'*. However, it's better to come up with your own class rights. Here is an example taken from our old Year 5 class:

- The right to have a writer-teacher.
- The right to take writing to and from home.
- The right to borrow ideas and phrases from other writers.
- The right to write about the things you care about and express yourself.
- The right to write in your own way.

- The right to make mistakes, cross things out and change your mind.
- The right to take time to think, to be unsure and to write freely.
- The right to experiment, take risks and break the 'writing rules'.
- The right to be shy.
- The right to a supportive writing workshop community.
- The right to have time to revise and edit your pieces.
- The right to publish your favourite writing into the class book-stock and beyond.
- The right to make a few mistakes when you're publishing.

These are the responsibilities our class came up with:

- Write as well as you can, not as much as you can.
- Work hard, take risks and try to achieve our class writing goals.
- Writing needs quiet and concentration. If you are in a conference, you need to speak in a low voice.
- Know where all the resources are in the classroom and what to do if you get stuck.
- Seek the views of other readers.
- Be good critical friends to your fellow writers during class sharing and peer conferences.
- Respect your reader by proof-reading for spelling, punctuation and paragraphing.
- Write using a double page: left-hand side for drafting and right-hand side for revising and trying things out.
- Maintain your *target list* by adding teacher comments. Try to achieve your targets by the end of each term.
- Don't disturb a teacher if they are in a writing conference.

Your first three weeks of writing workshop

Week One:

- Discuss the different purposes and reasons for writing. Why do we write? What moves us to write? You can use pages 4–6 to help.
- Introduce children to the routines of your classroom and how a writing lesson is structured into three parts: mini-lesson, writing time and class sharing.
- Explain where they can find resources and publishing materials so that they can be as independent as possible.
    - Explain how the class library is organised.

- Discuss the processes writing typically goes through to reach publication or performance (see page 47).
- Discuss any specific writerly vocabulary that you will be using together throughout the year.
- Discuss what children think their preferred writing 'habit' is. You can talk about the perceived advantages and disadvantages of different writing habits, such as being an *Adventurer, Planner, Vomiter, Paragraph Piler* and *Sentence Stacker* (see page 60 for more information on writing habits).
- Give out personal writing project books and explain how they work (see page 74).
- Discuss the class rules for writing workshop.
- Explain how your working wall can be a helpful resource during writing time.
- Teach some techniques for generating ideas for personal writing projects (see Part B for ideas).

Make sure you give children plenty of time to pursue their personal writing projects.

Week Two

- Introduce children to the idea that you will be pupil conferencing during writing time and start conducting pupil conferences to get to know your children as writers (see page 80 for more information).
- Introduce children to the idea that lessons end with class sharing and author's chair and begin conducting them (see page 71).

Continue to give children plenty of time to write in their personal writing project books.

Week Three

- Discuss and design your class publishing house and any independent publishing houses the children might want to set up (see next section).
- Discuss and choose a charity or cause the class is going to focus on and champion throughout the year (see page 37).
- Encourage children to publish their first personal project of the year into the class library.

Setting up your class publishing house

It is not enough for children to simply publish their work into the class library. As part of your three-week Welcome Project, we encourage you to consider what your class library stands for. What sort of texts do you want to publish for each other? What is your mission as a class? What type of writing is important to you all? This will be an ongoing discussion as new ideas for writing develop. Early in the year, you will need to establish your whole-class publishing house with its own mission statement. You will also need its name, slogan and logo. The logo must be clear and simple so it can be added to published pieces easily. For more information on class publishing houses, we can highly recommend Lee Heffernan's book *Back & Forth*.

It is important to let children know that not everyone within their community of writers might feel represented by the whole-class publishing house. Therefore, there should also be an opportunity for smaller, independent publishing houses to be established, run by groups or individuals in the class. These independent publishing houses will also need mission statements, names, slogans and logos. Independents should avoid encroaching on the whole-class publishing house. A poster of the different publishing houses, their mission statements and the names of the Commissioning Editors should be made available to the class.

If children wish to be published by a particular publishing house, they will have to meet with the Commissioning Editor of that house to seek advice on their manuscript before gaining permission to publish. Children will come to realise that a Commissioning Editor is a critical friend who will support and champion individual writers within the class and also tell you when things need untangling or changing. You may feel that your class needs a lesson on how to be a good Commissioning Editor. Obviously, their best role model is you as the teacher and how you conduct yourself during pupil conferencing sessions.

A publishing house example

We are Banger Books publishing! We publish books which *wizz* and *bang*. We like books that:

- Are well written
- Are original
- Are powerful and thoughtful
- Surprise and entertain
- Include a variety of people
- Encourage the reader to reflect
- Teach

Choosing your class charity, cause or interest

It's advantageous at the beginning of the year to spend some time with your children choosing together a local cause or charity that you are going to champion as a class for the year. Alternatively, it could be a special interest that your class gets known for writing about. Consider things that the children are passionate about, such as looking after people, animals or the environment. Once the area of focus has been established, allow children to use the class charity in whichever way they wish. This could be through their personal writing projects, but you might want to consider how it could influence their class writing projects too. You may even consider giving the class charity its own publishing house or section in the class library. Children can then decide on a number of activities they might carry out as a class to support their cause through the year. They might consider collecting or writing articles about the cause or writing in other ways about it.

Designing your working wall

We believe there are five things that classroom walls can't be without.

1 A poster detailing the community's writing rights and responsibilities (see page 33).
2 A diagram showing the recursive and flexible nature of the writing process (see page 47).
3 A poster showcasing the different reasons we are *moved* to write (see pages 4–6).
4 A poster describing the different writing habits (see page 60).
5 A chart recording the different mini-lessons that have been taught that week (see page 64).

Children's writing targets should also influence your working wall, posters and the sentence examples you put around your classroom. Anderson (2005) suggests that the effective use of working walls can increase children's attainment by around 13%. The claim is that effective working walls do the following:

- Act as a visual cue.
- Provide scaffold to learning.
- Teach when you're not available.
- Provide exemplars.
- Remind children of rules and conventions.

Books for writing projects

We recommend that children have at least two writing project books: one for class writing projects and a notebook for personal writing projects. Their personal notebook should be allowed to go to and from school. However, you may want up to four books:

- A book for class writing projects.
- A personal notebook for personal project writing.
- A portfolio book where children put a copy of any published class or personal projects. This book can stay with them for their whole time at school. It becomes a very special object which will be cherished forever. It will show them (and others) the development they've made as a writer over the years and will hold within it all the subjects they thought important enough to see through to publication (see page 111 for more information on portfolio books).
- A 'squirrel' book for storing excellent writing they find from their reading (see page 99 for more information). However, we find some children prefer to do this in the back of their existing notebooks.

We suggest that children only ever draft on the left-hand page and leave the right-hand side free as a 'revision and trying things out' page.

Conclusion

Key points from this chapter:

- It's important to take around three weeks, at the beginning of the year, to familiarise your apprentice writers with how you like to run writing workshop in your classroom and where resources can be found.
- During these three weeks, allow children to pursue personal writing projects and conduct regular pupil conferences to get to know your new fellow writers.
- Discuss with your class their rights and responsibilities as apprentice writers.
- Discuss and design your class and independent publishing houses.
- Choose a charity or cause your class would like to champion for the year.

4 | Will they remember writing it? How to plan a class writing project

When we shape our writing curriculum around genres, we give children access to the world and the fundamental reasons we are all moved to write.

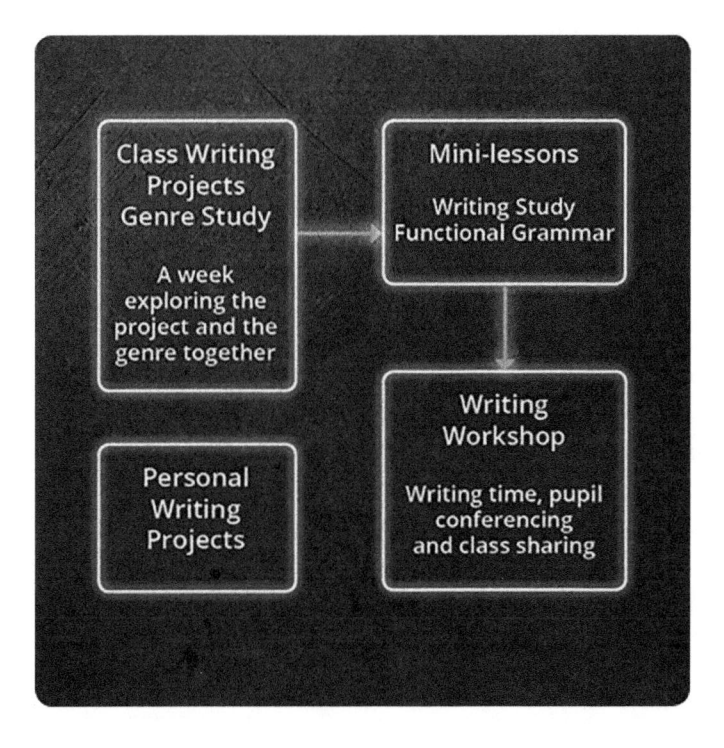

```
┌─────────────────────┐      ┌─────────────────────┐
│   Class Writing     │      │     Mini-lessons    │
│      Projects       │─────▶│                     │
│    Genre Study      │      │   Writing Study     │
│                     │      │  Functional Grammar │
│      A week         │      └─────────────────────┘
│   exploring the                        │
│  project and the                       │
│  genre together                        ▼
└─────────────────────┘      ┌─────────────────────┐
                             │       Writing       │
                             │      Workshop       │
┌─────────────────────┐      │                     │
│      Personal       │      │  Writing time, pupil│
│      Writing        │      │     conferencing    │
│      Projects       │      │   and class sharing │
└─────────────────────┘      └─────────────────────┘
```

Children want to write what they mean. We must therefore create the conditions for their writing to be meaningful. To do this, class writing projects centre around a genre and its purpose. Some of these genres will be known to your class from previous years, while others may well be a new experience for them. We suggest that you devote around two weeks to a poetry project and three weeks to any of the others. However, you need to be flexible. Through Real-World Writers, children are learning that they don't come to school to undertake writing *tasks* but instead to engage in authentic writing projects, so if you feel your class needs more time to complete a project, simply extend it. Part B of Real-World Writers provides you with 25 ideas for class writing projects.

Part A

How to create your own projects

Whilst Part B offers a variety of examples for class writing projects, you'll want to come up with your own too. A good place to start is with the children. Make sure class writing projects are life-directed. What sorts of things do your class want to learn how to write? What are they moved to write? Our match report project (see page 264), for example, was created in just this way. Our class wanted to learn about it so we provided it. Another place to look is your own writing. What sorts of writing do you enjoy undertaking and, importantly, why? And who for? The children in your class, coupled with your own writing passions, are always where good projects start. Whatever you decide to do, writing projects must be defined collaboratively with your class.

There are four important things to consider when developing a class writing project:

1 **Why does this type of writing exist?** Is learning about this type of writing going to feel meaningful and relevant for the children in your class? Are they going to believe it's worth learning about?
2 **What purpose will the writing serve for the children?** Will it allow them to teach, persuade, give their opinion, entertain, paint with words, reflect or make a record? Are you going to explain the value the writing project is going to have for them as developing writers?
3 **What is the final goal for the writing?** What is the intention and motivation going to be for the children? Who is going to read their published work or see and hear the performance?
4 **Do you have examples of the genre in action?** Have you written in this genre yourself? Can you share your process and the value the project has had for you as a writer? Do you have access to good examples created by children from other classes or in previous years that you can share? Do you have authentic examples from the world outside the classroom?

These points are also important considerations if choosing from one of our 25 suggested class writing projects. Year on year, your writing community changes. Their writing tastes and interests may be different each year, so take some time to browse Part B of this book and think carefully about which projects your class will want to do. Always ask yourself: in a year's time, will the sentences they wrote still mean something to them? In years to come, will they remember writing it?

What is the final goal for the project?

> *Ideally, no pupil should be given a writing task which does not yield them enough fruit in their own terms, so that they can feel it is worth doing.*
>
> **John Dixon**

Producing a writing product can, at times, be hard graft, so children will want to feel that their pieces are meaningful and will have an effect on someone or something. It's therefore important that you know where and how the children's writing is going to be 'put to work' once it is done. Here are some examples of distant goals for writing projects. We call it our publishing menu.

Publishing menu

- Read it out during class sharing times (in your own or in another class).
- Have a live debate or political discussion evening centred around the writing.
- Read it out during assembly.
- Have a slam poetry evening.
- Have a lunchtime or after school 'coffee-house' read-aloud club.
- Have a publishing party or a writers' picnic.
- Hold special writing celebration evenings or exhibitions where the community can be invited in to read, hear or see live/videoed performances.
- Put it in a frame or give it as a gift.
- Put it on your bedroom wall.
- Put it in the bathroom for people to read on the loo or while they're in the bath.
- Leave it in the car to read during traffic jams.
- Turn it into a presentation.
- Turn it into a film.
- Turn it into a piece of artwork.
- Add it to the class or school library.
- Send it to another school either here or abroad.
- Send it in the post to a friend or a family member.
- Take it home to share with the family.
- Mail it to a person who needs to read it.
- Send it to an expert, charity or association to see what they think.
- Collect it together with other pieces to make an anthology.
- Share with another class via their class library.
- Enter it into year group, school, local or national writing competitions.
- Send it to a local or national newspaper, magazine or fanzine.
- Publish it online.
- Publish it in the school newsletter or newspaper.
- Have a 'lecture day' where people can sign up to hear different speakers discuss what they've learnt during class topics.
- Put on a book or poetry sale. You can sell your writing – especially if people know it's going to a good cause. It can feel good knowing your thoughts, passions and ideas are worth money.

- Make an audio recording for the class library or school website.
- Suggest that it be used as an 'exemplar-text', when the writing is kept by your teacher to help teach next year's class.
- Ask if you can place it anonymously in local establishments such as libraries, places of worship, local history centres, museums, art galleries, train stations, bus stops, bookshops, corner shop windows, lamp posts, gates, fences, takeaways, retirement homes, cafes, coffee-houses, pubs, sports-clubs, dentists' or doctors' surgeries or on buses or trains.

How to teach a genre week

Class writing projects always begin with a 'genre-week'. Genre-weeks are usually made up of four or five lessons and cover the following:

1	Introduce the Writing Project	<= These sessions rarely take up the whole writing lesson and so, once finished, the children can continue to pursue their personal writing projects.
2	Look at Examples and Set Product Goals	
3	Discuss Poor Examples	
4	Start Generating Ideas	

1. Introduce the writing project

This lesson is about revealing the distant goal for the writing project. Share and discuss with the children what the purpose and audience is going to be for their finished writing products and take on any extra ideas, suggestions or questions the children might have. At this stage it's important to discuss who the potential readers are, get to know them and to make decisions about how you might 'address' them in your writing.

For example:

Our next writing project is going to be to write an advocacy journalism article about a charity which is important to you or your family. We are going to raise some prize money and the three best articles will win a cheque to send to the charity they've written about along with their article.

2. Look at examples and set your product goals

Often writers will talk about their finished writing being their 'product' – the thing they have created. Product goals are the intentions we have for our writing. The *'what will we have to do to make this an effective . . . ?'* These lessons help children discuss what writers have done well and find clues to what they can do and emulate. This is very different to the idea of 'success criteria'. Success criteria are often written by the teacher for the benefit of the teacher, whereas product goals are written by the whole class for the benefit of the future reader. Therefore, as a class, consider and explore who the audience might be and discuss what you can do to get the reaction you're looking for from your reader(s).

Research (Koster *et al* 2015) shows that it is advantageous to, as a class, decide what your product goals are going to be by reading a variety of examples. Examples help children see what it is they are hoping to achieve.

- First, give out and read an example written by you. Discuss with your children why and how you went about writing it. Ask them their opinion of it. What do they think makes it a strong or weak piece of writing? Part B of this book gives you lots of helpful hints and tips for writing your own texts for different writing projects. For more information on sharing your own writing with your class you can also go to page 137.
- It's then really important that children get to see and discuss a variety of good examples written by other children in previous years. Therefore, it's always good to keep an eye out for excellent examples and store them away for next time.
- It's also important that children discuss authentic and legitimate examples from the world outside school. Give out a variety of examples (maybe four or five) and allow the children to discuss which they think is the strongest piece of writing. The reasons they give will be a good starting point for writing your product goals. You may even want to ask that they put them in a ranked order.

By the end of the week, you will have your product goals on display. The goals are what you and the class have discussed as being necessary for their final writing products to be effective and meaningful, and you will refer to them often in the coming weeks.

How to create your product goal poster

Whilst reading and discussing the value of the effective examples, you can be contributing to your product goals poster. Here are the sorts of things you should be looking to include. However, product goals should represent the things you and the children think writers have done to make their writing successful and meaningful:

Purpose

- What would be helpful to remember about writing a . . . ?
- What would be helpful to remember when reading a . . . ?
- What are we intending this writing to do?

Content and Topics

- What sorts of topics are typically used in a . . . ?
- How could we play around with this type of writing? Can we include people or things that are too often ignored?
- How are you sure the topic you've chosen will appeal to your reader?
- How can you take advantage of your reader's passions, interests or concerns?

The Audience

- What do we know about our audience(s)? What are they going to want from this writing?
- What does the relationship between the writer and reader have to be like? For example, is it friendly, formal or colloquial?
- What sort of reaction do we want our readers to have to our writing?
- How do you ensure the reader finds you, as the writer, appealing?

How It Looks

- How can the writing be presented? What other modalities might be useful or required?

Style and Features

- What would be helpful to remember about writing in general?
- What sort of literary, linguistic or grammatical features are going to be useful?
- What sort of vocabulary might be useful?

Here is an example of our product goal poster for our advocacy journalism project with Year 5:

What we will have to do to make our advocacy journalism articles effective:

- *Raise awareness for your chosen charity and encourage people to donate.*
- *Charities typically involve people, animals or the environment.*
- *Your writing voice will want to persuade, sound knowledgeable and share a touching personal story.*
- *The examples used photographs, maps, contact details, information boxes and sub-headings.*
- *Pick a charity you can identify with.*
- *Come across as enthusiastic and earnest – pull at your reader's heartstrings. <u>Don't</u> sound desperate or aggressive though!*
- *The following will be useful: specific verbs, modal verbs, the subjunctive, subordination and quotations for interviews.*

- *A variety of modal verbs.*
- *Explain any technical terms using simple vocabulary.*

3. Discuss poor examples

Once you have established your product goals for the project, it's a good idea to explore writing which has failed to achieve the product goals. For this, we again recommend showing examples written by other children in previous years. You'll have to be sensitive here though! Obviously, don't share any details about the child whose writing you are examining. Discuss the writing examples against the product goals you established in the previous lesson(s). We find looking at poor examples is particularly effective with inexperienced writers as it helps them see what *not* to do when their time comes to start writing.

4. Start generating ideas

When we conducted our own research (Young 2019), we found there are three things which teachers can do to help children love writing. First, teachers can work to make children feel that when they write, they are going to be successful. Next, they can ensure children feel that they know what to do and how to do it. Finally, they can give children the responsibility to generate and choose their own writing ideas.

Each class project involves one or two lessons in which children are taught genuine writer strategies for generating ideas for writing. When we allow children choice of what to write about, they learn about writing without feeling they are being directed. Idea generation includes exploring their personal interests, knowledge, passions, thoughts or the texts they have read. In this way, children learn how writers take an original idea they care about and see it through to publication. Each writing project in Part B gives you suggestions for generating ideas for the different projects. More details on generating idea lessons can also be found in the next chapter.

Lastly, it's important to note that genre-study rarely takes a whole lesson and so once you've finished, you should invite your class to continue pursuing their personal writing projects. In fact, this applies to the end of all lessons. For more information on personal writing projects, go to page 74.

Avoid planning 'sugar rush' projects

A 'sugar rush' writing project is any project which involves the following:

- No agency being given to the children. Instead, the whole class is writing on exactly the same thing in exactly the same genre and in exactly the same way.
- Ignoring the fact that there is a class of children in the prime of their imaginative lives who are being denied the chance to share with their teacher *their own* imaginative topic ideas.

- Children are virtually encouraged to submerge their own voices and desires as they write for inauthentic purposes.
- There being no real intrinsic or extrinsic motivation for the writing to do well. It is just another arbitrary task disguised as being an 'exciting' one by the teacher.
- Huge amounts of time and effort being allocated just to teach the content knowledge necessary for children to access the project's stimulus.
- Perpetuating the erroneous belief that children don't like writing and so they need to be seduced or tricked into it by using gimmicks.

Some examples of such projects might be everyone writing a letter to Dumbledore; a diary entry from an evacuee; chairs 'quitting' the classroom and letters needing to be written to persuade them to return; 30 sets of instructions for a robot to make a jam sandwich, or 30 plus newspaper articles all about the discovery of a dragon's egg in the playground. These sorts of projects can feel attractive and can seductively leave you thinking they are effective. However, they are like writing 'junk food', and too much of it is bad for your writing community's health. They may provide your class with a sugar rush 'hit' of artificial enthusiasm, but this soon wears off, leaving behind only passivity and short-term value. This is because they are often too far removed from the real purposes of writing and deny children the opportunity to develop and realise their own writing voice and writer-identities.

However, far from saying children should be banned from being playful, writing imaginatively or from writing 'faction', we believe the point is that *they* should be the ones coming up with their own playful topics – not you. Faction, for example, as the word suggests, is the merging of factual genre writing with fiction (see pages 93–94). Children find writing faction incredibly pleasurable and you'll find many will choose to do so in their class and personal writing projects. For example, we've had in the past a child who enjoyed writing articles on how to take care of your pet ghost, the writing of F1 driver Lewis Hamilton's diary, a letter to parents in role as the demon headmaster and a magazine interview with a girl keeping ET at home.

Conclusion

Key points from this chapter:

- It's important for children to generate their own ideas and choose their own topics for class writing projects.
- Research tells us that writing goals are really important to children. Knowing the distant goal and the product goals for a writing project helps children produce their best writing.
- Evidence shows that by knowing these goals, children are more likely to work hard and be committed to a project.

5 | Teaching the writing processes

Teaching about the writing process is about teaching children how writers work and the strategies they use to craft their texts. However, there is no single agreed-upon writing process, nor is there a single set of strategies that all writers like or find effective. For example, some children like to use planning grids to plan whilst others like to draw. What we do know is that an individual's writing process involves going through a recursive, flexible and sometimes spontaneous undertaking which can, depending on the context of the writing, include processes such as generating ideas, planning (pre-writing), drafting, revising (evaluating) and editing (proof-reading) before publishing or performing. To illustrate, a writer's process can typically look something like this:

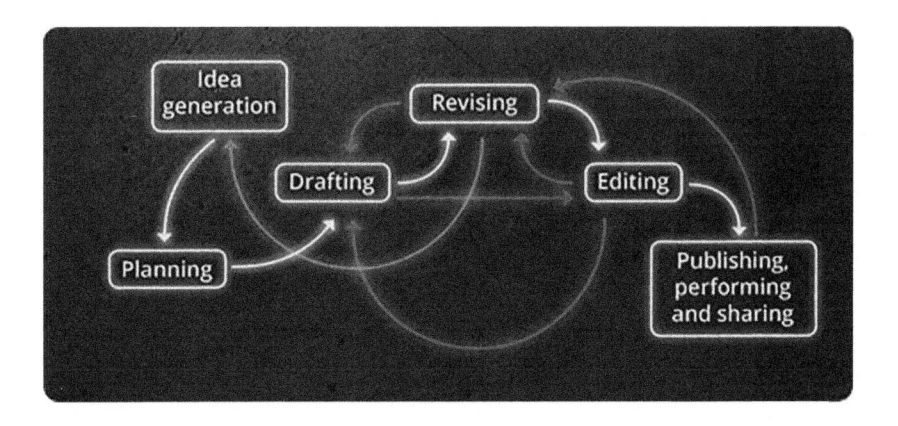

However, it's highly unlikely to ever look like this:

LINEAR MODEL

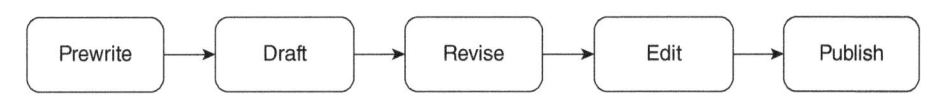

Prewrite → Draft → Revise → Edit → Publish

Many children are unaware of these processes, and so it's important that we share them. It's vital that each process be explicitly named, some of its differing strategies taught and frequently referred to in Years 3 and 4. More strategies can and should be introduced in Years 5 and 6 too. Here is a list of just some strategies that can be taught:

47

Generating Ideas
• Choosing, finding or being set a writing situation • Choosing a genre • Choosing a topic • Reflecting and thinking • Free-writing
Planning
Talking, drawing, physical and dramatic play, thinking, daydreaming, observing, reading, gathering notes from the internet, mindmapping, webbing, drawing diagrams or maps, tables, lists, notes and potential phrases, writing an outline, creating and/or filling in a planning grid or free-writing
Drafting
The different writing habits: • Discovery Drafting • Vomiting • Paragraph Piling • Sentence Stacking
Revising
• Re-reading to comprehend • Re-reading to discover new insights • Re-reading to compare • Re-reading to evaluate • Re-reading to fix problems
Editing
Proof-reading strategies: • Checking capitalisation • Checking use of vocabulary • Checking punctuation use • Checking spellings
Publishing and Performing
The various ways in which writing can be presented: • Paper based • Electronically • Film or audio • Live performance

Whilst writers' writing processes might include the items we've just outlined, no two writers' processes are the same and no two writers would write through these processes at the same pace, using the same strategies or in the same order. All writers work differently. Therefore, children need to find a writing process and a set of strategies that suit them best and allow them to produce their best writing. By the time children are in Years 5 and 6, they should be using their own preferred writing process and set of strategies.

It is vital that you have a writing-process poster, like the one shown at the head of this chapter, in every classroom. We suggest that it be Year 3 and 4's responsibility to teach the writing processes explicitly, and the vocabulary associated with them, and guide children carefully through the stages during class writing projects. This is done by setting whole class **process goals** (see page 69 for more information on setting process goals). By the time children are in Years 5 and 6, they are ready to use their own preferred writing process and to set their own process goals.

Through our writing workshop approach, apprentice writers will learn to regularly re-read their work as they compose, to make changes to their plans as they write them, to revise as they draft and perhaps to edit a sentence they have just written. All of this will begin to happen automatically and unconsciously if you teach it well in the lower-year groups. Through personal writing projects, even the youngest children are able to decide for themselves how they write best using their own strategies and set their own deadlines.

Generating ideas

When you write, ideas crazily spill from your head, tumble down your arm, into your pen and out along the crisp, white page. They are colourful, squirming, squiggly things that slide and slip through the nooks and crannies of your brain. Some of them crash against the walls of your head in roaring waves. Others come more slowly – each droplet of water a letter. Once you gain control of the sea – the droplets make out your idea.
Year 5 child

Research clearly shows that if children choose their own topics, their enjoyment of writing and therefore the progress they make is increased (Young & Ferguson in press). Without such agency, however, over time children become listless, indifferent, consumers rather than producers, reciters not writers, responders not composers, lacking in identity or voice, linguistically oppressed and ultimately not true to themselves. Additionally, a child's lack of knowledge about the subject she is being required to write about can be mistakenly translated as a 'problem' with writing.

However, simply giving children agency without instruction won't help either. Children may initially need to generate a whole raft of topics and ideas that they feel they could write about. In Part B, we provide strategies children can use for generating their own writing ideas. This concept works well because, when children write about what they already know or care deeply about, they have the information at their fingertips. They can then think about *how* to write instead of having to concentrate principally on *what* it is they are being asked to write about. Use of these techniques facilitates children's choice of writing topic, and so you won't have to spend time worrying about the children not having anything to write about. That's why writing can be a favourite subject for children and teachers alike. It is like nothing else on the curriculum. No other subject gives children such freedom to express themselves, and you have the chance to find out who they are. Remember too, that as teachers we can't and shouldn't pretend that we know what it is that children want to write about.

Top tips for generating ideas

There are five ways of approaching idea generation:

1 You can do it as a whole-class activity – taking ideas from the whole class and writing them up on flip-chart paper. Children can then choose an idea that resonates with them most.
2 You can put children into groups or pairs and they can generate ideas together.
3 Children can generate ideas independently in their books.
4 You can try out Peter Elbow's (1998) *free-writing* technique. This is the idea that there is no such thing as not having any ideas. If the mind is thinking – then it's talking to itself. This talk can be written down. *Free-writing* involves writing down whatever comes to mind for between 5 and 10 minutes and then sifting through what's been written to find any 'diamond' writing material.
5 Finally, don't underestimate the power of imaginative play. Children can play, with their writer's notebooks within touching distance, and when an idea strikes, they can quickly write it down.

Finding the diamond moment

One of the most important lessons we can teach children is the idea of finding a 'diamond moment'. Often, apprentice writers have too much to say in one piece of writing. Many children, whilst good at coming up with universal topics for writing, are unable to 'zoom in' on the quality within the topic. It's often too 'universal'. Too large. Too general. When young writers are asked to focus on the briefest of moments in a topic, one that is the most significant, their writing is often transformed.

To combat this issue, we use the analogy that a single writing topic is actually like a mountain of rocks. The writer's job is to find the one important writing idea – the diamond – within this huge heap of 'rocky' topic, and then hold, develop and polish it into a piece of 'shiny' writing. This process is vitally important across every genre, so this lesson is one that you should repeatedly refer back to. When you ask 'what is your diamond moment?' children can almost always identify it. Those who can't are often the ones you will want to work with first.

Here are a couple of real-life examples. In a piece about a day by the sea, a young writer writes vividly about her sudden discovery of a crystal. She tells of her excitement at finding something so beautiful and so special. This is the diamond moment she has picked out, and it makes her piece entirely memorable. Another example is a writer who has written a memoir about a trip to a safari park. She has written brief, conventional descriptions of some of the animals and has then picked her diamond moment – the unforgettable experience, with the lines *'with my heart beating faster and faster'* as well as *'feeling it slithering round my neck, rough and adorable. For a moment, though, I thought it was going to bite me.'* What this writer decided we didn't need to hear about was getting up, getting dressed, going downstairs, having her breakfast, brushing her teeth, getting in the car, driving in the car, parking the car, buying their ticket . . .

You get our point.

Planning

As Winston Churchill is alleged to have said, plans are of little importance, but planning is essential. Plans make visible and organise ideas. Children who are taught planning strategies and who then go on to spend time planning have been shown to produce more complete stories and enhance their writing performance (Young & Ferguson in press). Your role as the teacher is to make sure that the drafting stage goes as smoothly and as quickly as possible and gives children plenty of time for revision, because this is where many writing gains and developments can be made. When planning, children are considering purpose, audience and the genre of their piece. Writing study lessons are of course a good opportunity to share a teacher's or child's planning notes and to show good craft.

There are many strategies for planning and, over time, children should be given choice about how they go about it. In Part B of this book, our class writing projects provide you with an example 'planning grid'. However, these grids don't always suit all of the children all of the time. This is why it's important that you share with children other strategies like 'dabbling' or being an 'adventurer'. Once experienced enough, children can choose the way of planning which they believe gives them their best writing results.

Planning grids

By using the planning grids found in Part B, you make available to your class the typical journey writing goes through to be successful within a particular genre. For example, a biography *can* follow a journey of:

- Introduction
- Early life
- What led to the most important achievement
- Their main achievement

- What the person did afterwards
- Why the person is significant to the writer

There are obvious benefits and also limitations to providing children with such grids. Inexperienced writers have a reassuring road map they can follow to help them maintain the cohesiveness of their piece. However, for some children, a planning grid can limit any unique interpretations or innovations of the genre. These children might benefit more from 'dabbling' or 'adventuring' instead. Finally, it's important that children know that even the best laid plans can often go awry and that everything can be subject to change once they begin drafting.

Dabbling

A classic misconception about writing and writers is that they are struck by inspiration and then they write. This simply isn't true. Often writers will play around for a while, write a little and see what comes out of the bog of their writing mind. Dabbling is a helpful and an especially enjoyable way to plan. It's a process of playing around with drawings, words, phrases, thoughts and ideas on paper to develop an early writing idea. A great dabbler is children's writer David Almond. Remember, many writers begin tentatively when thinking what they want to write about and in what direction they want their writing to go. To aid this process, children should be given plenty of time to discuss their dabblings with their peers and with you. We discuss dabbling in more detail on page 98.

Webbing

When writing a non-fiction text about something they are expert in, children might find it difficult to organise their ideas. Webbing is a planning strategy that will help them think about how a topic can be split into sub-categories. When children have completed a web, ask them to be discerning by circling three or four of the sub-categories they would like to focus on. Explain to children that they will now be able to use their web to look for important questions their readers might want answers to.

Adventurer

With its links to Peter Elbow's (1998) *free-writing* technique, *Adventurers* are young writers who like to 'discover' their writing ideas through writing an initial draft before using it as their plan for a more formal second draft.

Talking and play

Do not underestimate the power of conversation and imagination when planning. We should encourage children to discuss and play with their ideas with their peers. They can be encouraged to take notes as they talk and play with one another.

Drafting

I do a kind of pre-draft – what I call a 'vomit-out'.
Calvin Trillin

A first draft is where children really begin to discover their intentions for their writing. As teachers, we often have a misconception that a draft is actually a writer's final crafting of their piece. This is rarely the case and so it's not helpful to teach this misconception to children. We mistakenly give the impression that drafting is a high-stakes affair and must (more or less) be the final writing product. In classrooms where this happens, children write tentatively and with tension and so don't produce their best. Instead, at this stage, children's focus should be on the quality of their composition and not their transcription. That's why we like Calvin Trillin's view of drafting – that it's 'a vomit out'. This is exactly what drafting should be. It's the transition from plan to an initial composition. This transition alone is challenging enough for children. One of the most important things to do as teachers is encourage fluency when children are drafting. Inexperienced writers simply need to concentrate on getting their ideas down easily and thoughtfully. To improve and encourage fluency, we suggest you have the following drafting rules on display:

Drafting rules	
Got a sticky or yawny bit? - Put a line under the bit you are unsure about. - Carry on.	**Don't know how to spell a word?** - Invent the spelling. - Put a circle around it. - Carry on.
Don't know what to write next? - Read it to a partner. - Get your partner to ask you questions.	**Not sure of punctuation?** - Put a box where the punctuation might need to go. - Carry on.
Think you have finished? Start or continue with a personal writing project!	

Encourage children to underline places where their writing doesn't sound quite right. These are what we call 'sticky' bits, where the writing doesn't run smoothly or cohesively or isn't saying quite what we want it to say. Children are also encouraged to underline any potential 'yawny' bits which may need to be cut. These drafting rules help young writers realise that a friend can often help them out of a writer's block and that you don't always need your teacher's advice.

These rules assist children's focus on their composition extremely well and help them write with ease. Because of the heavy burden writing can have on children's cognitive load, it is very important that, early on in their writing development, they attend to their composition separately from matters of transcription. If you ask children to focus on both at the same time, both too often suffer. Only once children are more experienced writers can they begin to combine the elements of drafting with revision and editing simultaneously. For more information about this, please see our typical writing habits on page 60.

As a writer-teacher, it is important that you share examples of your own drafts, so children can get an understanding of what crossings-out, false starts and invented spellings look like on the page and that this is what writers do and how they work.

We recommend that children always use double pages when writing in their books. The left-hand side is used for drafting and the right-hand side is for any trying out, revision or edits. Finally, it's our belief that children shouldn't be asked to write a lot but to ensure that what they compose is written with thought and care. We think a page or two pages is **plenty** for any genre and for any year group. We are all guilty of asking children to write a greater quantity than they need to.

Re-reading

A quick note on re-reading. Good writers re-read all the time. Writing involves reading. This is something you need to build into your class' writing routine. At first, you'll need to stop your class periodically and request that they read through what they've written so far (and perhaps share it with a friend) before continuing with their writing. Over time this should become part of their daily writing habit. It's also important that children re-read aloud rather than in their heads. This can be further explored through a mini-lesson on writing habits. To learn more about writing habits, turn to page 60.

Revising

> *Revision is a fun part of writing. Drafting is over, and now you get to play with your words. You've baked the cake, now you get to decorate it.*

Revising is, in many ways, the most important part of the writing process, and it takes time. Often, apprentice writers terminate the writing process as soon as they complete a draft, believing that once their initial ideas are on paper, the writing task is complete and they can announce 'I'm finished'. They often regard the encouragement to revise as a consequence of not having got it 'right' in the first place. We will need to break this misconception. Worse still, they may depend on you to revise and edit their work for them through written feedback, thereby learning very little. When revising a draft, children should act on the suggestions and conversations that have taken place with their peers, as well as with you during pupil conferencing. Writers rarely expect their writing to be right the first time. For example, Ernest Hemingway famously stated that the first draft of anything is s***.

Revision is best taught as part of your writing study mini-lessons. It's here that you can teach children about the different types of re-reading and improvements writers will make to their drafts. Your revision tips taught during writing study should be based on what professional writers have said they often employ in their work and what you do when you revise your compositions, such as searching for 'sticky' and 'yawny' bits, reconsidering openings and endings, trying out certain linguistic or literary features or poetic language or ensuring that other identified product goals have been included or at least considered.

By revising in this way, children are thinking more like mature independent writers. We suggest that revision in the earlier-year groups is done on the opposite page to the draft, using symbols such as asterisks or numbers to show where larger amounts of content has been added or changed. However, more experienced writers or children in the older years often outgrow these techniques and prefer to undertake a full second draft. This should be allowed to happen. Finally, we recommend that all writing revision should be done in a different coloured pen.

Trying things out: add, remove, move and change

If you're looking to give children a general way to revise any type of writing, then the four common types of revision will probably be most useful to have on display throughout the year and in all classes. These are **add**, **remove**, **move** and **change**. Add is writing in additional content. Remove is cutting out unnecessary or boring parts of the composition (this is often the most difficult one for children or for any of us to do!). Move is about changing the order of certain parts of a composition. Change means to upgrade or otherwise improve part of the draft.

Creating revision checklists

We suggest that as part of setting the product goals for your class writing projects, you provide the class with a revision checklist. These checklists are an opportunity to ensure children have attended to compositional elements that are going to make their writing effective and meaningful. This means your checklists will be different for different writing projects. Here, we have given you guidance on what sort of things a revision checklist should include and an example from our own practice when teaching our Year 5 class about memoir.

Memoir revision checklist Year 5

First time re-reading and improving	Second time re-reading and improving	Third time re-reading and improving	BONUS! Top tips from other professional writers.
Think! • What do you want your reader to feel? • Fix any 'sticky' bits • Fix any 'yawny' bits	Make your opening outstanding. Think: – Shock! – Question? – Action – Speech – Description Make your ending powerful and thoughtful. Think: – Advice and Learning – Character Feeling – Shock or Surprise – Uncertain – Hopeful and Happy	Try out the following things on your revision page. If you like them, add them to your piece: – Fronted adverbials – Subordinating clauses – Relative clauses – Brackets or dashes for parenthesis instead of commas	• Show, don't tell. Can you replace words like is, was, have, had, did? • Put an exciting moment in your writing into slow motion. • Personify a feeling or an object to give it personality. • Write a simile or a metaphor that you could add to your writing. • Check: does your writing create a film in your readers' minds? Think about wide angles and zooming in. • Check that you have a good variety of sentences. Have you used commands, statements, questions and exclamations? • Is there a mix of short and long sentences? • Some writers read their memoirs over 100 times!

The first re-read and improve was about giving children the opportunity to refocus on the purpose and audience for their writing. They also checked the overall text for cohesiveness.

The second re-read and improve, in the earlier example, was about attending to one of the product goals: ensuring a strong opening and ending to the memoir.

The third re-read and improve was about children showcasing their understanding and use of certain linguistic, literary and grammatical features mentioned in the National Curriculum for England. Encouraging the children to use their 'revision and trying things out' page to play with these features meant they could be discerning about which ones they wished to include in their final piece. This way, children were able to provide rich evidence of their understanding of these items for accountability and assessment purposes, whilst still having the ultimate authorial say over its inclusion. This was important because the enforced inclusion of specific features can actually make children's writing far worse.

The fourth re-read and improve was about giving children access to the sorts of revisions we or other hobbyist or professional writers do when constructing texts. In our example, you can see we offered children different ways of improving their memoirs.

Editing

In order to get quality proof-reading from your pupils, they first need to feel they've written something worth editing.

As we write, we all make mistakes. It happens, but we always try to correct them when we sit down to edit. Editing is an important and explicit stage in the writing process. Without it, all the children's hard work can be in vain, as their readers will find it hard to follow what it is they wanted to say. We will often say to our class that we read our writing four times so that our reader only has to read it once. And this is an important point. Knowing there is going to be a genuine reader at the end of this piece of writing provides the necessary motivation for children to proof-read with care and attention. Without that future reader, children often lack the drive to do the best they can. Unsurprisingly, research suggests that the most effective way to embed editing skills is by asking children to practise on their own compositions, and not through the completing of 'correct the punctuation' exercises (Fearn & Farnan 1998; Cunningham & Cunningham 2010). When asked why they are proof-reading, children will often reply with comments like:

- More people will read your writing.
- It improves my writing for the people who read it.
- I don't do it for you [the teacher] – I do it for my readers.
- I want my reader to read it all.
- I want everyone in the class to understand it.
- If I know it's not going to be seen by anyone, I wouldn't bother to edit it so well.

Editing checklists

Regular use of editing checklists helps children to become excellent proof-readers. The CUPS (Capitalisation, Use of vocabulary, Punctuation and Spellings) strategy ensures children don't over-burden themselves when editing and instead focuses them on one thing at a time. It is also important that, as a writer-teacher, you model how editing is done. All editing should be done by the child in their book using a different coloured pen so that the changes are visible, just as professional writers or copy-editors do. In writing study mini-lessons, children should be taught how proof-reading is a specific activity in which you read carefully word-by-word and hunt for errors, focusing on one or two types of error in each reading. You don't read in the usual way of reading for meaning. When checking their spellings, it's important that children have access to a variety of resources. These include spelling dictionaries, the 1000 common spelling words, electronic spell-checkers, online search engines and of course their reading books. Make sure you praise children in the class for how many errors they've been able to find. Children need to know that this is a positive thing and shows a job well done.

Finally, a couple of useful techniques which copy-editors employ is to read their writing from the end to the beginning. This ensures that you *don't* read your manuscript for meaning and instead focuses you on spotting and attending to transcriptional errors only. Modelling this to your class will be of huge benefit. Also, giving children a few days away from their writing project can sometimes be helpful before asking them to proof-read in preparation for publication.

Editing checklist Year 4

C	Capitals Remember to use capitals: • To start your sentences • For all proper nouns (names) • To start speech • For titles	
U	Use of vocabulary • Change your most boring words • Change the words you use too often • Choose your **verbs** and **adjectives** carefully	

P	Punctuation
	
	• For lists
	  Eggs, bread, milk, flour and sugar
	  Then she opened the lid again, lifted the pig out, and held it against her cheek.
	• For fronted adverbials
	  Enthusiastically, the class edited their work for commas.
	• For subordinate clauses
	  If you start a sentence with a subordinate clause, it will need a comma.
	• For speech marks
	  "Hey, watch it!" said an orange lump on a chair.	

S	Spellings • Circle any spellings you are unsure of. • Look up your spellings online, with your spell-checker, using a dictionary or by looking in your reading book.	

Top tips

- As children develop, they learn to use CUPS *as* they write. They do this if their writing habit is that of a 'Paragraph Piler' or 'Sentence Stacker'. They learn that vomiting and then having to do all your editing after writing is often not the best option. For more information about these writing habits, see page 60.
- It's better to get children to focus on just one aspect of CUPS a day. Children don't edit as well if asked to do it all in one session.
- Accept that some mistakes will sometimes go through to publication. This is just a fact of life.
- At the end of a writing session, you can give children around five minutes together to 'if in doubt, circle it out'. This is where they circle any unsure spellings ready for checking when they begin proof-reading.

Publishing

When young writers publish their work, when they send their work out into the real-world, and receive real-world feedback, they begin to value punctuation, grammar, handwriting, and spelling. Children need to write every day, to publish frequently, and to learn the skills of editing as they go along . . . the more children publish, the more they want to keep on writing and writing well.
Shelley Harwayne

Publishing, the too often forgotten part of the writing process in schools, is where children concentrate on their writing product and how the final piece will look and read. This includes aspects of multimodality. Children also make all the necessary revision and editorial changes to the piece. This is when we can say the piece is 'reader-ready'. Children must ensure that their handwriting and presentation of the work is of a high standard and that any spelling, grammar or punctuation errors have been corrected to the best of their ability. Children whose spelling is particularly poor and who cannot identify their own 'unsure' spellings very well should only be given around five common words to look up and change at any given time. Other errors can be corrected according to your judgement. Once these pieces are published, they need to 'get to work'. They should be published on the whole-class or independent publishing houses, within the classroom (see page 35 for more information on setting up your own publishing houses). They could also be performed out loud, shared with peers, other classes, friends and family for the enjoyment of all. However, they should also be sent out to other recipients or could be entered in local and national competitions. For more publishing ideas, go to page 41.

Part A

What about handwriting?

We know two important things about handwriting. When drafting, children need to handwrite with automaticity so that they are not having to consciously think about it. This leaves them with more cognitive space to think about their actual writing. This can mean writing cursively, printing or a combination of the two. The second important aspect of handwriting is that it must be legible for their readership. The best place for building up automaticity is in drafting, and legibility is best developed whilst publishing as this is where it can be given proper care and attention.

Children thinking about their favourite writing habits

When children are explicitly taught the writing processes and are given time to practise them in their class and personal writing time, they soon become fluent and experienced writers and will be ready to start developing their own writing habits. Our writing habits are our own ways of doing things. These habits can of course change depending on the type of writing we are doing. There are many benefits to children discussing and considering what their favourite writing habits might be. It will mean that they can write more naturally and quickly and to their greatest strengths. Here, we have outlined just some of the habits that might define you and the children as working writers. Allow children to experiment with these different habits in your Welcome Project weeks, then through personal project writing and, eventually, when they are experienced enough, allow them to use their preferred process in class writing projects too.

Adventurer	Planner	Vomiter	Paragrapher Piler	Sentence Stacker
Likes to write a draft first before looking at it and using it as a plan for a second draft.	Likes to plan in great detail, working out exactly what will be written and where it will go before they begin their draft.	Likes to write their piece out from a plan, before attending to revision and editing separately.	Likes to write a paragraph, re-read it, revise it and edit it before moving on to drafting their next paragraph.	Likes to write a sentence and ensure it is revised and edited just how they want it before moving on to the next sentence.

The writer and the secretary

Frank Smith (1982), in his book *Writing and The Writer*, uses the analogy of composition and transcription as if they were performed by two different people, the writer and her secretary, to help visualise the different processes that have to take place when one is writing alone. However, we often ask children to negotiate both these simultaneously when writing.

The writer (*composition*) has to attend to the following:

- Generating ideas
- Turning thoughts, opinions, feelings into words/sentences
- Using grammar in a functional way
- Vocabulary and tone choice
- Maintaining cohesion
- Thinking of the purpose of the text
- Keeping the reader in mind throughout

The secretary (*transcription*) has to attend to the following:

- Physical effort of writing
- Handwriting
- Spelling
- Capitalisation
- Punctuation
- Paragraphs
- How it might look (including multimodality)

When children are learning to write, composition and transcription can interfere with each other. The more attention you give to one, the more the other is likely to suffer. The problem is essentially a competition for attention.

If thoughts are coming too fast, then the quality of children's handwriting, spelling or punctuation is likely to suffer. If we concentrate on the transcription, the insertion of linguistic or literary features or the appearance of what we write, then composition will be affected and children may well produce impeccable nonsense. To avoid either of these occurring, we encourage the use of the earlier-mentioned writing habits which help children shift between these different and equally important focuses.

A quick note about Adventurers and Vomiters

Adventurer and Vomiter are likely to be the most popular habits of writing amongst early and moderately fluent writers, and this makes sense. These writers like it because it allows them to focus on one process at a time. Adventurers favour the Peter Elbow (1998) *free-writing* technique, the idea that you simply and quickly write whatever comes to mind and use this as the foundation on which to build a more formal draft. However, with increased experience, children often move away from these habits and instead begin to revise and edit their writing as they go – like Paragraph Pilers and Sentence Stackers.

Conclusion

Key points from this chapter:

- There is no single agreed-upon writing process. There are many habits and approaches to the writing process, and this can often depend on the type of writing we are doing.
- The writing processes are often recursive and typically include generating ideas, dabbling, planning, drafting, revising, editing and publishing and performing.
- Children need to be given increasing agency over their writing process as they become more experienced and should be able to use a writing habit and strategies that favour their process.
- It's important for children's motivation and enjoyment that they be given agency over the topics for their writing. Teaching idea generation strategies is therefore vital to the success of a writing project and developing independent writers.
- Only once children become fluent writers are they able to best deal with aspects of composition and transcription at the same time.
- Children shouldn't see revision as meaning they didn't get their writing 'right' the first time round.
- Children shouldn't be expected to attend to all aspects of editing in one session.
- In some ways, publishing is the most vital aspect of the writing process, but it is often the most neglected.

6 | How to teach an effective writing lesson

Using writing workshop

We defined ourselves as a class of writers. I relished our classroom culture and told anyone who would listen.
Leung & Hicks

Real-World Writers involves teaching writing in a reassuringly consistent and simple way. Research has repeatedly shown that explicit instruction in the writing processes is one of the best ways of teaching apprentice writers (Graham & Perin 2007; Graham & Sandmel 2011; McQuitty 2014; Koster *et al* 2015; Wyse & Torgerson 2017). Therefore, the writing workshop approach, with its focus on children practising what writers really do, developing self-regulating strategies, and giving children resources and techniques to help them undertake the different writing processes largely independently, makes it a highly effective writing approach. In essence, a writing workshop is an approach which encourages children to become involved in developing as writers. Independently does not, however, mean working in isolation. The collaborative element of the writing workshop can and should invigorate, enliven and promote a sense of socialising about writing and create a community of writers working and learning from each other as they write.

A typical writing session should be split into three parts: a **mini-lesson**, **writing time** and **class sharing**. Writing sessions begin with a mini-lesson – a lesson that is short, wholly practical and of long-term use to the apprentice writers in your class. The children will often be able to apply what they have learnt that day in their writing time. Remember, keep it simple and ensure children get to write every day.

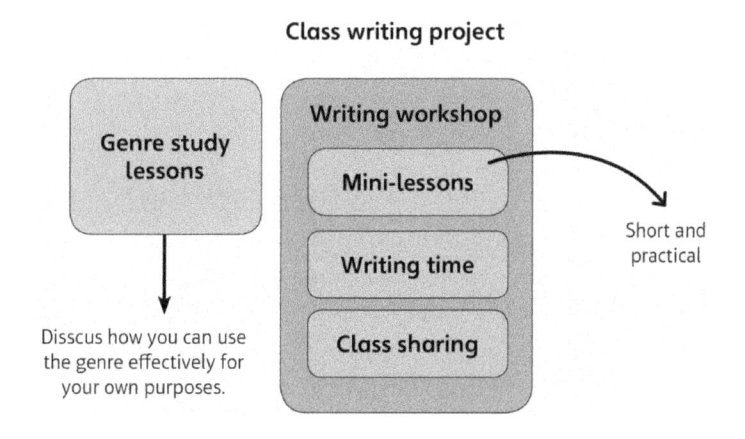

Class writing project

- Genre study lessons
  - Disscus how you can use the genre effectively for your own purposes.
- Writing workshop
  - Mini-lessons → Short and practical
  - Writing time
  - Class sharing

Part A

We suggest that a writing lesson takes around one hour to an hour and 20 minutes:

10–15 minutes mini-lesson
30–45 minutes for writing time
15–20 minutes share time and author's chair

Donald Graves (1983) states that not allowing children to write every day is a sure-fire way to make them hate writing. You need to protect writing time not only from outside interruptions but also from yourself as the teacher. Don't try and eat into that 30 to 45 minutes of writing time. Writing every day is important because children get to know that they'll be carrying on with their writing project the next day, and this helps maintain momentum and motivation. They are in a constant state of composition, and it's this concept of ongoingness that helps children to start to think and act as writers do. They continue thinking about their writing and will be mentally composing and considering it even outside of writing time. They will live the writer's life.

Mini-lessons

What lessons will have a practical, lasting, positive influence on student writing?
Nancie Atwell

Mini-lessons precede each daily writing session and aim to provide children with the knowledge, strategies and resources to write with more self-regulation and with a greater understanding of how writers and the process of writing really works. Mini-lessons should typically last only 10 to 15 minutes. A good mini-lesson is one that children will remember and return to throughout their year of writing.

There are two broad types of mini-lesson to choose from: **writing study** and **functional grammar study**. Writing study lessons focus on an aspect of the writer's craft or how to use a specific resource or writing strategy. Functional grammar study is about children understanding how they already use grammar and punctuation in their writing projects in powerful ways, as well as how they can learn new aspects of grammar, from real examples, to suit the type of writing they are currently undertaking.

Writing study

Writers learn by learning about writing.
Frank Smith

Research shows that teaching writing strategies and craft knowledge is the single most effective way of improving children's writing outcomes (Young & Ferguson in press). It is therefore imperative that you spend time helping children deepen their understanding of the writing processes. Writing study lessons help you teach children about how to generate ideas, plan or dabble, draft, revise, edit and publish effectively. Writing strategies such as those taught in writing study lessons are vital because ultimately they save children time. They allow children to get down to the act of writing quickly and confidently and learn, increasingly, to be self-regulating writers. Children often know what they want to write about but not necessarily how to do it. This is where the writing study lessons come in.

Writing study lessons are the difference between saying *'this is how I want you to start this story'* and saying *'what are the different ways you can start a story?'* The first provides children with no long-term significance, whereas the latter provides children with knowledge useful for future projects. The first promotes learnt helplessness, the other self-efficacy and self-regulation.

Using examples of great writing

Another approach to writing study is to read and discuss good snippets of writing and to make links between what the example has done superbly well and what children want to achieve with their compositions. This need only be a short extract. For example, it might be some dialogue between two characters from *Wind in The Willows* – where you really get an understanding of the personalities of the characters through how they talk to one another. Once this understanding is discussed, you can invite your children to try this out too during writing time. We would argue that one of the best places to find excellent examples is in children's own writing. You should certainly feel comfortable sharing children's excellent craft because not only does it feel attainable for the rest of the class but you also have the author in the room. *They can explain to their fellow apprentice writers how they did it, in a child-friendly way.*

Here is an example of a writing study mini-lesson we gave our Year 3 class:

Finding your best line

When revising, did you know it is really helpful to be your own critic when it comes to looking at your writing? Let me read you some of my writing and we'll underline which you think is my best line.

- Why have you chosen that sentence?
- Is it because of the descriptive language or the style?
- Is it because of a character or setting description? Or is it because of the description of some action?

On my trying things out page, I'm going to take this best line and turn it into a paragraph by expanding on it, using more descriptive language and painting the moment with words.

I would love for you to try this technique during today's writing time. You could even exchange your writing with someone else in the class to see whether your partner agrees that you have chosen your best line.

Functional grammar lessons

> *Grammar is style.*
> Patty McGee

We know that formal grammar teaching doesn't improve children's writing. However, we can't simply ignore grammar. So how best to teach it? To put it simply, functional grammar lessons are about children seeing how grammar is authentically used by writers and being invited to try it for themselves. Grammar lessons like this are essential for showing children the *hows* of writing. Punctuation and grammar use is a skill to be developed, not simply content to be taught.

The first place you and your pupils need to go for grammar advice is books. If they are unsure about a 'grammar rule', they should automatically go to the book they are reading. Another useful technique is discussion of a prepared text which does not achieve its intentions as a result of poor grammar use. The act of reading requires understanding how writers use grammar to enhance their meaning. Children will learn that if they ignore grammatical conventions, readers might not understand their text.

Grammar lessons through writer's craft: the research headlines

- Teach one item at a time and invite children to apply it that same day in their real writing.
- Use short examples from real literature and from children's own writing.
- Encourage children to look out for and squirrel away good examples from their reading (see page 99).
- Effective teachers of grammar have a 'let's see what this does' as opposed to a 'right/wrong rule' attitude.
- Don't expect children to transfer knowledge from grammar exercises into their writing.
- Functional grammar lessons are not only the key to good writing, but teaching in this way results in a deeper understanding of grammar for formal testing.

(Fearn & Farnan 1998; Graham & Perin 2007; Myhill 2018)

Here is an example of a mini-lesson we gave Year 6 on replacing *and* with a semi-colon for rhythm.

> ### Replacing *and* with ; for rhythm
>
> Sometimes writers will use a semi-colon to join two ideas together in one sentence instead of writing two separate sentences, as long as the ideas are clearly connected. Show children the examples you found in the class library.
> Ask children:
>
> - Can you see what the writers have done in these examples?
> - Why have they used semi-colons in this way?
> - As the reader, what do you think of this technique?
> - Have you ever used semi-colons in your own writing?
>
> Before we start writing time, with the people on your table, try to find any examples of a semi-colon being used in the books you are reading at the moment.
> Today, look out for an opportunity to use a semi-colon in your writing.

Planning your mini-lessons

At the end of any mini-lesson, you want one thing: for your children to say *'I can see what writers are doing–I can do that too!'* Mini-lessons have to be carefully thought through to ensure they will be relevant to your class at that particular stage in their writing process and for the type of writing they are currently undertaking. The individual best placed to know what your children need to develop as writers is you. Over time, it will be vital that you make your own judgements about what your class needs instruction in. You should ask yourself questions, such as the following: What are my children trying to do in their drafts? What is their image of good writing? What can I tell them in a mini-lesson that might help move their writing forward? What am I always repeating in pupil conferencing? What are they simply not doing? What writing process do they understand the least? What does the curriculum need to see them doing? You should also ask your class what *they* believe they need a mini-lesson on.

There are two ways of knowing you've planned a good mini-lesson. Firstly, it is responsive to what your children need and what you are seeing during writing time. Secondly, you're teaching them something that is going to be useful to them time and again. When you know which areas you would like to focus on in your teaching, follow these stages:

Part A

1. **Introduce the topic and its purpose:** This can be anything from a writing strategy or skill to an item of grammar or a literary technique. Always share the purpose with the class before moving on to any formalities or rules.
2. **Share examples:** Look at examples from published writing (including your own or the children's compositions).
3. **Provide information:** Provide information about the topic and how it can be used in writing. Clarify any misconceptions that the children may have.
4. **Invitation to practise:** Children are invited to try out the topic discussed during writing time that day.
5. **Assess learning:** Ask the children how they got on. You should ask this at the end of writing time. *Was the mini-lesson helpful today? How did you use it? Anyone have a good example they can share?*

The importance of giving 'writing tricks'

Whatever you choose to do in these mini-lessons, you should ensure that you teach everything in context and in a way that will empower your children in relation to their writing intentions. We suggest that you teach these lessons in the spirit of quick '**tip giving**' or the revealing of a '**writer's trick or secret**' before writing time begins. Doing this will change your perception of the lessons and stop them from turning into exercises. Instead, you create a climate where children feel they have been taught something valuable by an experienced writer-teacher.

How you know you're going to teach a good mini-lesson

When we give direct instruction and invite children to apply what they've learnt in that day's writing, we can't help but move children's writing forward. Progress in writing happens before our very eyes and, for a teacher, is obviously very satisfying. You know you're teaching a good mini-lesson if you're trying to help children write what they really mean. You'll probably start out by saying something like:

- When I write . . .
- Yesterday, I couldn't help but notice that . . .
- When some writers . . . they'll . . .
- Why do authors use . . .
- I've noticed recently that . . .
- I wanted to show you how . . .
- I thought today we could try . . .
- We need to show that we can . . .
- Remember when we wrote our . . . well now I think we are ready to . . .
- I know that last year you . . . well this year . . .

Writing time

There are usually four steps children go through during writing time. The following could be put on display:

> **Writing Time To-Do List**
> 1. Think about the mini-lesson.
> 2. Decide what your process goal is.
> 3. Get writing.
> 4. Once finished for today, continue with your personal writing project.

Setting process goals

Writers set themselves deadlines. They sit down to write knowing what it is they want to achieve in that couple of hours, day or week. Through writing workshop, you and your class will learn to do the same thing. Writing workshop teaches children about the whole writing process. They then use this knowledge and the appropriate resources to navigate the writing processes and so complete accomplished, accurate and personally significant pieces of writing. They are gently guided through the process by you. For example, you can suggest a process goal for that day's writing session. However, every writer writes at a different pace. Therefore, we need to let go of the idea that all children can and should finish a writing project or process goal at exactly the same time. You will need to be flexible about the process goals you suggest. We explain how here.

> Examples of process goal setting in LKS2:
> - Over the next couple of writing sessions, you will need to have a plan for your instructional text ready.
> - Using your plans to aid you, you will have the next few writing sessions to draft your instructions.
> - I am giving you this writing session to work with your partner on revising your instructional text ready for publication. If you feel that you may need another session because you have a lot of revisions to do, please let me know.
> - If you feel ready, I have put aside this writing session (and tomorrow's session if we need it) so that you can proof-read and edit your instructional texts to make sure they are 'reader-ready'.
> - Today is the day! This writing session is for you to publish your instructional texts into the class library.

Part A

> Examples of process goal setting in UKS2:
> - *You have 12 writing sessions to write your short stories and prepare them for publication.*
> - *It's day 3 of 12. I would suggest that many of you ensure you start drafting today if you are going to meet our publishing deadline.*
> - *You have 2 days left until publication day. Make sure your manuscripts are 'reader-ready'.*
> - *This is your last day. Your short stories must be ready for publication tomorrow. If you don't think you are going to make the deadline, come and speak with me.*

Setting process goals in LKS2

At the start of writing time, you should be setting a process goal you want children to complete. For example, *'to get a plan together for your information text'*. A process goal can last for a number of writing sessions, meaning all children have enough time to achieve the goal successfully. Importantly, there will also be enough time for you to verbally provide feedback to children on how they are getting on through pupil conferencing (see page 80). As every class writing project follows this reassuringly consistent routine, children will begin to use what they have learnt year-on-year about the writing processes and will use the same strategies when undertaking their personal writing projects (page 74). They quickly become experienced writers. Once experienced enough, they can be encouraged to write at their own pace, using their preferred writing habits (page 60), and can set their own deadlines.

Setting process goals in UKS2

In UKS2, we suggest that you do not include setting a specific process goal at the beginning of writing time. Instead, children should be allowed to complete their writing at their own pace, using their own preferred writing process, over a number of sessions. This gives all children, regardless of ability and support requirements, ample time in which to publish their finished product to the best of their ability from a position of strength. Importantly, there will also be enough time for you, as their teacher, to provide pupil conferences and see how the children are getting on with their writing.

Whilst we suggest that you don't set specific process goals for your whole class in UKS2, this doesn't mean you shouldn't set an ultimate deadline. As you can see in the examples in the table shown earlier, you should be reminding children of how much longer they have left before the final deadline for the project. You can also give them a rough idea of how far along they should be in the writing process to ensure they can make that deadline. Some teachers share deadlines by posting them up on their working walls whilst others suggest that children write a to-do list.

Completed the process goal for the day? Children should pursue their personal writing projects!

No more will you need to hear 'I'm finished!' during writing sessions. We recommend that once children have completed the process goal for the lesson, or series of lessons, they continue writing by undertaking their personal writing projects. This means children are always undertaking meaningful work during writing time. We know that the more opportunities and time children are given to write, the quicker their development. For more information about personal projects, see page 74.

The importance of being flexible with your process goals

It's important that you be flexible with your deadlines. For example, you may tell your Year 4 class that they have two days to complete their drafts for their short stories but soon realise that many of the children would appreciate another writing session. Simply give them that extra session.

So what do I do during writing time?

1. Ensure that you regularly sit amongst your class and write alongside them for the first five minutes. You'll be surprised at how this modelling settles your class down to write and encourages them to be independent.
2. Start conducting pupil conferences (see page 80).
3. Stop the children at regular intervals to remind them to re-read their writing out loud and also to share what they have been working on with their peers.
4. Teach another mini-lesson. Don't be afraid to teach an additional mini-lesson when you see a great opportunity to do so. You may find yourself repeating the same advice to various children during conferencing. Why not stop and give this advice to the whole class?
5. You may read or hear an example of really excellent craft. Share this with the class and encourage them to try it out too.

Class sharing and author's chair

At the end of each writing session, children should be given the opportunity to talk with their partners, in groups, or with the whole class about how their writing pieces are coming along. They should share what they like about the piece and its particular strengths but also give advice and strategies when they feel difficulties have arisen in their peers' work. They can also learn from good examples of writing from others around the classroom.

It's essential that this time be made before the end of a writing session. It is an opportunity for children to talk about their process, their ideas and where they are taking their writing and to get feedback from a potential audience. As a community, you should be asking questions like 'What did you learn about writing today?', 'What techniques did you try?', 'What worked really well for you today?', 'What do you love about a person's piece?', 'What did you find hard today?' and 'What do you feel you need a mini-lesson on tomorrow?'

After children have had a discussion amongst themselves, there should be time made for 'author's chair'. This is where children can come to the front and share extracts from their finished or ongoing compositions. Author's chair works best when you follow this kind of routine:

1. Give children time to consider what they might like to share. Alternatively, you pick children to come to the front of the class.
2. Ask them to 'warm up the text' by explaining a little bit about the background behind it.
3. Ask the child whether there is anything in particular they would like the class to listen out for or any advice they would like to receive.
4. Then, allow the writer to read their whole piece or a particular extract of the writing.
5. Once the piece has been read out, invite children in the class to explain what it was about.
6. Ask what struck them as being interesting about the piece, whether it reminded them of anything from their life or anything they have seen or read, and whether they have any questions for the writer.
7. Your last question should be whether anyone in the class feels they would like to give some advice. This is also an opportunity for you, as the writer-teacher, to give some advice on the writing piece too. This is a powerful part of the sharing because all children can listen and apply the advice you have given to their future writing projects too. To keep things fresh, it is also beneficial to have the occasional draft book ceremony, where children display on their tables their favourite example of dabbling, planning, drafting, revising, editing or published work. This has hugely positive results on children's writing and shouldn't be underestimated.
8. Instead of whole-class Author's chair, you can have children share with their partners or across tables. Children can still follow the typical sharing routine once they have internalised the process.
9. Finally, there is also the concept of 'process shares'. This differs from sharing the writing itself. Instead, children describe or show an aspect of their writing process and how they go about writing in a certain way. For example, you might have a child explain how they go about writing a character description.

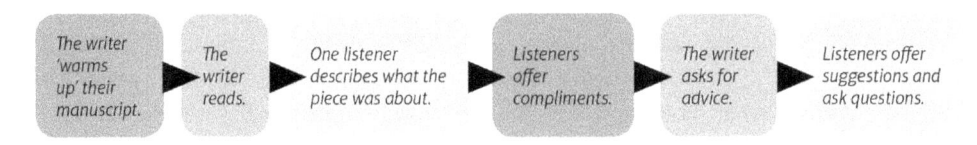

The writer 'warms up' their manuscript. → The writer reads. → One listener describes what the piece was about. → Listeners offer compliments. → The writer asks for advice. → Listeners offer suggestions and ask questions.

Conclusion

Key points from this chapter:

- A good writing lesson follows a consistent routine of **mini-lesson**, **writing time** and **class sharing**.
- It's vital that children be given the opportunity to write every day.
- A good mini-lesson is one that is short and is responsive to what your class' learning needs are at the time.
- Research makes clear that the most effective writing instruction includes teaching writing study mini-lessons (Young & Ferguson in press). Writing study involves teaching techniques, strategies or aspects of the writers' craft that children can use independently to navigate the writing processes or to make their writing more effective and meaningful.
- Formal grammar lessons do nothing to improve children's writing. Instead, teach functional grammar lessons which invite children to try out the learning point in that day's writing time.
- As children become more experienced, they should be given agency to set their own deadlines.
- Always allow time for class sharing and author's chair.

7 Setting up writers' notebooks and personal writing projects

Giving young writers genuine choice is the best way I know to create an environment where they can flourish.
Ralph Fletcher

Setting up writers' notebooks

Children will keep their own writer's notebook to be used both at home and at school. The notebooks are where they can work on their personal writing projects. Clark's (2016; 2017) reports into writing state that children who write at home are five times more likely to progress beyond school expectations in writing than those who do not. We certainly found that the level of commitment and quality of the texts our class wrote in their notebooks was extraordinary. By using home-school writing notebooks with your class, you can take advantage of this level of engagement and quality of writing in school.

Early on in the term, share your own writer's notebook with your class. Explain that it has stories, poems, opinions, knowledge, memories, words, phrases, drawings, clippings – some of your life in it because you keep it beside you always. Ask the children to think about events from their lives which hold memories for them. You can then give each their own personal home-school notebook to be a bridge between writing at home and writing at school. Tell them that, as you have done, they can 'squirrel away' in the back of the notebook snippets of excellent writing from their reading to draw on later (see page 99 for more details).

A notebook is like a safe, warm and comfortable greenhouse where personal projects can take root, germinate and grow. However, children should know that not everything they write down has to be published or even fully drafted. They don't necessarily have to write in the ways they do in class writing projects. For example, they can abandon pieces or simply 'dabble' on an idea without following it through. Sometimes they will never get around to turning their little bit of dabbling into anything, nor should they feel they have to. Not everything that is written in a notebook turns into something significant or needs to be shared.

To-do list for setting up writers' notebooks

1 At the beginning of the year, get children to draw an 'ideas heart' in the front of their notebook (see page 185).
2 At the beginning of the year, ensure children leave some space in the back of their book for collecting potential writing ideas. As a writer, you simply must make a note of promising writing ideas before you forget them. Writing ideas are like dreams. They are vivid the moment you have them but if you try to remember them later, they elude you – unless you've written them down.
3 Give children the opportunity (either at home or at school) to personalise and decorate their notebook.
4 Teach children how to find their 'diamond moments' (see page 50).
5 Ensure parents know that this is their child's notebook and that there isn't an expectation for it to be marked or scrutinised by you as the teacher or by them.

Personal project weeks

If we don't let children write for themselves, we miss out on knowing them as writers.

As discussed in Chapter 2, we suggest that there be four occasions in the year when children are given three weeks in which to pursue **personal writing projects**. Personal projects are a central and visible part of Real-World Writers. They should never be an add-on. As Chamberlain's (2015) research asserts, writing with agency and seeing their own topics as valued and valid subjects for writing within school is a huge motivation for children and creates in them a sense of volition to develop themselves as authentic writers. Personal projects give children freedom, time and space to write and publish a portfolio of purposeful, informative, reflective, poetic, maybe strange, experimental and memorable pieces of writing that mean something to them and to the community of writers to which they belong. Reading them gives teachers a sense of motivation and pleasure themselves.

Most importantly, personal project time provides the arena (albeit in the classroom) in which children are able to write as writers do in the outside world, bringing to it their own purposes, ideas, intentions, audiences, and all that they have learnt about the craft of writing in its widest sense. It's also a place where children can write away from some of the demands of class writing projects. They can write about topics and use the writing processes more spontaneously.

We would like to emphasise that giving children full agency to choose their own topics and ways of writing does not mean that your lessons will become suddenly loose and without structure. In fact it's quite the opposite. The kind of authentically creative and genuinely independent work we want our apprentice writers to do relies on organisation of resources and command of ideas and involves not just innovation but also application of knowledge and skills. This is where you as the teacher will need to continue putting in your hard work, teaching, support and advice.

No more 'I'm finished'

Effective writing teachers understand that writing is not easily or quickly mastered. Children need opportunities for repeated practice. Of course, this does not mean mechanical drills and empty exercises; it means daily and sustained engagement with writing that is enjoyable and purposeful. Personal projects mean children can write every day. Remember, children can continue with these projects any time, for example after their class writing is completed for the day. Never again will you hear a child say 'I'm finished, what do I do now?' They will always know they can be working on their personal writing, where the resources are and what you expect to see in terms of quality. Even the very youngest children are capable of this kind of independence.

Expectations for personal project weeks

Children need to be aware of the different reasons they are *moved* to write. They should be able to answer the question: 'What has moved you to write about this?' If they can't answer this question, they may not have the motivation to see the writing successfully through to the end. The writing process is like cutting through thick jungle. It can be hard work and it's tiring. And we only undertake it with pleasure and commitment if it's writing we care about.

Not surprisingly, research shows that if children enjoy and care about their writing, they will work harder at it (Young & Ferguson in press). This means that they will take personal writing time incredibly seriously and hold it in the highest possible regard. Teachers should do the same. It is also worth saying that, whilst children are afforded a great deal of autonomy during these times, you should expect the routines, expectations and behaviours which you have established in class writing project sessions to be well maintained when undertaking personal projects too.

'Hot topics'

It is important to note that in a session you will probably only encounter a small number of what Graves (1994) calls 'hot topics', that is to say, pieces that are extremely successful and memorable. Do not be discouraged by this, particularly early on. You cannot expect children to always be the new Maya Angelou or Shakespeare! Most children will be simply practising the craft of writing until their 'hot topic' comes along. Professional writers dry up and fail from time to time, and of course it's the same for children. Failures are a necessary part of the process. Consider how much writing an author will burn or throw away – it will not see the light of day – so be kind to your children!

Routines for personal project weeks

The routines for personal project weeks match those for class writing projects. Begin with a **mini-lesson**, perhaps one based on a need you have observed within the class. **Writing time** follows, and the session ends with **class sharing**. Continue to conference individuals during the writing time. Direct instruction and high-quality teaching continues as much as it does during class writing projects.

Keeping a writing register

We have found that maintaining a daily writing register is very useful for keeping track of the progress of individual children and also checking that they are undertaking writing in a variety of genres. Keeping a writing register is important for a number of other reasons too. It helps sustain children's motivation and commitment and shows them that you are interested in helping them see their projects through to publication. And it allows them to share their ideas aloud so that others may be inspired. So how is it done?

Call each child's name and record their topic or title. If it's the first time you've heard about the idea, ask the child what their final goal is for the composition and what's moved them to write about it. Do they plan to publish it in one of the class' publishing houses? If so, which one? Then ask what their goal is for that day's session. What are they hoping to get done by the session's end? The child will tell you very briefly where they are currently at, whether it is generating ideas, planning, drafting, revising, editing or publishing. Simply make a note of this. Some children may tell you that they've decided to abandon what they were working on last time and have instead started exploring a new project.

Children abandoning projects

Discarding a project is fine. However, it is important to keep a tab on children who continually abandon projects as they are often the ones who would benefit from some intervention and maybe some writing advice on how to stay with a particular idea. There are several reasons that children abandon a project:

1. They aren't really that motivated by their subject.
2. They want to continue but have got stuck and don't quite know how to realise their intentions.
3. They have been distracted by another idea that, at present, feels more exciting and worth pursuing!
4. They've realised they don't know enough about the topic.
5. It feels too personal or inappropriate for the classroom context.

All of these situations do happen, but children will sometimes return to previously abandoned topics later on in the year.

Publishing personal writing

Not all writing needs to become published writing. When children have completed a number of personal writing projects, they can choose one piece for formal publication. This should be a piece of writing that fits the class publishing house criteria or alternatively can be written for one of the child-run independent houses set up by small groups or even individuals to represent their particular interests. Each independent publishing house will have a mission statement, a name, a slogan and a logo and will avoid encroaching on the whole-class publishing house. A poster giving details of the mission statements and editors of each publishing house supports and champions individual writers within the class. Children should meet with the designated editors to get their opinion and advice before publishing into the class library on their imprint. However, it may be that the child has a different audience in mind and may want to take the writing home or give or send it to someone. See page 35 for more details on publishing houses.

Keeping the momentum going

Children need to keep in touch with their projects to maintain momentum. They should be able to check in with these pieces every day. If this can't always be achieved in the classroom, then it's imperative they be allowed to take their compositions freely between school and home.

Dealing with children's sensitive topic choices

We know that teachers may feel anxiety about the possibility of some children disclosing sensitive issues in their own lives through, for example, the writing of a story, poem or memoir. We should, however, regard this as a positive aspect of personal project writing. Children may have a real need to share these issues with an adult, and in fact we've found that some children find it easier to write about them than to talk about them directly to an adult in school. The teacher will then be in a position to know how to proceed in an appropriate and sensitive way. Children are not of course asked to share their personal writing with their peers if they are reluctant to do so. Incidentally, children are capable of knowing for themselves what they do and do not want to write about and you, as a professional, can trust your judgement on whether it is appropriate to intervene. Learning what is appropriate to share in print, as with speech, is not only an important writing lesson; it's a life lesson.

A couple of tips from experience

Of course there must be space for talk during writing time, but there must also be a time for the writing to proceed. In other words, don't let personal writing time become an opportunity for children to just socialise with their friends. There comes a point – even for adult professional or recreational writers – where you have to say 'Right, enough procrastinating – it's time to get to work'.

Personal project time is not drawing or art time. However, that's not to say that children can't draw or create artwork to support the publication of their piece, nor is it to say that drawing isn't a valuable aid for generating and planning ideas. The point is that drawing isn't the end in itself, and you need to teach children that though it's fine to draw, the purpose of it is to lead to a potential composition. See pages 106 and 123 for more information on drawing leading to writing.

If possible, organise your timetable so that personal reading time is sometimes immediately followed by personal writing time. This can allow ideas from reading to flow into writing (see page 93).

Key points from this chapter:

- Writers' notebooks help grow quality writing.
- Personal writing projects provide an arena for children to write as writers.
- Children need to find the 'diamond moment' to focus on in their writing.
- Children need to have in mind the distant goal for their writing. Where do they want it to end up?
- Children should set themselves a process goal for the writing session, although they may not necessarily achieve it.
- Set up classroom publishing houses, both whole-class and independents.
- Using a writing register helps you and the children keep track.
- Keep the momentum going by ensuring children check in with their pieces often.
- Personal projects are held in high regard by teachers and children.
- Personal writing notebooks should be allowed to go to and from school freely.
- Substantial time is allowed for personal projects throughout the year.

8 Meeting children where they are

Giving effective pupil conferences

The conversations with the writers in my classroom feels satisfying, genuine and useful.
Nancie Atwell

The research literature (Calkins & Ehrenworth 2016; Young & Ferguson in press) makes it clear that giving specific verbal feedback which is immediate and relevant and allows children to attend to learning points whilst actually engaged in writing is more effective in helping children move forwards in their writing than 'after-the-event' written feedback. Rich verbal responses, both by teacher and peers, are always crucially important; reading, sharing and talking about writing is an essential part of writing for pleasure and being in a community of writers. Conferencing is one way of talking about writing. In addition, the exchanges you have in the conference can be used to make assessments of and for learning. In a good conference, you literally can't help but teach something, and children can't help but learn and apply it.

What are the purposes of a conference?

When young writers know someone cares about their words, it changes how they relate to you as their writer-teacher. Conferences can be amongst the best, warmest, most purposeful and productive interactions you can have with the young writers in your class, but they have a more important purpose than that of simply improving the written product. The huge significance of giving children strategies and techniques for instant application in their written piece is that you will be helping them become *better writers*, developing the writer within as well as the writing, and children will soon understand and appreciate that this is your aim. During the conference, you will be giving them a little more writer 'craft' knowledge to take forward into new writing projects – and also into their present and future lives outside the school gates.

Good conferencing allows children to have agency, become self-directing and feel greater motivation in the act of writing. Think of each conference as a conversation, in which you are the trusted and sympathetic adult who will help and advise without being judgemental. When teachers act only as judges, children's writing is focused on what the teacher wants. As a result, the writing is nearly always tentative and unambitious and children learn less. Your aim should be to build up a writer's pride in their own work and the motivation to improve it through self-regulation. Never be afraid to give practical advice. You yourself may not be the best writer in the class, but you are the most experienced!

So much depends on the tone

Children need to feel secure in a teacher's presence and assume that they will be interested in the writing, responding in the first place to *what* has been written and not to *how* it has been written. Children can become self-conscious about errors in the earliest stages of the writing process. This means they are less likely to take risks as a result. You won't therefore be concentrating on transcription issues unless the conference is taking place at the editing stage of the child's writing, and you won't be seeking to 'fix' the writing by imposing your own ideas as to how the piece should go. Instead, you will listen sympathetically and with interest, give suggestions and guide the children towards making their own reflective and informed writing decisions. Best of all, you will know that you are giving responsive, high-quality, focused and direct instruction to individual writers in a very short space of time (a conference can sometimes take less than a minute).

You will be drawing on your own experience and insights as a 'writer-teacher', who writes when possible alongside the class and who is therefore able to talk to pupils as 'writer to writer'. We cannot stress enough the importance of sharing with honesty the difficulties you yourself have encountered in writing and the positive solutions you have found. This puts you in a position of empathy, and you should, when possible, draw on these personal experiences when conferring with children.

How to conduct a conference

A good conference has a definite structure. This is important, because knowing where you are going in a conference means you can be time-efficient and keep your focus on the pupil. In the first part, you ask the most simple, brilliant and inviting question it is possible ever to ask to open the conversation: 'How's it going?' In response, the child talks about their piece and sets the agenda for the conference by identifying a difficulty or an uncertainty.

You take in what the child is saying and then tease out more information through questioning. On the basis of what you have been told, you get what Anderson (2000) calls a 'line of thinking' about the pupil's intention which helps you make a decision to teach one or, at the most, two specific things. In the second part, you teach these things about the writing, making a writerly suggestion or giving them a strategy to try. You then encourage the child's self-direction and leave the conference. The example below will show how this works.

Conference conducted with a pupil in a Year 5 class at the start of one of her personal writing projects

T: How's it going?
P: Well, I want to write a piece about my grandma, and so to start with I've been trying to make a whole list of things about her that I could put in. [Talking about the writing]

T: (scans list) There are lots of ideas here, aren't there? I can tell she's quite an unusual person, isn't she? And I sense that you're really proud of her, and you'll probably want to put that over to your reader. [Responds briefly with interest to content; gets a line on the pupil's intention as a writer]

P: Yeah. I'd like people to know she's great and she's done some brave things, but I'm having trouble with getting it into a plan, don't know where to start and what order to put stuff in. And what sort of ending to write. [Reflects; states problem and sets agenda for the conference]

T: Mmmm, so you've got lots of information and it's hard to organise it all. I know how that feels! Well, I can tell you something other writers often do when they have this problem. They focus on the most interesting thing about that person and they just write about that. So you could try that. You just said you wanted people to know about her courage, right? Well, how about picking the thing that shows that most clearly about her? [Sums up the problem, makes a teaching decision, refers to mentors, gives a writerly suggestion]

P: (thinks for a while) Mmmm. I suppose that would be when she ran in the marathon and she never gave up even when she got so tired she nearly couldn't breathe!

T: Great! That sounds really dramatic! I'd certainly like to hear more about that and so will all your other readers. So what will you do next? [Encourages self-regulation]

P: Well, I could plan it – like a story maybe? Beginning at the start of the race and then the middle could be what it was like when she was running, did she talk to anyone and things like that. And then the ending when she nearly didn't make it, or something? [Pupil becomes self-directing]

T: Sounds good to me! So I'll leave you now to get on with your plan. [Supports pupil's self-direction]. Was that helpful?

P: Yeah! Thank you so much!

Practicalities

- Conferences can take place at any stage of the writing process.
- Each conference should be short (no more than a few minutes).
- If you can, go to the children and sit beside them, rather than have them come to you. A small foldable stool is useful here.
- Aim to see all children at least once during the week, but give priority to those who request a conference or are in most need of one.
- Children can 'listen in' to a conference being held with another child and can conference each other.
- Set high expectations for the behaviour and noise level in the class while you are conferencing.
- Always end a conference with 'was that helpful?' Say it loud enough for others to hear. Children then begin to see that having a conference with you is no bad thing!

It must be said that conferencing is a skill to be learnt and developed, but through regular practice you will become adept at asking the sorts of questions which will draw out the information you need and enable you to give your pupils the kinds of advice which will help them as writers.

Here are some examples of the *kinds of questions* you can ask.

1. 'Invitation' questions:	2. Open-ended 'research' questions to find out more about the writer's intentions and to **help you make a teaching decision:**	3. Teaching something writers do:	4. Process questions and comments to help with carrying on the writing:
How's it going? How can I help? What are you doing as a writer today? What's working well? Tell me about your piece. What's tricky that you need help with today? Scan the writing and comment briefly on what's been done well.	Can you tell me a little more about that? What do you mean when you say . . .? What's the big idea in your piece/diamond moment/focus? How do you think you will start your draft? Have you thought about what we discussed yesterday in the mini-lesson? What made you add in a bit right here? What do you want your reader to feel at this point?	Well, when this happens to me, what I'll usually do is, . . . One thing writers do when they're revising is, . . . When I'm writing a story I usually try out several different openings and choose a favourite, . . . You could give that a go. One strategy that might help you is, . . . Remember we talked in the mini-lesson about how to treat your setting like a character? Think about how writers make time pass, in a fairytale for example. I know that feeling! Sometimes what I do is. . . . Do you have any good writing squirrelled away in your writing notebook that might help you? Something writers do when they don't know what to write next is to picture it on a cinema screen. Add some visual detail; show your reader what's on the screen.	Which bit are you going to work on next? I'll come back in a bit and see how you've got on with that. Try that out and see what you think. Focus on getting the plan finished by the end of the session. What if you tried . . . on your revision page? Well, maybe it's finished then. . . . (This is a great response when children say 'I don't know what to write next'. They will immediately say no and will say why. This is what you suggest they write next!)

Encouraging children to request conferences

At the beginning of the year, children who have not been taught writing through a Real-World Writers approach may at first distrust conferences. They will often say 'I'm fine'. It takes time for children to realise that you're a sympathetic and experienced writer who can give them advice or help them out of a bind in a non-threatening way. If they are urgently in need of a conference and you are already occupied, the routine is: 'underline your sticky bit, tap me on the shoulder to let me know you're in need of some advice, sit back down, and carry on with your writing until I can attend to you'. However, if you're regularly finding yourself inundated with requests, then something is amiss with how your writing classroom is running. When this happens, it's worth reflecting on what's going wrong and making changes quickly.

Goal-setting conferences

Goals or targets can be set with the children during conferencing. However, the best way of getting children to attend to a specific product goal for a writing project is simply to invite them to try out some ideas on their 'revision and trying things out' page. For more information on target setting go to page 88.

Conferences which set a challenge

You can use a conference to set a challenge for the writer: for example, to write in a genre they do not normally choose. This is done with the aim of further developing the child as a writer and can be part of their writing goals or targets.

Peer conferencing

Children need to understand the four main reasons conferences take place: wanting help, wanting advice on what to write next, wanting to share and wanting feedback. They must listen carefully to each other's requests in the conference and respond appropriately. Writing takes a huge amount of concentration and effort. Whilst the power of peer-working and talk is very much part of writing workshop, children also need to understand that any talk with peers about their work should be focused, considered and quiet. You may, if possible, want to create a space in the classroom where quiet peer conferencing can take place.

Common conferences

Settling on an idea:

- Broad topics can be difficult for children to handle. An early writing conference can be key here, when you can encourage the child to make some general statements and then proceed to something more specific and personal. For example, one boy in the class wanted to write generally about cricket. After conferencing, he decided that he would write about hitting a six for his team's cricket final. This was his 'diamond moment' and his finest hour!

Planning:

- Children will often ask whether they have to include everything that's on their plan. Encourage them to decide how they feel about this themselves as their writing proceeds.
- Sometimes children will be concerned that their plan has ended up being their first draft. You can reassure them that this often happens and that it's quite acceptable.
- Children may sometimes be concerned that their plans are sparser than their peers'. Explain that, if they have talked through their plan with their talk partner and neither of them can see any gaps in their ideas for the piece, then they need not worry.
- Children may ask whether they can take their plans home to work on. We have always found this to be of huge benefit and can be encouraged.
- Children may say they want to change their writing idea or plan. We give children time to plan again, particularly if they are willing to put some time in at home or use other free time to do so.

Drafting:

- When a child says they don't know how to begin, it's often the case that they just need to 'tell' it first. As Michael Rosen (1998) has pointed out, if you can say it, you can write it. Simply asking them to *say* how they would like the writing to start is usually enough of a nudge to get the writing going. We might also give them several suggestions. If they are writing narrative or memoir, we might draw their attention to the types of openings authors typically use and encourage them to experiment on their 'trying out' page with a possible type of opening: *question, action, dialogue, monologue, shock/surprise, description*.
- If the piece has little organisation or logic, ask the child in conference to fill in a planning grid to show where they want their piece to go and to remind themselves of their own intentions. They can then use coloured highlighters to group and re-arrange their information ready for a re-draft.

Part A

- If a child says they don't know what to write next in a narrative piece, it's often because they aren't sure how to move between space and time. They may simply need advice on paragraphing or possibly using a time adverbial to change the direction of their piece.
- Children might ask *'How much have I got to write?'* We always find giving children a limit to the amount they can write (particularly for class writing projects) is advantageous. It's often unnecessary for children to write more than a couple of pages at the very most, even in Year 6. In reply to the question, we will often say *'until you've written everything you've wanted to say'*. This seems to put children at ease. It's good to address the misconception that more writing is better writing.
- If children aren't sure how to end their piece, you can suggest the types of endings authors typically use (*speech, shock/surprise, advice, character feeling, action, uncertain, hopeful/ happy ever after*), and they can then experiment with different endings on their revision and trying out page.
- Sometimes children might just ask your opinion on how their piece is going. You should feel able to give an honest assessment.
- Always tell the child what a professional writer (or you yourself) might do in their situation.

Revising:

- When conferencing during the revision stage, it is always a good idea to encourage the children to simply experiment with revising on their 'revision and trying out page'. If they like what they've created, they can add it in to their main composition.
- You can encourage children to do a complete rewrite if their revisions are very extensive.
- If there is a particular linguistic feature, writerly technique or aspect of grammar you would like to see a child try out, it's always better to ask them to do it on their revision page. They can then make the decision as to whether they want to include it in their composition.

Editing:

- When children first start to learn about proof-reading and editing, they need to understand that you have to read your piece in a completely different way. You should read it almost like a robot, one word at a time, in order to spot errors. You may need to model the technique alongside them. It's always good to have a talk partner or whole group proof-read their pieces together too.
- Finally, giving children a few days away from their writing project can sometimes be helpful before asking them to begin proof-reading it in preparation for publication.

Conclusion

Key points from this chapter:

- Conferences are conversations between writer and writer.
- For conferences to be effective, children need to see you as a trusted fellow writer who is there to help them develop their pieces and not simply judge or correct them.
- Drawing on your own experiences as a writer-teacher when giving advice is advantageous to developing young writers.
- A good conference will have a definite structure, will promote self-regulation and will leave the child with something practical to apply straight away.
- Always end a conference with 'was that helpful?'

They do the hard work so you don't have to

Marking and target setting

Target setting

After a significant conference, you may ask the child to write any compositional or transcriptional targets onto their 'writing target' list. These could be placed in the back of their books, on their desks or in their trays. Whatever you decide to do, they should be easily accessible. They will refer to their targets whenever they finish drafting or editing a piece before handing it in to you and they should try to achieve these targets by the end of the term. The combination of using revision and editing checklists and their writing target list is extremely effective in encouraging children to be self-regulating. You can easily and quickly see patterns in children's writing target lists too. Some teachers will create a class writing target list and have it on display. However you choose to do it, the patterns you see should inform your functional grammar or writing study mini-lessons. Finally, don't make it your responsibility to add to the children's target lists, particularly in the upper years. Instead, get them to make a note of it.

Celebration

It's an important part of community life and of building up children's sense of self-efficacy and confidence that everyone celebrates the achievement of class and individual people's writing goals. Learning to write isn't a competitive pursuit. Goals should be celebrated regardless of a person's experience. We are all developing our craft together.

> Example Writing Target List
>
> Name: _____
>
> 1 *Look at every word, circle those I'm not 100% sure of, and look them up.*
>   Date: 9/20
> 2 *Capital letters on the first word in each sentence and in my title.*
>   Date: 9/20
> 3 *Full stops and capital letters (including all proper nouns).*
>   Date: 9/20
> 4 *Adjectives before nouns: no comma between the final adjective and the noun.*
>   Date: 10/20
> 5 *Listen for and avoid any repetition of conjunctions*
>   Date: 10/20
> 6 *Keep a consistent tense: all past or all present*
>   Date: 11/20

Written marking

Research (Calkins & Ehrenworth 2016; Fisher *et al* 2010; Jean *et al* 2013) indicates that *swathes* of 'after-the-event' written feedback is neither efficient nor effective. As Dylan Wiliam (2011) says, feedback like this is often the equivalent of telling an unsuccessful comedian that they need to be funnier, with Harold Rosen pointing out that 'any idiot can tell a genius they have made a spelling mistake' (Graves 1983 p. 188).

It is our hope then that reading a piece of children's writing will be enjoyable because of the variety of texts you receive and that it will be manageable because children's compositions come in at their own pace rather than all at once. Before handing in a finished composition, children are responsible for editing their own writing against the class 'Editing Checklist'. Do not do this work for them. Consider having a system in place so children know when and where to hand in finished drafts and edited pieces ready for marking.

Finally, just consider the following point from Jeff Anderson (2000): do we take children's paintings and with a red pen comment all over them? We don't. So why do we feel this is OK with their writing?

For more information on assessing children as writers, go to page 111.

A Possible Marking and Feedback Routine During Writing Weeks	
Generating ideas, dabbling and planning	• Provide responsive teaching through mini-lessons. • Pupil-conference throughout this stage.
Drafting	• Provide responsive teaching through mini-lessons. • Pupil-conference throughout this stage. • Only mark drafts when they are finished and as they come in. Children will hand these in steadily over the course of the writing weeks. Mark the writing for two or three **compositional features only**.
Revision	• Provide responsive teaching through mini-lessons. • Pupil-conference throughout this stage. • Children attend to any suggestions you've given them. If they are unsure, they can try out your suggestions on their 'trying things out and revision' page.
Editing	• Provide responsive teaching through mini-lessons. • Pupil-conference throughout the week. • Only mark proof-read compositions when they are finished. Children will hand these in steadily over the course of the writing weeks. Mark the writing for two or three **transcriptional issues only**.
Publishing	• The piece can contribute towards any assessment you are required to give and a photocopy should go into the child's writing portfolio.

Conclusion

Key points from this chapter:

- If you are giving children compliments on their writing, it's better to say it directly, writer-to-writer, during pupil conferencing than to write it in their book.
- Don't mark the children's writing once it's published. Mark it while it's still in process, after drafting or editing, so children can actually attend to your suggestions.
- Use written feedback sparingly; follow up in conferencing.
- Always set writing targets in collaboration with the child and not on their behalf. Children work harder on their targets when they've set them themselves. If the child can write the target down themselves, all the better. Don't write it for them.
- If a child is regularly ignoring an aspect of the writing process or an item on a check-list, sometimes you need to make it a specific focus by setting it as a target.
- If you see an opportunity to set a future target during a conference, take it.
- When you're noticing writing issues across the class, respond by teaching a mini-lesson or by setting a whole-class target.

10 Oh, for literature's sake! How to build reading–writing connections

If we want to attract children like bees to the idea of writing for pleasure, we must treat our classroom as a field and fill it with the sweetest of nectar – good literature. As teachers, we are in the business of creating and modelling environments where children learn the behaviours of life-long readers through our teaching of reading for pleasure (Cremin et al 2014). Basically, our classroom must feel like an inviting library. A place where people come to write and read together. And as we have discussed in our introduction, the promotion of reading for pleasure is vital to the success of our young writers. Therefore, it's surely imperative that we look at the ways these two pursuits meet. What does *literacy* for pleasure look like? Surprisingly, there is very little research on how reading and writing influence each other. However, what we do know is:

- Giving children ample time to read enhances the quality of their writing.
- Allowing children to write in *personal* response to the texts *they* have chosen to read significantly enhances their comprehension of the texts.
- The more children are given an opportunity to write, the more their reading comprehension improves.

(Graham et al 2018)

If we want reading to raise the quality of children's writing, we should give them the choice over the books they might want to take from in their writing. It's important that we teach writing and reading in a connected way and so show children how all writers will use *their* favourite literature and other reading to influence their writing. When writers do this, it's called intertextuality. This is the idea that writing (and therefore writers) will be influenced or inspired by things read, watched or heard. We must first let our young apprentice writers know that this is an utterly natural thing for writers to do and then encourage them to do it for themselves. Children don't only show their comprehension when they write in response to the books they're reading; they give something of themselves to the text too. A fair exchange of ideas is made between the reader and what's read.

In this chapter, we describe some of the best ways of bringing reading and writing together and how you can encourage intertextuality in your classroom. The two most important things to take from the chapter are, firstly, that the children in your class must be allowed to write in *unique* response to their personal reading or, should they wish, to a whole-class shared book and, secondly, that the books children choose to read may be important to them in ways that we as teachers can't initially see. A failure to recognise these two points will result in children only ever being receivers of texts rather than the dynamic creators of a writer and reader self-identity. A literary identity.

> *Yes! Yeah! I want to do it. I just find it very enjoyable and I love reading – so I think it all comes together–I love to read my own books – and it's something I always try to do and I love writing in that sort of way.*
>
> Year 6 Child (Young 2019)

An Example of Intertextuality in Action!

Daisy is in Year 3 and has written a short story called 'Norris'.

She was initially moved to write because she wanted to write about a backpack (she had recently bought a new one and brought it to school). It also came from her hearing *A Huge Bag of Worries* as the class read-aloud. Style-wise, her story makes use of quirky, fantastical little details from Chris Riddell's *Ottoline* books. She also uses some of the 'voice' from the *Clarice Bean* and *Judy Moody* books she loves reading in class so much.

Norris' magic rucksack had been put out in a 'yard sale' – a plot line she has taken from the film *Toy Story*. Daisy has recently been really immersed in *The Worst Witch* audiobooks and also watches the CBBC adaptation of it. These books use a more old-fashioned vocabulary and an 'objective narrator voice' with lots of speech to advance the plot, and this was the style of writing Daisy was now replicating. She also took the names Sweetpea (from *Princess Poppy*) and Drusilla (from *The Worst Witch*) for her own unkind characters.

Daisy carries on telling the story of how Norris was going to retrieve her backpack. Norris and Mimosa decide to put up posters, and this gave her a chance to describe a variety of characters and places on the high street. This particular idea came from a book called *The Fairy Hairdresser*. This is a series of books where the first page always shows a high street inhabited by a fairy tale character waiting for a haircut. Daisy and her two younger brothers are regularly dragged down to the high street by their mum at week-ends. Incidentally, Daisy's mum is also a hairdresser.

Building a reading-writing community by reading aloud

> *The real author of the narrative is not only he who tells it, but also, at times even more, he who hears it.*
>
> **Gérard Genette**

One of the strongest supports you can give your community of apprentice writers outside of writing workshop is to share books. Read texts aloud. If they're short, read them twice. Make time for conversation. Encourage your class to react and discuss what's being read without too much guidance on your part. Remember, children are always ready to turn into story not only their personal experiences but also what they hear and read.

This of course all begins with building an excellent class library. Your library, and all the texts which sit within it, become additional members of your class. To be an effective teacher of writing, you need to know your literature. Your library stock should include poetry, plays, magazines, newspapers, leaflets, information texts, 'faction' texts, picture books, a wide variety of children's literature, your own writing, and the children's own published writing too. Over time, children can start contributing any books from home that they think would serve the class library well. This way, the library really does represent an extra member of the class and its unique personality.

Allow reading time to lead into personal writing time

When children are treated as writers, they gain the ability to read like writers. They hear writing ideas coming from the page. They can even get into written conversation with the book they hold in their hands. By providing time for children to write when they are reading, we give them an opportunity to think on paper about what they are reading.

You don't need us to tell you that any teacher worth their salt allows children to have time for personal reading. We typically give children 15 minutes of reading time at the start of the school day and another 30 minutes of reading time after lunch. Often, we will read a couple of poems just before lunch and then have 30 minutes for our class-read at the end of each day. Children are then asked to take their book home each day and continue reading before bringing it back the next day. Any little pockets of time during the week are also devoted either to more personal reading or else reading aloud poetry or any news or magazine articles which might interest the class.

As we know, giving children ample time to read enhances the quality of their writing; allowing them to write in response to the texts they've chosen to read significantly enhances their comprehension of them. What many of us don't consider is how powerful it is to allow this reading time to lead into some personal writing time. When we do this, children begin to make links. They begin to write in natural response to what they've read. It's a normal and utterly enjoyable process. We also know this is an extremely effective way of teaching both reading and writing (Graham *et al* 2018). Volitional reading leads to volitional writing (Parry & Taylor 2018). Over time, the two begin to merge and it's the most wonderful sight. Comprehension and creative response become one.

Children will respond in lots of different ways. They may simply want to write down why they liked the book, they may dwell on the things that surprised or confused them, they might write down all the things they learnt, what the book made them think about, what they noticed, something about the book they want to share with others or a review, and they may even write about what their friends might think of the book. Then they may use their response, consciously or unconsciously, as a trigger for a story, a poem, a piece of non-fiction or some faction.

Here we show just some of the things young writers will do when given time to write in natural response to what they are reading. It is adapted from the work of Wayne Tennent and his colleagues (2016).

Part A

What Is It Writers Write When They Are Reading?			
Connect With the Book Write using what they know about the book so far. Write something that connects with the themes of the book. Relate parts of the book to their own lives and experiences and write about it.	**Suggest** They may write because they're inspired to make logical, plausible or inventive suggestions as to what could happen next in the book or about a character's personality and intentions.	**Question** Their writing may be a way for them to question the text. They may write in direct opposition to what the book is saying. They may write to share their opinion of the text.	**Clarify** They may rewrite the text in their own way to help them confirm or better understand what's going on.
Summarise They may write summaries for themselves or to share with others. They might write down things they've learnt.	**Think Aloud** Write a few sentences or a paragraph to talk about their thoughts so far.	**Visualise** Draw about what they have read.	**Reader in the Writer** Develop their own text inspired by or in personal response to what they have read.

The importance of personal response

Children's personal responses should be honoured, validated and considered to be of worth. This is not always the case in school. Expressing a personal response, particularly in writing, isn't always legitimised. Whilst at school, many children don't learn that readers will have unique and personal responses to the texts they read. They don't learn that their own lives, thoughts, opinions and memories have a direct impact on how they interpret what they are reading. They are therefore even less likely to know that they can have a personal response to their reading *through writing*. Too often they are asked to simply replicate the teacher's response or voice. The adult's point of view and response to a text is often used, maybe unconsciously, to shape a child's response. Yet when children give a personal response to a text, it stretches them as readers, stretches their comprehension and demands much of their writing. They certainly do not need to be required to respond to decontextualized comprehension skill prompts or sets of questions.

When children write and then share their response to a text, all of a sudden they are exposed to a wide range of understandings, thoughts, opinions and creative reimaginings. No longer should they feel they have to write what they think their teacher wants to hear. No longer do they need to write in response to their teacher's comprehension of a text. It is important to remember that an imaginative written response to literature can also be a personal *critique* of the text (Benton & Fox 1985).

The rest of this chapter will focus on the ways in which we can help children to express their personal responses to what they read, hear and watch and to use them in their own writing.

A personal response can be deepened, refined and shared through writing

> *Through others we become ourselves.*
> Lev S. Vygotsky

During the first few weeks of the year, you will want to be sharing and discussing poems, tongue twisters, riddles and picture books and encouraging children to reflect on the following questions recommended by Michael Rosen (1998):

- Does this writing remind you of anything from your lives?
- Does it remind you of anything else you've seen or read?
- What do you have in common with this writing?
- Why might the author have been *moved* to write?
- Does anyone have any questions they would like to ask the class?

This way, you are already showing children that they can have and express a personal response to a text. This, in turn, can encourage playfulness with thoughts and ideas, and it's this that leads to writing. A few weeks into the year, children will be thinking along the lines of:

- What's the one thing I want to write about this book?
- Cor, I would love to nick that for my writing . . .
- I would love to have a go at writing something like this . . .
- That's reminded me of something . . . and I'm going to write about it . . .
- Why don't I draw, jot and dabble with ideas that come to mind as I'm reading or listening. Maybe it'll turn into some writing – maybe it won't . . .

The reason we suggest you start with poetry is that it always has a feeling of 'universality'. There is always something within a poem, or a line, or a word which sparks in us our own experiences, thoughts or ideas. In poetry, we can always find something of ourselves. It's in this way that you're showing children that you can have a personal response to text. This, in turn, can encourage playfulness with thoughts and ideas that can lead to writing. Once this begins to happen, you can encourage children to write things like *'Inspired by'* poems. In our experience, the best poetry book to introduce children to this idea is *Love That Dog* by Sharon Creech. Then you can begin reading whole novels together, asking just the same questions as earlier. Show your love of language beyond narrative and share newspaper clippings from the local paper, pieces of non-fiction and your own writing compositions (both finished and in process). In relation to non-fiction, you'll start saying out loud things like: *'Isn't that amazing'* or *'That's really sad'*, and the same questions as mentioned earlier will continue to apply. Children can begin to write *their* personal responses to the non-fiction you are sharing. For more information on children's personal response in non-fiction writing, go to our chapter *Thinking through writing: writing across the curriculum*.

Memoir writing

As we read, we unconsciously make connections to our everyday lives and experiences, our feelings, our personal characteristics, our philosophies and morality. Unfortunately, whilst at school, children's unique and personal responses to the texts they read can be undervalued. They are unlikely to learn that they can have a personal response to their reading *through writing*. Too often they are asked to simply comply with and replicate the teacher's response. One way to show children the possibility of weaving their own lives, thoughts, opinions and memories into their writing is through personal narrative or memoir (see page 187), which is of course the writing of personal response.

Once children know that they can story-tell incidents from their own lives, they can weave these same techniques into stories, poems and even non-fiction; they learn that they can rewrite their personal experiences in an utterly fictional way. Autobiographical fiction, non-fiction and poetry will flourish. After all, this is often what professional writers do.

Through memoir teaching, children learn that writing can allow them to share their personal thoughts, feelings, opinions and lives.	The consequence is that children learn that personal responses to their reading can be a source for writing ideas.
Through good reading teaching, children learn that they have personal responses to what they are reading.	They use these personal responses to inform their ideas for fiction, memoir, poetry and non-fiction writing.

We like to use Michael Rosen's *Quick! Let's Get Out of Here* poetry or Jean Little's fictional notebook *Hey World, Here I Am* because children are always easily inspired to find, write and share their own anecdotes in response to these often universal childhood thoughts and memories. Incidentally, here we can sow the seed that we often use hyperbole and artistic licence when we retell our anecdotes to others. The 'facts' of our real-life experiences can be transformed into other things that might happen. Memoir writing then helps children become better story writers, and story writing can also aid memoir writing. (See page 187 for more information on memoir writing.)

Even a single word can elicit a personal response. For example, take the word 'transformation'. Give the definition to your class and ask them what the word makes them think of from their own lives. Does it remind them of anything they've seen or read? Their answers to these two very simple but rich questions can provide them with potential writing ideas.

Finding writing: unearthing writing topics together

Many of us have been guilty of preparing a book-planning 'unit' by reading the book to ourselves and deciding what writing tasks we want children to do in response to it. But this deprives children of the chance to decide this important matter for themselves. They are kept on what Donald Graves (1983) called 'writer's welfare' because they are never taught how writers will use a book *they* have read to inform their writing. Obviously, this needs to be modelled, as many of your children won't know how this is done, but your ultimate aim must be that children begin to do this important work on their own – with their own reading. A good place to start is with a whole-class writing project which focuses on a single text in order to teach the strategies and techniques authors use to generate ideas.

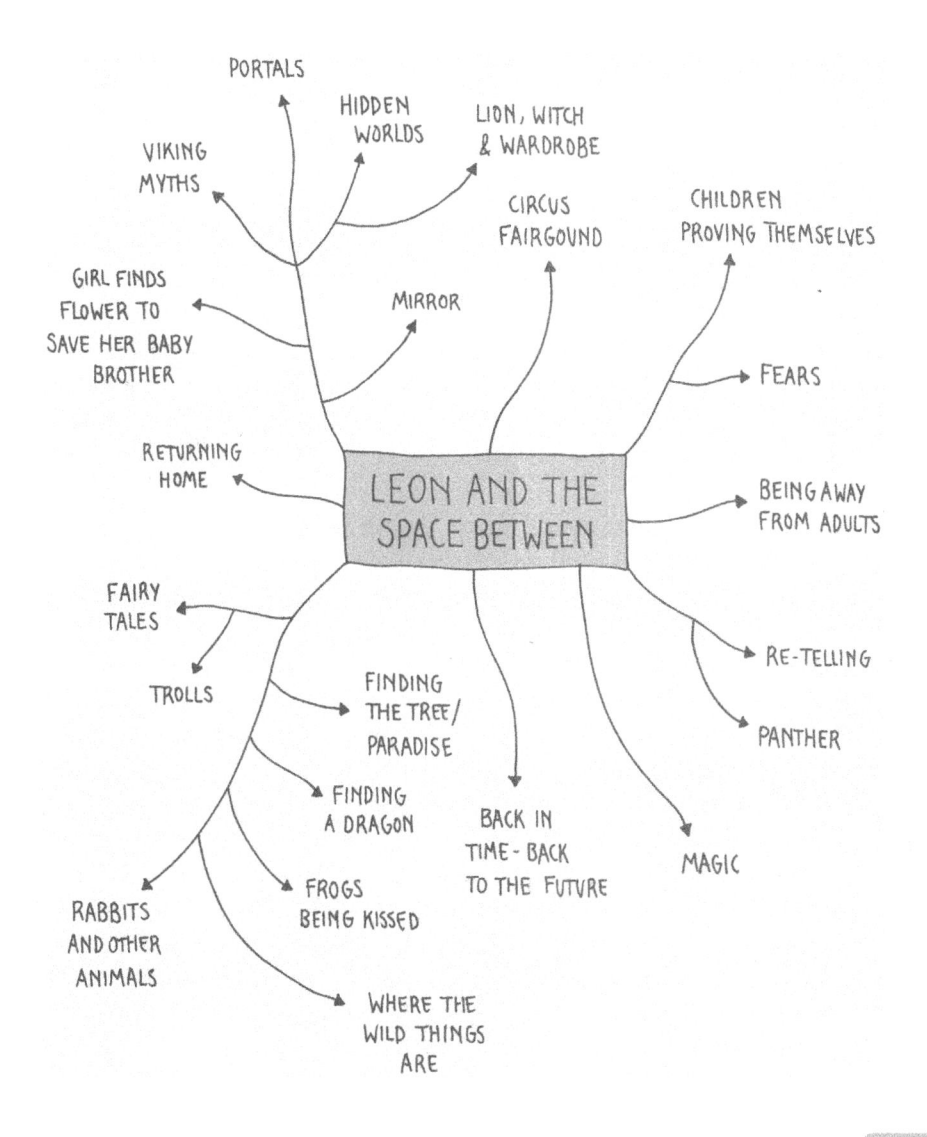

LEON AND THE SPACE BETWEEN

- PORTALS
- HIDDEN WORLDS
- LION, WITCH & WARDROBE
- VIKING MYTHS
- CIRCUS FAIRGOUND
- CHILDREN PROVING THEMSELVES
- GIRL FINDS FLOWER TO SAVE HER BABY BROTHER
- MIRROR
- FEARS
- RETURNING HOME
- BEING AWAY FROM ADULTS
- FAIRY TALES
- RE-TELLING
- TROLLS
- PANTHER
- FINDING THE TREE/ PARADISE
- FINDING A DRAGON
- BACK IN TIME - BACK TO THE FUTURE
- MAGIC
- RABBITS AND OTHER ANIMALS
- FROGS BEING KISSED
- WHERE THE WILD THINGS ARE

Part A

Here is an example of a whole class coming together and answering the Michael Rosen questions. These are their responses to reading the picture book *Leon and the Space Between*. You can see that, as a community of readers and writers, they had many personal responses to the text and generated an abundance of potential writing ideas to explore. The children not only heard how others were interpreting the book's themes but also learnt that you can use others as a source of writing inspiration if you need to. And once the technique had been modelled, the children were able to use it for themselves for the rest of the year. No longer did we have to read the same 30 pieces with largely the same response, and perhaps more importantly than that, nor did the children in the class. Instead, they learnt even more about the book, their peers, the true purposes of reading and of course writing.

You and the children can generate ideas from a text as a whole class, in small groups or as individuals.

Finally, don't underestimate the power of imaginative play. Children can play in response to what they are reading, with their writer's notebooks within touching distance, and when an idea strikes, they can quickly write it down.

Learning to dabble

> *For me, the creative process has to be imperfect, messy, playful, often child-like, often weird. I can't plot or plan too closely. When I start a new story, I usually have a few notions or images. . . . I use notebooks, sketchbooks, pens, pencils, coloured pencils. I scribble and doodle, experiment and play. I allow words and images to flow from my hand onto the page and I'm often amazed by what appears there.*
> **David Almond**

Something changes in your classroom once children are taught how to dabble. Reading and writing seem to mesh together. By now your class library is well established – librarians have been assigned, books from home have found their way into the classroom and children are publishing into the class library on their very own publishing house (see page 35). You and they have been performing and discussing poetry every day. You're all enjoying the class read-aloud. The class are talking about books, recommending books, and now, they are ready to start taking from these texts aspects of the writer's craft, maybe similar themes, language, forms. And making them their own in their own writing.

Personal notebooks are a place for children to undertake personal writing. At the beginning of the year, it's always valuable to teach your class how to use these notebooks (see page 74 for more details). To help them, we show them our own. But how do writers (like us) use their writer's notebook to *'mine'* their reading for potential inspiration for writing?

'Mining' your reading is a way of finding writing. Many of you have done it – you read a passage or a line in a book and it conjures up your own interpretation, inspiration, memories or an idea for how that writing could be used for your own purposes. Well, this can easily be taught to children. 'Dabbling' is often part of a writer's writing process. It's that special space between generating an idea and coming up with a formal plan (if that's indeed how you write).

Build reading–writing connections

As you can see from the earlier quote, children's writer David Almond often talks about his 'dabbling' process. You can model and encourage children to 'dabble' as they read.

Teaching children about dabbling starts like all good writing lessons, doing it all together. For example, show them your dabbles from a picture book you've read. Then maybe read it to the class and ask them to draw or write anything that particularly strikes them. Read it for a second time and ask them to write down any phrases they thought could be great lines for a poem or a story. After this, discuss the things you have noticed, and talk about your drawings a little with one another. Finally, ask the children to try circling their favourite things from their dabbles and give them 10 minutes to turn it into 'something' 'anything'. This is what we call a 'quickwrite'. Quick writing teaches children the habit of getting down to the act of writing quickly and in a low-stakes way. It becomes natural for them to get started. They no longer have to fear the blank page.

What it's about/what I'm thinking

On another occasion, you could ask your children to make two columns in their notebooks before reading them a short-story, picture book, poem or newspaper or magazine article. The first column can say 'what it's about' and the other 'what I'm thinking.' Once modelled and practised together, the class will be able to use this technique for themselves whilst they are reading independently or together. They can consider questions or say things like:

- Did I re-read any parts of the text because it was just so well written?
- Do I want to stop to read any lines that I liked to the people around me because they are just so good!?
- Do I have the urge to copy any parts into my personal writing project book for safe keeping?
- This has given me an idea!
- I could write something like this!
- This has reminded me of something from my life!

Dribbling

A dribble is a story written in only 1 to 20 words. A great way to get children going on a writing idea is for them to write a dribble. A good dribble can often turn into something more once it's given a bit of time. Children will often return to their dribbles in personal writing times throughout the year and turn them into something more.

Being squirrels: inviting children to search and store

Imitation is not just the sincerest form of flattery – it's the sincerest form of learning.
George Bernard Shaw

Very early on in the year, we set some children a challenge to do at home. We ask them to find a line or a passage from a book that has really struck them. We set no other parameters. Children are free to discuss the task with people at home, use the book they are currently reading or use an all-time favourite. We do this not just because it's a great way of getting to know the children in the class, but it prepares them for the work we are going to do that year. You want the children in your class to read texts and exclaim 'I want to write like that!'

Together, over the course of the year, we will all search for great writing in the texts we are reading. We will act like squirrels, nesting it away for the time when we might need to borrow or learn from it. Children enjoy the challenge of supplying the class with a healthy stock of great writing. This is particularly useful if there is a learning point you know you want to cover with the children. Let them know beforehand so that they can prepare. For example, 'We are going to be looking at how writers write great setting description soon, so keep a lookout for any good examples during your reading'.

Over the course of the year, children will be ready and able to supply the class with excellent examples of titles, characters, settings, object descriptions, poetic lines, unusual ways of seeing things, plot ideas, story openers or endings, and voice used in non-fiction, all stored in their writing notebooks.

Instead of looking at a single example chosen by the teacher, the children will look at a wealth of examples that they themselves have found. They will even continue collecting extracts when they are at home. They will begin composing their very own excellent examples which can be shared across the whole class too.

Having a whole-class 'squirrel' book that lives in the library can be a good model for some children and shows them how they can start their own. It can act like a scrapbook. So during reading and personal project time, encourage children to do the following:

- Write 'what it's about/what I'm thinking' dabbles.
- Write down any 'I wish I had written that' lines.
- Write down any spectacular passages.
- Write down any interesting vocabulary.

Finding stories within stories

In every story there hides a hundred other stories.

A great idea generation technique to teach children when undertaking narrative writing is to find stories within stories. The best way to do this is to ask the children to choose two or three books they've recently read or that are particular favourites. Ask them to write down the main plot of the stories, the settings and the main characters. Then they can start looking for connections. Where can they mix and match these elements to create a whole new story?

Hey! Picture this . . .!

In her book, Mary Roche (2014) encourages teachers to beam the images from a picture book up onto the whiteboard while they read the book aloud to the class. This allows children time to respond to the images, which in a good picture book, often provide a different or complementary narrative. Children can be encouraged to share their thoughts with each other, build on each other's ideas and co-create meaning in a democratic, semi-formal process. Roche calls this approach Critical Thinking and Book Talk or CT&BT. It's this kind of discussion that children are so good at channelling into their own exciting and creative writing projects.

Spotting gaps? Use literature

Readers need to read and hear language used skilfully by master writers. The topic for mini-lessons is always dictated by the needs of your class. If you have noticed a deficit or an issue in your class' writing development, a mini-lesson is where you attend to it. Choose pieces of literature or other writings to illustrate the specific technique or strategy you want the children to apply in their compositions and invite them to use it that day during writing time. You should be able to begin a mini-lesson by stating *'the reason I'm showing you this text is because I've noticed that as a class we're not . . .'*. Discuss what the writer has done and how they achieved it. At the end of any mini-lesson, you want one thing: for your children to say *'I can see what the writer is doing – I can do that too!'* This, of course, is radically different from the insistence that children include certain grammatical, linguistic or literary 'features' in their writing whether they enhance the text or not.

Seeing is believing

> *Children . . . will read stories, poems and letters differently when they see these texts as things they themselves could produce.*
> **Frank Smith**

In class writing projects, teachers will typically provide children with exemplar texts with which to learn about a genre. When using exemplars, we can too often be sucked into ensuring children identify the 'features' of a genre instead of focusing on its intentions. A good way to avoid this is to include texts written by yourself or by children you've taught in previous years. Children particularly like hearing about the craft of other young writers as it feels attainable and real. Go to page 42 for more information.

Sharing is caring

It's important that whenever children discuss with us what they've learnt about writing from their reading, we make this public knowledge and give the child time to explain how they made the reading–writing connection. Children need to know it's more than acceptable to try and do what a writer they admire has done, for example things like ideas, characters, style, language, vocabulary or structure. They should of course consider other children's writing. Children need to learn that wanting to copy something a classmate has done really well and has been praised for by others in the writing community is not wrong and is a compliment to any writer.

For example, during 'author's chair', we should ask children where they found the inspiration for their writing. As writer-teachers, we too can share where we have made reading–writing connections in our own writing. Believe it or not, the children's writing will often inspire *you* to write something – tell them so! Finally, when a child's writing reminds us of other authors' work, we can share that connection with them – they'll thank you for it.

Finding a mentor author

Often, when we read a book, particularly if it's from one of our favourite authors, we begin to pick up and use their voice in our own writing. It's important to encourage children to do the same thing. Ask them to choose a writer who they are loving at the moment to be their 'mentor'. Can they copy aspects of the writing or steal parts of it to make it their own? It's worth asking the children what they think is missing from the class library. What sort of writing do they think is under represented? Try challenging them to write it themselves!

Books about writing

It's important that children have an opportunity to be exposed to books about writing. Here is a collection of titles we have found particularly useful and of interest to children. These books can be an excellent way of introducing mini-lessons about the writer's craft too.

How Writers Work: Find a Process that Works for You by Ralph Fletcher
A Writer's Notebook: Unlocking the Writer Within You by Ralph Fletcher
Before They Were Authors: Famous Writers as Kids by Elizabeth Haidle
How to be a Young Writer by Oxford Dictionaries and Christopher Edge
The Best Story by Eileen Spinelli
You Have to Write by Janet S. Wong
Dear World, How Are You? By Toby Little
The Word Collector by Peter H. Reynolds
The Dot by Peter H. Reynolds
How a Book Is Made by Aliki
How This Book was Made by Mac Barnett
My Worst Book Ever! By Allan Ahlberg

What Do You Do with an Idea by Kobi Yamada

Beautiful Oops by Barney Salzberg

The Pencil by Allan Ahlberg

The Story Machine by Tom McLaughlin

How to Write Your Best Story Ever! by Christopher Edge

How to Write Poems by Joseph Coelho

How to Write a Story by Simon Cheshire

Singing for Mrs. Pettigrew: A Storymaker's Journey by Michael Morpurgo

What Is Poetry? by Michael Rosen

Thirteen Secrets of Poetry by Adrian Mitchell

Such Stuff: A Story-Maker's Inspiration by Michael Morpurgo

Conclusion

Key points from this chapter:

- Build a class library which is full of high-quality literature, picture books, poetry, plays, non-fiction, magazines, newspapers, pamphlets, your own writing and children's published texts.
- Give children ample time for daily reading, little and often to keep up momentum. Children should continue reading at home every night and take their book to and from school every single day.
- Encourage children to discuss their personal responses during class read-alouds.
- Encourage children to write *Inspired by . . .* poetry in response to picture books and poetry being read aloud.
- Generate a variety of writing ideas inspired by the texts you've read together.
- Allow children to generate ideas from their reading in groups and, when they are ready, independently.
- Teach children how to write down their own experiences as stories through memoir writing.
- Teach children how to keep a writer's notebook and how to dabble whilst they read.
- Create a culture where the class 'squirrels' away great writing they've read.
- Teach children the technique of finding stories within stories.
- Use great writing to teach mini-lessons.
- Share your own and other children's writing from previous years.
- Encourage children to share and discuss their reading–writing connections during class sharing.

Thinking through writing

Writing across the curriculum

Writing is one way in which we try to solidify the knowledge we gain from reading, listening and our experiences. Therefore, the whole curriculum can provide wonderful opportunities to further develop your community of writers. Everyone can learn to write in new and interesting ways. Devoting some time to writing in other areas of the curriculum gives children a real opportunity to consider their own thoughts and insights about topics and to exercise their critical thinking and self-expression skills. However, too often children are simply asked to 'bark back', as best their memory will allow, what they've learnt in previous lessons. Children are often restricted because they can only write as well as their retained 'background' or 'content' knowledge will let them. They simply become reciters – not writers. However, with the right approach, lessons in other parts of the curriculum can *move* children to write like no other. Children, through writing, can be given intellectual freedom. They can, through the creation of text, re-invent what they have learnt and gain a richer perspective on the world, themselves in the world and how others might perceive the world. Let's remind ourselves of the reasons children are moved to write in the first place and put them in the context of writing across the curriculum.

Teach

What's being learnt can move children to teach others by sharing their experience or knowledge. Also, they may write as a way to teach themselves and to better understand their response by 'writing to learn'. Writing can be our own teaching, as it can provide us with time to think, form our own ideas and so learn more and learn deeper. Within a community of writers, these responses can be shared and so everyone benefits.

- I know a lot about cheerleading and I think it could help out the other girls in the class. (PE)
- I recently went camping with scouts and learnt how to make and look after a fire safely. (Science)
- What surprised me about rivers. (Geography)

Persuade or influence

What's being learnt can often move children to want to share their thoughts, opinions and personal response to the topic with others.

- I don't think the Egyptians could have built those pyramids on their own – I think Aliens did it! (History)
- I think gingernuts are the best biscuits for tea dunking. (Science)
- My family are trying to cut down on the amount of meat we eat to help the environment. (Science)

Entertain

What's being taught can often connect children to stories or passions from their own lives or from the lives of people they know. Telling and writing stories, both real and imagined, are often the way children learn things best. Story-telling can be discovery learning. These stories can be highly entertaining too. Beyond that, some children can be moved to write in role or to create narratives like historic, sci-fi or realistic fiction.

- Finding slugs on grandad's allotment. (Science)
- Viking gods versus Marvel comics. Who would win? (History)
- Escape the volcano! (Geography)
- The story of the sandwich and the digestive system – Warning! Includes poo. (Science)

Paint with words

What's being learnt can move children to show their artistry, their ability to paint images in their readers' minds, to see things differently, to play around or to simply have fun with the subject.

- Goodbye dear friend: the rise and fall of a snowman. (Science)
- Dad, if you keep on like this, you're going to cough up a lung! (Science)
- What if the internet never happened. (Computing)

Reflect

What's being learnt can move children to write in order to better understand the new subject, their response to it or their place in the world. Just as we encourage children to have a personal response to their volitional reading (see page 93), we should encourage children to share their personal response to new content learning too. It may remind them of something from their own lives.

- I wish I lived by the sea. (Geography)
- I just don't understand it. Why did they treat them so badly? (History)
- To fly with the Bird: wanting to be with Eziabella Bird. (History)
- Talking with Dad about climate change. (Science)

Make a record

What's being learnt can, at times, move children to write in order to remember. This can be an emotive record or a record for utterly functional purposes.

- Which melts ice quicker? Salt, sand or chili powder? (Science)
- How to take care of a baby. (PSHE/Science)
- Things I learnt in topic today.

Read–Sketch–Write

We believe the best way to invite children to write in other areas of the curriculum is to use the 'Read–Sketch–Write' writer's strategy. Invite children to read to learn some information on a topic you're currently studying. As they read, invite them to sketch what they are learning about *and* their reactions to it. Once they feel they have enough information or an idea, they can start writing. If you've made the reasons we are moved to write clear – perhaps through a poster on the working wall (pages 4–6), children can then make their own decisions about audience, purpose, content and genre. They will decide which genre will best fulfil their urge to write and they will be working just as writers do in non-school contexts. Of course it doesn't have to be Read–Sketch–Write at all. You could replace it with *watch, listen, experience* but the basic premise remains the same. Too often writing in other areas of the curriculum is assigned just so children can prove to us that they have remembered the content knowledge we've transmitted to them earlier.

Genre-hybrids

As teachers, we must always be careful that our teaching of genres does not result in a loss of creativity for children. We need to ensure that it's children who are controlling their intentions for their writing and that any so called genre 'features' don't end up controlling the child

(Kress 1994). For example, not all of the children's writing examples shown earlier sit neatly within one genre and we as teachers don't need to act like the 'genre police', where we spend our time identifying and ticking any features being used. Writing is often enhanced by the fact that it can serve more than one purpose at a time. For example, a biographer will rarely write without a personal response (either positive or negative) to the subject, and so their writing will carry not only information but also opinion. The poets from the trenches of WWI weren't just painting with words but were also teaching us about the consequences of war. You can't say that when Piers Torday wrote *The Last Wild* he wasn't also teaching us and giving his opinion on the destruction of our planet. Children can and will do this too in their writing and this is a positive development. It allows children to create their own unique meanings to what they've learnt and will, in all likelihood, mean they have a deeper understanding and response to the subject as a consequence.

Subject-specific class writing projects

We believe that since children write every day and in a variety of genres, you can be free to teach the foundation subjects as the disciplines that they are intended to be. In Part B of this book, we provide you with class writing projects which are subject-specific genres. These include:

- People's history (page 279), historical account (page 289)
- Biography (page 284), autobiography (page 195)
- Science report (page 259)

We also provide genres which are regularly used within other writing disciplines such as geography, history, science, art, design, computing, social studies and citizenship.

- Information (page 237), instructions (page 244)
- Explanation (page 248), discussion (page 254)
- Persuasive article (page 275)

The advantage of teaching these genres is that children learn how ideas and experiences are exchanged, how they are subjected to criticism, where misconceptions can be corrected, where new lines of thought, reflection and inquiry can be set up and, perhaps most importantly, how to share a reaction to what you have learnt. They like to engage in the same behaviours as professional writers in these disciplines. This is obviously a move away from simply asking children to regurgitate information delivered in a lesson. When children are asked to do this, the subject knowledge may appear to be learnt, but at the cost of an utter divorce from being *moved* to write for purpose, audience and pleasure.

If you read the opening chapter for the earlier projects found in Part B, you'll see that they give children agency over what they write. The projects encourage them to find something that not only is meaningful but will also give them sufficient motivation and desire to see the writing through to publication. No longer will you need to read thirty identical science reports, thirty information texts about Roman villas or thirty biographies of Mary Seacole.

K-W-L

Another way to generate opportunities for writing is to sometimes produce a K-W-L chart. This is where, as a class, you write:

K: What we know **W:** What we wonder **L:** What we've learnt

You can then invite children to find a writing topic which has particularly struck them and which they may wish to engage further with. Individuals or groups may be inspired to research a topic and produce a piece of writing that answers a specific class question asked in the 'what we wonder' section. Additionally, you may see this as an opportunity to produce a shared piece of writing. Instead of having the children individually sum up the topic of the lesson, you could construct it collaboratively. The benefit of this of course is that children not only learn what good writers do but also learn to expect printed works, even within the disciplines, to be imaginatively and thoughtfully crafted.

Personal response can enhance non-fiction writing

Within all non-fiction there also lies, somewhere, a story that can be told. Children can find writing in other areas of the curriculum difficult because they are often asked to use new and limited knowledge within the challenging craft of writing. They are often denied the chance to draw on their personal responses to the subject because it's seen as not in keeping with the 'type of writing done in these subjects or disciplines'. This is a big misconception.

With the invention of the internet and knowledge being instantly accessible, gone are the days where writers are only interested in dishing out facts within their non-fiction writing. It's often not enough to simply inform. Personal response, personal anecdote and painting with words are not only acceptable, but actually enhance this type of writing. See for yourself. Pick up a contemporary children's non-fiction text and you'll be surprised to find the author doing more than just transferring dead facts. See in how many ways they are *moved* to write on their subject. By allowing personal response to enter cross-curricular writing, it also means that, as a class, you are subject to a kaleidoscope of understandings about the topic being studied and everyone benefits as a result.

Publishing houses

Don't forget your publishing houses (see page 35). They can be a great source of motivation for undertaking writing within the foundation disciplines. The great thing about your independent houses is that every year is different. They reflect the particular quirks and interests of your class that year. You may have a cluster of history buffs, another group of budding scientists or a troop of eco-warriors. They can create a publishing house to represent their particular passions within the foundation subjects and topics.

In Foundation Subject Lessons	
Read–Sketch–Write ⬇ **Acquire new or use existing knowledge** ⬇ **Moved to write** ⬇ **Choose a genre** ⬇ **Start writing**	**Study subject-specific genre** ⬇ **Acquire new or use existing knowledge** ⬇ **Start writing**
• Through reading or other experiences, children gain 'new knowledge'. This **new or existing knowledge can become writing:** 'I've found out something interesting and want to share it with others'. 'I already know something interesting and I want to share it with others'. • **Writing to re-imagine new knowledge:** 'How can I see this knowledge from a different perspective?' 'How can I share it in a completely different way?' Sharing knowledge through genre-hybrid, 'faction', painting with words or narrative – including memoir. • **Writing to learn one's own response:** 'What is my personal response to this new knowledge?' 'What are my thoughts and opinions?'	• Learn a genre specific to a certain discipline (e.g. historians, geographers or scientists). • Undertake independent study within the subject. • Share new knowledge with others using the genre.

Conclusion

Key points from this chapter:

- There are a variety of ways in which children can be *moved* to write in the foundation subjects. These include teaching, persuading or influencing, entertaining, painting with words, reflecting and making a record.
- When children are only asked to regurgitate newly acquired knowledge, the result is an utter divorce from being *moved* to write for purpose, audience and pleasure.
- A useful technique to use across the curriculum is the *Read–Sketch–Write* technique.
- When children hybrid genres, it can often enhance their writing *and* their understanding of the topic or subject taught.
- It's important in your writing to share a personal response to what you've learnt.
- Children like to engage in the same behaviours as professional writers in the subject-specific disciplines. Let them write as historians, geographers and scientists.

12 Assessing your writers

It is possible to carry out your teaching so that assessment can be undertaken in a low-stakes way. We have suggested throughout that, alongside high-quality instruction, children be allowed to work through the writing process organically, at their own pace, producing a variety of pieces independently and for pleasure. The usual alternative employed in schools at present is to hand out a writing task to children and give them limited time to complete it in a high-stakes, pressured environment. Evidence suggests this won't get you the best results (Hoffman et al 2003; Au & Gourd 2013; Barrs 2019).

Keeping writing portfolios

A child's portfolio should include:

- Children's formally assessed and published class writing projects.
- Any published personal projects that children have chosen as their most pleasing and successful texts. You can assess some of these too if you wish.

When children have edited their class writing projects and made them ready for publication, you will have an opportunity to formally assess them. Once assessed, you can talk to the children, in conference, about any possible improvements that could be made, as well as any writing targets they should attend to in future projects. Children should write these targets into their books and then publish their piece. The conferences need not take very long and can be done over a number of writing sessions. Editing and publishing sessions are a particularly useful time to meet and conference.

Writing progression scales

Here, we have attempted to describe and so make explicit what children's development in the common genres can look like throughout primary school. We encourage you to examine children's progress for yourself and see what patterns you notice over time. Let these observations inform your teaching, as they have done for us.

Progression in Story Writing

Early writers

It is useful to see the stories written by early writers in a similar way to their drawings. Their drawings are usually dominated by people or objects. Once these items are drawn, children will often verbally describe some action associated with the object or character in the drawing. The same process is evident in children's writing too.

When asking early writers about their planning, you are likely to be given a general statement of what is going to happen in the story. Planning won't necessarily come naturally to beginning and inexperienced writers, though they might like to talk at length before they write and 'tell' the drawing to a trusted adult or peer.

Early writers will often write retellings of the TV, films, internet media or games they have been exposed to. Alternatively, they will write about things from their own recent past. The chosen characters will often be borrowed from popular culture or may be their friends and family members. It may be that they are yet to experience the pleasure of placing themselves in a fictional story. Their familiarity with the characters means they often don't feel a need to develop them. Instead, they use their writing as a way to 'play' with their characters. They are playing with figurines but on paper.

Their stories are usually limited in scope and are often quite literal retellings, possibly including some basic description, and may sometimes lack a clear dilemma or conclusion. The stories may be written simply to amuse themselves or for the pleasure of sharing what they know about their favourite narratives from popular culture. They may often write for an immediate audience and not consider publication for a wider readership.

In conferences, these beginning and inexperienced writers will typically provide more information about the story verbally than is shown in their writing or in their drawings. Older children at this stage will really benefit from the chance to retell or 'play out' their stories with a trusted adult. These retellings will often exceed their writing ability and they may find putting these ideas on paper challenging, but will nonetheless be motivated to do so. They will require regular reassurance and praise, maybe even after each sentence.

Early writers of narrative often need help with giving their story a clear beginning, middle and end or at least some kind of structure. They can find it hard to manage a whole writing project, so encourage them to talk a lot, draw a lot and break their story down into manageable chunks. Helping children formulate a possible ending before they begin writing can be really helpful here.

At this stage of their development, you can expect to read many 'chain of event' stories, including what happened and who was there, rather than why. Children will also find it difficult to move broadly over place and time and so will tend to include everything that happens in between main events, even if irrelevant for the reader.

There will be little re-reading of the text for setting description and character motive. If children do revise their work, it will be to add in yet more action since this can be seen by the writer as making a story more exciting or interesting.

Fluent writers

Fluent writers' main concern is that their stories are exciting, maybe humorous, exaggerated, interesting to their friends and likely to get an instant reaction. They will set up questions in their narratives that readers will be keen to know the answers to, and they will have understood the need to develop a plotline.

Fluent writers can use exemplars and planning grids to plan and write paragraphs, but their ideas often lead the structure of their writing and so it can lose cohesiveness. They may also like using story maps, drawing their ideas with connected arrows or using a story arc. Once they have completed the planning process, they will appreciate being able to discuss it with their peers. They will be able to use transitional phrases and move between time and place, though not always smoothly.

Fluent writers will sometimes choose plot lines that are too complex for them to control, resulting in their narratives being rushed and maybe clichéd. This probably reflects their reading habits, since they are now beginning to take on longer chapter books and will want to replicate the style for themselves. Fluent writers begin to consider their readership beyond their teacher and are now much more interested in their peers' opinions of their writing.

These fluent writers will begin trying out techniques noticed in their reading. They will focus on creating a strong opening and will often give a basic description of setting, although this isn't usually sustained throughout the narrative. Their character depictions will continue to rely largely on description of physical features and may well lack dimensionality. They may continue to use generic characters from popular culture, but may now be venturing into first-person narratives. Their main concern is still with action and event, and they will need to be encouraged during conferencing to start considering the motives of their characters. Longer pieces may finish abruptly, due to a lack of stamina or being uncertain how to formulate the ending.

Experienced writers

More experienced writers begin to see that narrative writing can be a form of escapism – a way of placing themselves in fictional situations and perhaps to 'socially dream'. They begin to weave what is true to their life, or what they wish were true, into their fictional characters and fictional worlds. At this stage of writing development, children's obsession with plot begins to move towards character-driven narratives. They extend their writing beyond simple physical description to how individual characters might behave, what they think, how they feel and how they converse with others.

They will plan using planning grids and appreciate the importance of having an ending in mind, even if this is not to be set in stone. As always, they will appreciate being able to discuss the plan with their peers.

Experienced writers are able to weave plot, setting and character description and dialogue together as they construct their narratives. They are now beginning to understand how narrative can be an effective way in which to express yourself and your own feelings. They are able to write cohesively, use transitional phrases and move between place and time with ease.

Experienced writers are beginning to view their role as writer in similar ways to that of a film director or a camera operator, panning their words across the screen to reveal to their reader what is occurring. Their settings are beginning to be written in such a way that they become additional characters in their stories. They begin to pay particular attention to openings and endings and will revise them repeatedly until they are satisfied with the result.

Children's writing at this stage really begins to be informed heavily by their reading choices, and their own writer's voice and personality is starting to show. Children may consciously or subconsciously begin to place themselves or the people they know in their characters. They will also begin to experiment with creating original characters, using dialogue appropriately to push the story forward or to reveal important messages about the character.

Experienced writers can use 'show not tell' effectively. They will begin using rhythm, rhyme, alliteration and other sound effects appropriately and perhaps unconsciously. They have stamina for writing, but at times write pieces that are too long and rambling. They are often reluctant to cut these pieces down during the revision and editing stages of the writing process!

Advanced writers

Advanced writers begin to complain that the planning grids are limiting and say they want to devise their own way of planning that gives them more freedom. They are likely to use their personal writing notebook to collect notes from their reading about possible characters, settings and plots. They may collect favourite lines, poetic moments, effective dialogue – anything they think may one day be useful to them.

Children at this stage will have their own stance as a writer; they write and then read their own writing with a sense of purpose and audience. They have a well-developed writing process and their own ways of working.

These writers will write strong openings as well as genuinely interesting and unexpected endings to narrative pieces. They will choose topics that are honest and which invite them to express strong feelings and show their personality. They are now casting a wider net and allowing a range of fictional genres to enter into their writing. You will begin to see more examples of realistic, political and historical fiction. They may write on social issues that matter to them either implicitly or explicitly. You may also find they are more subversive and want to push the boundaries of what is conventional within literary traditions.

Advanced writers will readily manipulate fantastic sentence constructions, poetic and figurative language, ideas and words from the books they are reading and use them for their own purposes. They are taking regular opportunities to 'paint with words' within their stories. There is a real variety in sentence use, structure and type and this is beginning to develop quite naturally. They have embedded the concepts of character development and setting description into their writing habits. This includes creating and sustaining empathy with their characters, using internal reflection and making links between their growing understanding of people and their wider knowledge of the world.

You may well find at this stage of writing development that children are inventing characters who are older than themselves. Their settings may be personified and reflect and affect their character in profound ways. A character's mood will have a direct impact on how the setting is seen and described. Their stories will usually offer a message or something to think about. They will imitate their favourite writers almost unconsciously. Finally, they are able to use flash-backs, create tension, atmosphere, character flaws and symbolism, hint at wider meaning and give clues as to what might happen next. They can also tell more than one related story within a single narrative piece and present different points of view.

Progression in Memoir Writing

Early writers

Early writers will often find memoir the most comfortable genre to write in, and they will thoroughly enjoy sharing anecdotes and vignettes from their lives. With this said, their oral retellings will often be far more vivid than their written pieces. This is because they will still see the writing of personal narrative (such as memoir) as recounting, rather than as a type of story-telling. This will often result in 'and then' retellings that focus solely on who was there and what actions took place when.

When conferenced, these beginning and inexperienced writers will typically provide more information about their subject verbally than they show in their writing or indeed their drawings. Older children at this stage will often require regular oral retelling with a trusted adult. These retellings will often exceed their writing ability, and they may find putting these ideas to paper challenging but will still be motivated to do so. They will require regular reassurance and praise, perhaps after the writing of every sentence.

Beginning and inexperienced writers of memoir will feel they have to include every part of the experience they have decided to write about. This can include mentioning or listing things which are largely unimportant. They find moving between place and time difficult.

Fluent writers

Fluent writers can use exemplars and planning grids to plan and write cohesive paragraphs. However, their ideas seem to lead the structure of their writing, which as a result can lose cohesiveness. Fluent writers will sometimes choose subjects for their memoirs that are too large for them to control. They lack a focus or a 'diamond moment'. For example, children will write about their 'day at Thorpe Park' as opposed to a particular significant moment during the trip.

These writers can begin to get tangled in long, complicated pieces that are difficult to manage. This usually reflects their reading habits, since they will be beginning to read longer chapter books and so will want to replicate these sorts of stories for themselves. Fluent writers begin to consider their readership beyond their teacher and are now far more interested in their peers' and others' opinions of their writing. Where writers in the earlier stage tend to see their writing as an extension of themselves, by this stage they have a greater need to make their writing work for others. They will often want to write down episodes that will get a response from their peers. Other children's pieces will spark in them a desire to express an anecdote of their own, on the same subject.

These fluent writers will begin trying out techniques they have noticed in their reading. They will give basic description of settings, particularly in the opening scene, but this may not be sustained throughout the memoir. Their character descriptions will continue to largely rely on physical features. Longer pieces may run out of steam or finish abruptly, due to a lack of stamina or being uncertain about how to end.

Experienced writers

More experienced writers can now attend to memoir as story writing. They will consider plot, character development and setting description.

They see their role as a writer in a similar way to that of a film director or camera operator, panning their words across the screen to reveal to their reader what is occurring. Their settings start to be written in such a way that they, too, become additional characters in their memoirs. Experienced writers are able to understand that story and memoir blur and that writers will often use artistic licence, bending the truth or using hyperbole to tell a better story.

Their writing is starting to be informed heavily by their reading choices and their writer's voice and personality is also beginning to show. They may show an interest in reading and writing realistic fiction at this stage. They may consciously or subconsciously reveal parts of themselves in their memoirs: their hopes, fears and thoughts about their lives, past, present or future.

Experienced writers can use 'showing' rather than telling effectively. They will begin using rhythm, rhyme, alliteration and other sound effects appropriately and perhaps unconsciously. They will have stamina for writing but at times write pieces that are too long and rambling. Children at this stage are often reluctant to cut these pieces down during the revision and editing stages of the writing process. They will begin focusing on a topic, give weight to significant moments and develop characters and settings. They will readily revise their titles, openers and endings. Their memoirs may begin to reveal deeper significance about the events they are recounting and their thoughts about them.

Advanced writers

Advanced writers begin to complain that planning grids are limiting and say that they want to devise their own ways of planning which give more freedom. They will have their own stance as a writer; they write and read their own texts with a sense of purpose and audience. They have a well-developed writing process and their own ways of working.

They will write strong openings, as well as genuinely interesting and unexpected endings to memoir pieces. They choose topics that are honest, express strong feelings and display their personality. They may well use the themes and techniques of memoir as the inspiration for non-fiction writing, including persuasion, explanation, discussion, information and instructional writing.

Advanced writers will readily manipulate fantastic sentence constructions, poetic and figurative language, ideas and words from the books they are reading and use them for their own purposes. They will imitate their favourite writers almost unconsciously.

They have embedded the concepts of character development and setting description into their writing habits. This includes creating and sustaining empathy with their characters and making links between their growing understanding of people and their wider knowledge of the world. Their memoirs will usually offer a message or something to think about, will contain flash-backs and will tell more than one related story or shared multiple perspectives within a single memoir.

Progression in Non-Fiction Writing

Early writers

Beginning and inexperienced writers will often write about the books, TV, films, internet media or games they have been exposed to. Alternatively, they will write about things from their recent past. They may run the risk of choosing an attractive topic but one they know too little about. Alternatively, they will know a great deal about their subject but will assume too much knowledge in their reader, resulting in an unclear text. Their information pieces may sometimes turn out to be more in keeping with personal narrative and vignette.

When conferenced, they will typically provide more information about their topic verbally than is shown in their writing. Older children at this stage will often require lots of talk with a trusted adult. These verbal explanations will often exceed their writing ability, and they may find putting their knowledge to paper challenging but will be motivated to do so. They will require regular reassurance and praise, maybe after the writing of each sentence. They will use technical vocabulary relating to their chosen topic, but may also assume that their reader will understand the terminology without explaining it.

These writers will find 'chunking' their information into sections difficult. They are likely to throw their information at their reader in a long list of facts, without any kind of orientation. They will often fail to finish non-fiction texts adequately.

Fluent writers

Fluent writers will know what makes a good topic for non-fiction. They will know that they need to have some depth of knowledge to share with the writing community They will often write at length about their subject but fail to always keep the reader in mind, resulting in a lack of clarity or cohesion.

Fluent writers may begin to play more with modality, picking up on how non-fiction texts are designed in the books they read in the class library. They may begin to add captioned pictures, diagrams, tables and other non-fiction devices, including bubble writing, 'key facts' and 'did you knows'. They are now able to divide their topic into sub-topics and use headings for cohesion. They may also begin to merge non-fiction genres together. Their endings will draw conclusions, suggest ways forward or ask questions of their readers.

Experienced writers

Experienced writers are now motivated to ensure that their readers understand their information clearly. They will classify their subject of choice before moving on to discussing its nuances. They are also beginning to include descriptions as well as definitions for technical vocabulary that their readers may not know. They may include information collected from a variety of sources, including personal experience.

Experienced writers may begin to use formal and informal voice as well as figurative language and comparison when describing phenomena. They will take part in writing 'faction' and will begin to naturally mix non-fiction genres together. They can maintain their focus on their topic, give weight to significant moments and develop their own and others' thoughts on a particular subject. They will also begin to reveal their personal response to their subject, providing personal anecdotes and feelings about their subject that really bring an extra dimension to their writing. They conclude their pieces well, leaving their reader with a final insight to meditate on.

Advanced writers

Independent and advanced writers begin to complain that planning grids are limiting and say they want to devise their own ways of planning. They are willing to delete the parts of their writing that impede the cohesiveness of their piece and will add content at the request of their peers or teacher. Independent writers seek the opportunity to play around with non-fiction genres, deliberately turning them on their head in new and creative ways.

Advanced writers' non-fiction writing is usually able to lead their audience the whole way, keeping them on track and ensuring that their thoughts and ideas are easy to follow. They can write formally or informally with ease, even within the same piece. They will use examples to imply relationships between different phenomena or to clarify their point. This includes using figurative language and use of imagery as a means of explanation or description. They will also use other sources to back up the points they want to make. They may quote sources and provide a list of references for the reader.

Independent writers will re-organise material to improve sequencing. They have complete control over their writing and use subtleties and nuances of language that evoke all the senses and leave their reader genuinely in awe, entertained, thrilled, persuaded and informed, often all within the same piece. Their conclusions will ensure that possible actions, challenges or implications are all considered by their reader.

Advanced writers are able to write with an individual style and voice in non-fiction texts. They can explain with clarity and express depths of meaning using figurative language or personal narrative.

Reporting on children's progress

Using these descriptions enables you to assess individual pieces of writing, but more importantly, they give you the ability to profile a young writer at a particular point in their writing life and record the progress and development of both the writer and their writing using a portfolio of their work. It also enables you to give valid suggestions for how the young writer can develop next year with their new teacher. Here, you can see an example of what such assessment could read like. The example shown could be typical of a 9–11 year old writer. You'll see that it begins by addressing the writer herself.

You've read over 40 books this year Emma. Your favourite one though has been *One*, a story about conjoined twins. You naturally took to this because you loved finding out about other people's lives. One of my favourite pieces that you wrote this year was your flash fiction 'I Remember'. You created a moment in time about a Native American girl and a cowboy who were swept up in the troubles of different cultures. It was powerful stuff and involved dreams, flash-backs and discord. It was complex and layered – and easily some of the best composition in the year group. You always have a way with words which places the reader exactly in the moment. You're a very talented writer. Thank you for a wonderful writing year.

Emma is an experienced writer. She has a clear writer's voice. She writes and reads with a real sense of purpose and audience. Emma can write strong leads/openings alongside genuinely interesting and unexpected endings to narrative pieces. She often chooses topics which are honest, have strong feelings and show her personality. Emma is now casting a wider net and allowing a range of fictional genres to enter into her writing. She can handle writer's block and has strategies to work out where to go next. She can use humour appropriately, take risks and engages in wordplay. Emma is always willing to give writing advice during Class Sharing. I like that she will 'magpie' ideas from her reading and adapt them for her own purposes in her writing. There is a real variety in the sentences Emma uses and this includes all the grammar and linguistic features taught this year. She has embedded the concepts of character development and setting description into her writing habits. In poetry, Emma is able to give more subtle meaning and not write so literally. Her paragraphing often goes beyond those suggested in our planning sessions. In non-fiction, Emma can inform, persuade and entertain her readers, ensuring that her meaning is clear and cohesive. When revising, she focuses not only on what she is saying but how she wants it to sound. Emma is now willing to delete parts of her writing which are irrelevant or unsuccessful to the cohesiveness of her piece and will revise content at request of her peers or myself. This can involve taking a whole new angle – elaborating here, slowing down the action there. She is diligent at finding and fixing transcription errors in her writing. As a result, fewer errors are making their way into her published pieces. There is evidence she is regularly using spelling strategies.

For Emma to develop further, she should consider character development becoming the main driver to her stories as opposed to plot. She should also be deliberately stretching and 'hybriding' genres in new and interesting ways. Looking to go beyond the usual text types to create something fresh from a different perspective, this could include using narrative or 'faction' to discuss a political or historical subject. Because she is so talented, Emma's writing should continue to act out on the world – looking for opportunities for her writing to go beyond the classroom.

13 | Supporting early, advanced and EAL writers

How to support early writers

Every child deserves to be treated as a writer. Never assume the world is divided into people who know how to write (professional and recreational writers and grown-ups) and those who don't (children). The purposes of writing are utterly inclusive. All children, regardless of their needs, have something to say in terms of knowledge, memory, feeling, interest or experience and so they also have something to 'write'. Every child can write, even if it is only mark making and verbal explanation to start with. If children can say it, they can write it. Very young writers do this quite happily and when asked what their marks mean can often explain with complete clarity. What stops children from writing as they get older is often a preoccupation with correct spelling, being required to write about something they do not know much about or are not engaged with, being asked to navigate all the processes of writing simultaneously, and the lack of a future audience for the piece.

Early writers can be of any age; what we mean is that they are 'early' on in their experience of writing. Adjustments can be made to support children with SEND and with EAL who are also early writers. See page 111 for more details on progression descriptions.

For early writers, we suggest that the writing process be simplified to the following three stages:

Planning ▶ Drafting ▶ Publishing

You can expect children's writing process to progress over time as follows:

1. Story-telling > Drawing and talking > Writing
2. Talking > Writing
3. Moving toward conventional planning, dabbling and revision
4. Planning, revising and basic editing

How to set up writing workshop for early writers

Working alongside an adult

It is important for all children to see adults writing for real purposes and being *moved* to write. By watching and working alongside an adult, children can see that writing is worth doing. It is particularly beneficial for early writers to work alongside a sympathetic adult co-writer. This includes taking some time to read aloud and *tell* stories with each other before they begin writing.

An adult can co-write on a computer with the child or allow the child to write. Slowly wean them off these strategies once they are motivated and ready to write independently. It is important they have a reader in mind at the earliest moment in the writing process. It could be their best friend, the class, another class, their teacher or a family member. What is important is that they are writing for someone.

Generating ideas

Telling stories

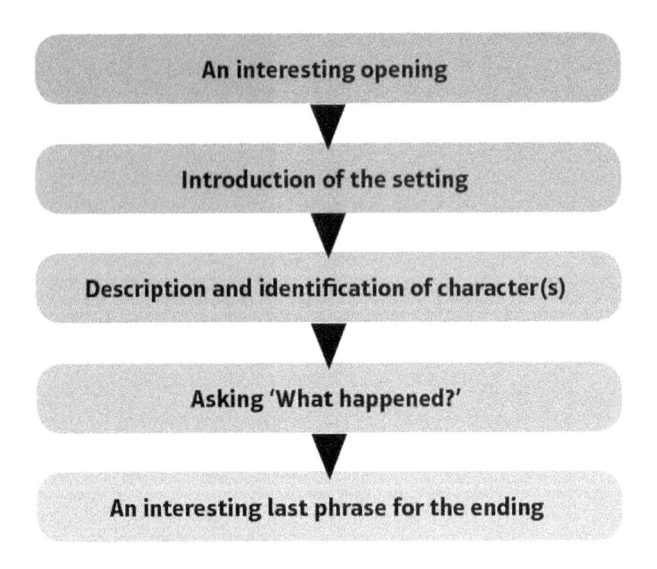

```
        An interesting opening
                 ▼
       Introduction of the setting
                 ▼
 Description and identification of character(s)
                 ▼
        Asking 'What happened?'
                 ▼
   An interesting last phrase for the ending
```

Play and story-telling can take place either alongside or instead of a drawing. The stories you tell and encourage the children to tell are often about true personal experiences. You can create a really strong bond with all the children in your class by doing this, but particularly in relation to the sorts of writers that you will be working with intensively. These children will soon realise that they also have stories to tell. When telling stories, particularly with early writers, the above sequence will help them learn about the linguistic and genre patterns and features of narrative and memoir.

The importance of personal writing project books

To become fluent and experienced, early writers need to be writing more than anyone else in the school. Therefore, encouraging a child to write in their personal writing project book is vital. They should be carrying it around with them everywhere and filling it up, often with drawings but sometimes with writing as well. Personal writing project books should be going back and forth between school and home.

Parents or caregivers can assist writing being undertaken at school by supporting the following at home:

- Tell stories to one another.
- Encourage their child to treat their personal writing book like a scrapbook by sticking in interesting artefacts.
- Encourage their child to draw in their personal writing book.
- Together, write down any potential writing ideas.
- Write in it together.

Treasures from home

Personal writing project books can be accompanied by artefacts and pictures from home, including playthings. Children can then use dramatic and imaginative play as a source for writing.

Planning

Drawing

Children can plan or rehearse for writing by drawing. In our eagerness to see writing on the child's page, it is easy to dismiss these picture stories; but do so at your peril! Drawing a topic immediately allows the teacher and the child to discuss what the drawing is about, teasing out lots of information and then dabbling with key words, phrases or ideas. Writing captions over the picture and labelling the who, what, where, when and why onto a photocopy can certainly be seen as an early version of planning and helps set many children up for drafting. Another big advantage to drawing is that it focuses the child's attention on a single moment in time, that 'diamond moment', rather than creating a long repetitive 'and then . . .' story or memoir.

Talking

Children become less reliant on drawing as time progresses. This is a significant developmental shift. Talking about their ideas will eventually replace drawing them and precedes conventional planning. Encourage children to write down any spoken 'dabbles' onto paper before they lose them. This is a sign of early planning.

Drafting

Something to be tolerant of is the extent of a child's writing stamina.

Paragraph Piling and Sentence Stacking

Some children find navigating the writing process quite challenging. You can make the process more manageable by encouraging them to draft, revise and edit paragraphs one at a time. It is the same with the process of Sentence Stacking, but instead of composing, revising and editing a whole paragraph, the child goes through this process for each sentence.

Spelling

> *There is little point in learning to spell if you have little intention of writing.*
> Frank Smith

Early writers often believe spelling to be their biggest obstacle. To limit the impact of this, all children, but particularly early writers, should be encouraged to use 'temporary' 'invented' spellings if they need to whilst drafting their pieces, using whatever knowledge they have of letter-sound correspondences. The important thing for children to realise is that once they know even a small number of letter-sound correspondences, they can invent any spelling they like. The idea here is to get them drafting happily and smoothly.

If you can, make available a letter-sound board. Children can then see the letter-sounds displayed, often with a matching picture. Children should also have access to a 100/200 or 1000 common word spelling list. Over time, you will want to move children away from using letter-sound correspondence to counting and writing down the syllables they can hear in the word that they want to spell.

Revising

The earliest sign of a child being ready to revise their composition is when they begin to alter their drawings to reflect what they are about to write. Encourage children to alternate between their writing and drawing, making changes to *both*. Children then further develop their revision skills by attaching extra information, often to the end of their pieces and usually as a result of talking with a peer or an adult. Often this information will not make sense structurally but should be seen as an important developmental step.

Eventually, you can begin to discuss with early writers where their writing is leaving you 'reader hungry'. This is where you can feel your belly rumbling whilst they are reading – because your belly wants more detail from them to leave you satisfied!

Mini-conferencing

Early writers often need you to repeat back the sentence they have just written. When this happens, children will often reply with more information. This is where the revision 'gold' is to be found. After a child says something extra to you, they will often return to their piece of writing and add that information in.

Editing

This stage should come last and should not be too overwhelming for the child. Work on tentatively introducing the basics to children, like capital letters and full stops, using a personalised editing checklist. Notice and celebrate the conventions any early writer uses independently and any errors they spot and correct. These are added to a list glued to the inside front cover of a child's writing book. An example is given here:

> **Things Anna can do:**
> 1. Write her name on her book.
> 2. Write the title in her book.
> 3. Write the date in her book.
> 4. Begin each sentence with a capital letter.
> 5. Use speech marks.
> 6. Use a question mark at the end of a sentence.
> 7. Use a full stop at the end of a sentence.

Publishing

Publishing does not make an appearance in our early writers' process, as early writers often do not like the idea of having to copy out what they consider to be a finished piece. Instead, the chosen final draft can be taken straight to publication by an adult helper. When publishing, it is wise to correct the child's invented spellings so that the piece can be read by them and others easily. You should also support a child's writing by asking them to sit in the author's chair and read their published story out loud to the class. To help you, consider enlisting the aid of parent-helpers who are often very happy to help type up and publish children's manuscripts for them. Incidentally, knowing that one of these helpers will need to understand their manuscript gives children extra focus when editing their writing too.

How to support advanced writers

You will sometimes come across children who have huge experience and skill in the craft of writing. These children need to be developed and supported too. Here are some suggestions you might want to pass on to such writers to experiment with.

Create a community of authentic writers

- Create a small peer workshop environment in which you as the teacher can write with other mature, experienced writers.
- Consider ways both home and school writing can merge and influence one another. For example, these children will need to feel they are living a literate life. They should be encouraged to take and use their writer's notebook everywhere they go.
- Allow children the freedom to use their own writing processes and ways of producing and publishing their final written product.

Genre experts

Encourage these writers to move away from simply taking part in the class writing project as normal, and instead ask them how they could actively hybridise or subversively manipulate it. You may even want to share with them pages from Part B of this book before they begin writing.

Connecting their reading with their writing

- **Collecting:** words, sentences, poetic moments, themes, trying out types of openings and endings, metaphors, characters as metaphors, collecting psychological or philosophical ideas to become plots, characters or settings for narrative writing.
- **Acting like a film director:** In narratives, use flash-backs, multiple perspectives and changing perspectives; consider 'camera angles'; use delay; try out different chronology and use of tenses and consider pace.
- **Reading for pleasure and 'with rigour':** Build a reading for pleasure culture in the classroom and home. Provide children with books and exemplars that could showcase particular teaching points and provide 'rigour'.

Developing their narrative writing

- Help children understand what psychological or philosophical points they want to make through their narrative first, then building or disguising this idea within their characters, settings, objects and events. For example a plot, character and setting that deals with *fear*.

Or the philosophical idea that *the end always justifies the means* or *people and the environment must be able to live peacefully together.*

- Give children time to dig deep into the consciousness of their characters. Encourage some of their writing to be character rather than plot-led. Even mature and experienced writers will too often make up a character to advance their plot and don't try to explain and authenticate them. Therefore, they should interrogate their character until they know everything about them and why they do the things they do.
- Know about and use a variety of story arcs.
- Help children appreciate that narrative is made up of structural units of 'description', 'dialogue,' 'monologue' and 'action'. Children need to be able to develop these units in both an individual way (almost as pieces of poetry or art in themselves) and as part of the collective whole.
- Encourage children to see the descriptions they use as always being affected by the mood of their characters and their present feelings. For example, a character would describe all the details of a party differently depending on whether they were in a good or a foul mood.
- Children can check the variety and length of sentences by actively looking at pace and flow.
- Children's writing could deal with the abstract as opposed to the concrete. It's the difference between *autumn* and *that specific autumn day* or *happiness* rather than someone's *specific* happiness.
- They can be encouraged to revise their piece multiple times. No aspects should be left untouched or underappreciated.
- Suggest to children that they could write part of their piece from another character's perspective. Remember, character can include personified setting too. Alternatively, children could try to write the same piece but from the point of view of a different person (first, second or third).
- Encourage children to experiment with chronology. The stories could be photocopied and paragraphs cut and moved around (for example, placing their ending at the beginning of their narrative). Children can also experiment by writing alternative openings and endings and choosing a favourite.
- Show, don't tell. You could encourage children to cut out words like *is, was, are* and *were* as these encourage telling, and replace them by showing your readers what is happening instead.
- Be playful and silly with words. Use puns, alliteration and repetition.

A quick note on non-fiction

- Children should seek the opportunity to play around with non-fiction genres and deliberately mix different non-fiction genres together.

- Children should classify their subject of choice before moving onto discussing its nuances.
- They can turn non-fiction genres on their heads in new and creative ways. They can take part in writing 'faction' and can also include rich poetic descriptions as well as definitions for technical vocabulary that their readers may not know.
- Children can begin to use the formal *and* informal voice as well as figurative language when describing phenomena.
- Children shouldn't be afraid to reveal their personal response to the non-fiction subjects they write about; providing personal anecdotes and feelings about their subject really brings an extra dimension to their non-fiction.

Mature and experienced writers who may lack confidence

There are children who are mature, experienced writers yet struggle to settle on a piece. These children should be a high priority for daily conferencing. If they have a particularly strong draft, you can encourage them to share it during class sharing time. Encourage the rest of the class to ask questions to give these children the chance to reveal information they know but have failed to include in their piece.

Supporting writers with EAL

The principles of effective practice as outlined in Chapter 1 naturally support writers new to English. For example:

- Children feel reassured by the consistent routine of mini-lesson, writing-time and class sharing (see page 63).
- They feel reassured by the consistent meta-language that is used to describe aspects of the writing process and the writer's craft.
- They have daily time in which to practise speaking, reading and writing in English.
- Because they are choosing their own writing topics, they are able to write from a position of strength. You can talk together about the content of their writing, thus helping you get to know them and supporting their language learning and vocabulary development.
- They can be encouraged to use drawing as a means of sharing what they are writing about with their peers and encourages conversation.
- Class working walls and other resources should include a visual representation or diagram of what any writing is saying, ensuring all children can access the resource.
- Children learn, through daily class sharing, how to work together and talk with one another. We recommend that children new to English write and talk with *two* others as

- opposed to being one in a pair. This not only gives them more opportunity to listen to others but gives them two people to engage with.
- In author's chair, children can read out their writing or have someone read it for them if they are too shy. This increases their feelings of confidence and being a valued member of the writing community (see page 71).
- Children learn about conventions and grammar quickly through daily mini-lessons and can be invited to try them out during that day's writing time (see page 66).
- They can be given lots of opportunities to write and talk in both their first language and in English. Their first language can then make a valued contribution to the writing community too.
- Through personal writing notebooks, children's home languages can enter the classroom easily and their English learning can also be seen at home.

Conclusion

Key points from this chapter:

- Real-World Writers is an inclusive approach and supports even the most inexperienced and early writers.
- Telling stories to an adult and drawing are good sources for the generating of ideas with early writers.
- For early writers, drawing can be a great technique for planning.
- Early writers can struggle with the demands of the writing process. This means they should focus on composition and transcription separately.
- It's vital that early writers be allowed to use invented spellings whilst they draft.
- Advanced writers often need specific support and particular instruction.
- Advanced writers should be encouraged to actively subvert and manipulate class writing projects.
- Advanced writers need to be pushed in their development of narrative by considering the psychological and philosophical background to their writing, digging deep and interrogating their characters, treating each paragraph they write as a work of art in its own right, and experimenting with chronology and different perspectives.
- Advanced writers should be encouraged to bring their personal voice into non-fiction.
- The principles of effective practice as outlined in Chapter 1 naturally support writers new to English.

Growing a school of extraordinary writers

Advice for writing coordinators

We know from research that having a consistent approach to the teaching of writing across school is vital to children's pleasure and academic progress (Young & Ferguson in press). The *Writing Is Primary* (2009) project explained the importance of having a dedicated writing coordinator in school. Alongside this, a school needs 'writing champions'. These are staff members who are positive advocates for writing and for young apprentice writers in the school. They seek ways in which to give writing a high profile in school, the local community and beyond. It's useful for these writing champions to set up a special interest group. Ideally, this would be linked to the school's or a local teachers' writing group (see page 138).

It's important to recognise that an evidence-based writing approach such as Real-World Writers is going to be new to many at your school. There will be excellent practice taking place in every classroom in the school and it needs to be listened to and shared. What's good is that many will be able to 'see themselves' and some of their practice outlined within Real-World Writers. However, schools rarely have a unified, consistent approach or a complete understanding of the best practices for teaching writing. Therefore, expect this approach to take some initial time and effort to implement, but remember, any meaningful effort never feels like a struggle!

One thing that might make Real-World Writers challenging to implement (at first) is that many teachers are not confident in their writing teaching. For example, they may have hang-ups carrying over from how *they* were taught to write or they may never have seen teachers teach writing effectively. This is why we suggest you take your time with implementation. Try introducing practices slowly and get together regularly to assess the impact they are having as a school.

Another exciting but initially daunting aspect of Real-World Writers is the new roles that are assumed by both the children and teachers. Children have more responsibility and ownership over their writing than teachers will be used to. Teachers have a more democratic role, spending a great deal of time working and giving instruction to individual children or small groups rather than directing the whole class all of the time. They will be planning and teaching more responsively to the needs that arise in the writing workshop throughout the week. These new roles can feel strange at first, but with practice they will become positive, affirming and highly effective. It's vital that the benefits of a consistent approach are supported and articulated with clarity by senior management. They must be convinced of the benefits for improvements in writing teaching to become realised within the school.

What's important in developing writing for pleasure and raising attainment across a school?

- Developing a shared understanding of why we are *moved* to write, of the recursive nature of the writing processes and what good writing is.
- Your school policy needs to be more than a list of generic statements about writing. It should give specific examples of what your school considers to be good practice and how children's development as writers takes place over time.
- Staff need to appreciate the benefits of a reassuringly consistent whole-school approach to writing and have a shared vision of what good writing teaching looks like.
- Full engagement of the headteacher and senior leadership in the process of practice improvement. We know this improves children's educational outcomes.
- Focusing on the affective domains of effective practice, namely self-efficacy, agency, motivation, volition, writer-identity, self-regulation and writing for enjoyment, satisfaction and pleasure (see page 9).
- Networking, continued professional development and teachers teaching teachers.
- Teachers do not have to believe they are excellent writers but they must confidently model writerly behaviours to their classes. All staff must identify as teachers who write in *some* way, even if some acknowledge reluctance and apprehension. *All* staff and children are on a writing journey together.

What needs to be done

- Produce an agreed definition of what 'writing' is and what it means to be an apprentice writer.
- Create and share a whole-school strategy for teaching writing.
- Undertake classroom trials and action research. This includes reporting on new approaches, resource evaluation, staff role-play and peer-observations.
- Teachers could read and share examples of practice at **www.writing4pleasure.com**.
- Know how class writing projects progress through the different year groups, ensuring children build on their knowledge and skills from previous projects learnt (see page 29 for an example).
- Develop teachers' understanding of what it is like to write in a writing workshop environment and to develop their own practice as writers. This is best achieved through a special interest group or setting up or joining a teachers' writing group (see page 138).

What you're going to need from senior leadership

- They need to buy into and understand the importance of having a whole-school strategy for teaching writers. They need to give you their full engagement.
- Enshrine the importance of developing writers in a formal school policy.
- Appoint a writing coordinator and recruit at least one member of the teaching staff to the role of 'writing champion'.
- Provide Continued Professional Development for all staff, particularly peer-led CPD. Allow opportunity for new practice to be regularly reviewed and discussed. Allow teachers to observe teachers.
- Be willing to make a long-term commitment and make significant changes in practice slowly.
- Encourage teachers to set up or attend a teachers' writing group and join it themselves.

Join our free professional development website

If you feel you need training or advice, please do get in contact with us or visit our website at **www.writing4pleasure.com**, where you'll find lots of free resources and examples of research-rich practice from other schools. The website also includes a free teacher and whole-school audit which you can complete to help you decide what aspects of writing teaching you might need to focus on. This can then help inform your school improvement plans and staff training.

The benefits you can 'sell' to teachers and senior management

Here we share the concrete benefits of teaching through the Real-World Writers approach.

- You have a clear whole-school approach and system for teaching writing which children will internalise and apply quickly. This means what is taught in one year aids teachers and children in the following year(s).
- Planning time is significantly reduced (see page 63).
- Marking is more manageable and enjoyable (see page 89).
- You create highly motivated and self-regulating writers. Children enjoy learning to be writers and are enjoyable to teach.
- Through mini-lessons, teachers are able to teach in response to the needs of their individual class. Responsive teaching is efficient and therefore highly effective (see page 64).
- Teachers get to meet regularly with every child, giving them tutor-like individualised instruction and targets (see pages 80 and 88).

- Early identification of individual learning needs is possible, with targets set quickly and regularly monitored.
- The approach is based on evidence supported by both Ofsted (2009, 2011, 2019) and the DfE (2012).
- The approach is based on what scientific evidence says are the most effective writing practices as well as case studies of what it is best performing teachers of writing do (Young & Ferguson in press).
- Teaching the foundation subjects can be free of the need to devise associated writing assignments. Topic lessons can be shaped differently and more authentically (see page 104).
- Teachers feel they are teaching in the right way: teaching children how to be actual writers instead of simply producers of writing.

Questions that are worth asking yourself

1. How does a child's knowledge and development as a writer progress through the school years?
2. Do children know and enact the different reasons we are *moved* to write? (see pages 4–6)
3. How are you preparing children for a possible (professional, recreational or functional) writer's life after they leave school?
4. How does developing as a writer in your school positively impact on children's personal development?
5. How is children's development as writers connected to other parts of the curriculum? (see pages 91 and 104)
6. How does the school encourage the affective domains of writing for pleasure? (see page 9)
7. How does the development of writers in your school reflect and honour the local community?
8. How are class writing projects sequenced and organised? (see page 29)
9. How do children understand what and why they are writing?
10. How are children with SEND and with EAL supported in developing as writers? (see page 121)
11. How are advanced and highly experienced writers supported? (see page 126)
12. What do teachers need expert subject knowledge in to teach writing effectively?
13. What pedagogical knowledge do teachers need to teach writing effectively? (see page 16)
14. How do you check pupils' understanding and set future writing goals?
15. How do you ensure key knowledge and skills about being a writer become part of children's long-term memory?
16. What will children have to show for themselves at the end of their time with you?

Finally, when aiming to develop a school of extraordinary writers and to deliver world-class writing teaching, everyone needs to be on board. Some teachers will understandably be worried about change, perhaps fearing that their existing ways of working will be threatened or that they may not be capable. Such teachers need to be reassured by SLT and by their other writer-teacher colleagues. However, you cannot let teacher resistance deter you from developing an approach based on the principles outlined within this book. Real-World Writers will transform your apprentice writers as they begin to write with purpose, pleasure and power and learn what it means to write for real.

Conclusion

Key points from this chapter:

- It's imperative that your school has a designated writing coordinator.
- You need to work closely and over time with senior leaders to ensure success.
- Other staff members should declare themselves 'writing champions' whose role is to find opportunities to maintain writing's high profile in school, within the local community and beyond.
- Many teachers, for a variety of reasons, are not confident in their ability to teach writing. You'll have to take school change slowly and continuously evaluate the effectiveness of that change.
- Join or set up your own teachers' writing group. More information can be found in Chapter 14.
- Visit our website, **www.writing4pleasure.com**, and download our teacher and school audit to find out what aspect of writing teaching your school might need to attend to first.

15 | A guide to becoming a writer-teacher

Teachers who perceived themselves as writers offer richer classroom writing experiences and generate increased enjoyment, motivation and tenacity among their students than non-writers.
Teresa Cremin & Sally Baker

As you may have noticed when reading other chapters, developing yourself as a writer-teacher will be beneficial to the success of your classroom practice. You will talk with your apprentice writers, suggest strategies for them to try, set process and product goals together and advise them on their compositions. You will be doing this through pupil conferencing and mini-lessons, but it will also happen naturally through the creation of a community of writers. Being a writer-teacher does not mean you have to be good at writing, but it does mean that you join and become a member of your community of writers, writing alongside the children when possible.

Why be a writer-teacher?

- There is no way of helping children to see themselves as writers if you yourself are not interested in it. You must demonstrate to your community of writers that you believe writing to be interesting, utterly possible, enjoyable and satisfying. Teachers who are not themselves members of their class writing community cannot effectively model how to be part of it. In essence, if writing is important to your life, children will think it is important to their lives. You have to show that you have personally experienced writing's benefits.
- Just as it would be difficult to teach children to play the tuba if you've never played it yourself, you are going to find it harder to teach writing and how to be a writer if you don't do it yourself.
- Writer-teachers write in the hope of better understanding how to build writing communities. For example, by creating or joining a writer-teacher group, you know how a writing workshop behaves and what it feels like. When teachers and children write together, everyone in the writing community sees everyone else as a learner and a teacher.
- Writer-teachers write to ensure they can talk with children about writing authentically and from a position of empathy and experience. Children trust and listen to you when they know they are about to learn something from a fellow writer rather than from a

teacher. They trust that the advice, tip, trick or secret you're about to give is coming from someone who has been there themselves.
- We underestimate the influence school policies or assessment arrangements have on our teaching of writing. There is no better way to understand the consequences your writing pedagogy has on your apprentice writers than to write yourself under the same conditions.
- In a more traditional way, through shared writing, writer-teachers model and make visible the normally invisible processes that occur whilst writing by showcasing the inner dialogue that writers often undertake whilst crafting.
- Writer-teachers model how writers' reading material can often move them to write for themselves.
- Writer-teachers write to share their own writing goals with their class and the variety of ways in which they are *moved* to write. This can help generate agency and showcase the power of personal writing projects.
- It helps you see how you rely (either positively or negatively) on your own history of being taught to write. It's too often the case that our childhood writing experiences provide us with no comfort or encouragement in writing now as adults.
- Most importantly, writer-teachers write because of the pleasure it affords them and because they want to share this pleasure with their class.

How to be a writer-teacher

I immersed myself in writing for pleasure, and brought my pleasure into the classroom. The effect was palpable. I saw my lived life become an educative experience.
Doug Kaufman

The hardest thing in becoming a writer-teacher, particularly if you lack confidence or are tentative about the idea, is to shake off how you yourself were taught writing. The first question, then, is to ask why *don't* I write? The shadows of our writing past can lead us to believe that writing is a mythical gift that is simply bestowed upon lucky people. We can also believe that all writing is high-stakes and always has to be highly accomplished. The real fact of the matter is that it can be quick, easy, low-stakes, successful and done for fun. It is a craft. If you're nervous about setting up a notebook or becoming a writer-teacher, here are a few things to try:

1. Write a list of reasons you *don't* write. Then try and attend to them.
2. Don't ever assume you can't write or that you don't write well. You're an apprentice writer alongside the children in your class. You want to improve too. Accept and celebrate the fact that some children in your class may well write better than you. Take and learn as much from your community of young writers as you give to them.
3. Don't always put high expectations on your writing endeavours. You don't have to write with a view that it will be seen by anyone. It's good to ignore the 'phantom reader' who you feel is judging your writing. A reader beyond yourself doesn't have to exist if you don't want them to.

A guide to becoming a writer-teacher

4 Get yourself a notebook. The more notebooks you have, the better, and in a variety of sizes.
5 Have a notebook with you at all times and always within touching distance. Don't ever say to yourself that you'll remember that writing idea and write it down later because you'll always forget it.
6 See writing as being like doodling. Try out dabbling as a technique (see page 98).
7 Write dribbles. Dribbles are pieces of writing that can only be a maximum of, say, 20 or 50 words.
8 Take inspiration from children. A good place to find writing ideas is in children's compositions. If you like a subject or idea a child has written about, why not use it as a template for your own writing?
9 Write on your phone using a note-taking app. A good way to start is to write a little something the moment a writing idea strikes.
10 Write down lines or phrases you like from your reading or from the things you hear people say.
11 Write up funny anecdotes or episodes you talk to your friends about. Usually, the stories we share with friends or loved ones are also things we can write about.
12 Consider starting a journal. You don't have to write in it every day, only when something significant comes to mind.
13 Try using Peter Elbow's (1998) 'free-writing' technique. This is where you write non-stop, whatever comes to mind, for 10 minutes. Then comb this writing for anything you think might be worth developing further.
14 Find a writing habit which works for you (see page 60).
15 If you don't like where your writing is going, abandon it and move on. Regard it as simply practice.
16 Have a moment in the day where you sit down and write *something*.
17 Purchase books about writing. We can certainly recommend:

   a *A Writer's Notebook: Unlocking the Writer Within You* by Ralph Fletcher: HarperCollins
   b *Discover Your Own Literacy* by Donald Graves: Heinemann
   c *Bird By Bird: Instructions on Writing and Life* by Anne Lamott: Anchor Books
   d *Writing Without Teachers* by Peter Elbow: Oxford University Press
   e *100 Ways to Improve Your Writing* by Gary Provost: Penguin Books
   f *The Art of Fiction: Notes on Craft for Young Writers* by James Gardener: Vintage Books

14 Join or create a writer-teacher group.
15 Join our writer-teacher Twitter community by using the hashtag #WritingRocks

How to share your writing with your class

When we write live, in front of our class, we give children the impression that they are simply to copy what we have written. And probably the impression that writing comes easily. Live writing is done under pressure and is often phoney (Hillocks 1986). However, when sharing an example of your writing with your class, you can engage in rich discussion with them about your intentions, how you kept an eye on your audience, the craft decisions you made and the strategies you employed. In turn, they can ask you questions about it. So how do you discuss your writing with children?

1. Talk about the purpose and audience you had in mind when writing. What did you want the writing to achieve or do to the reader? How did you want people to react?
2. Children will want to get into a conversation with you about your writing. They want you to tell them how you developed the piece. Where did you get the idea? How did you do that? Why did you do that? Share with them the writing tricks, tips and secrets you used to make the piece happen.
3. They may want to emulate your intentions and the spirit of your writing and to try out the strategies and techniques that you used, but with their own writing ideas.
4. An exemplar written by you can give children a feel for the writing project they are about to engage in and what it is going to look like as a product at the end. They are able to see for themselves what the ultimate goal for the project is.
5. Be sure the show how your writing looked at different stages along the way towards publication. This helps children understand how writing develops over time and processes.

Creating a writer-teachers' group

The perfect place to start if you're considering setting up a writer-teacher's group is by reading *Introducing Teachers' Writing Groups* by Jenifer Smith and Simon Wrigley or by joining an existing group. You can find out whether there is a local group near you by contacting the National Writing Project at **nwp.org.uk**. Another good resource is to join us on one of our writing retreats for teachers. To find out more, go to **www.writing4pleasure.com**.

Early on, establish a regular time and place to meet. Some groups like to meet once every week while others will meet once every half term. Next, send out an invitation. It's good to send out an initial invite to *all* staff explaining the structure and a brief rationale behind the group and to send out regular reminders about your next scheduled meeting.

This is a good routine to follow during group meetings:

1. **Writing time.** Start with a short writing exercise or some free-writing to get people warmed up and ensure everyone has engaged in some writing. Popular exercises can be found on the National Writing Project website. Alternatively, there are a lot of idea generation techniques in Part B of this book.
2. **Sharing time.** Invite the group to discuss and share any of the writing they have undertaken or are currently undertaking since the last meeting. People can also discuss their process and ask for advice on their developing compositions.
3. **Discussion time.** It's good to end the session by discussing how your development as writers is impacting the ways in which you teach your apprentice writers in school. People can also share good teaching practice from their classrooms.

We recommend that it's always a good idea to bring cake to meetings! Once people get comfortable with the format of the meetings, it's good to devote one to discussion of your own writing histories. Invite group members to think about how they were taught writing. First, how many people in the group consider themselves to be writers? Of those, how many attribute this to having a good writing teacher? How many good writing teachers did they have over the course of their whole education? For those who don't consider themselves writers, why might this be the case? What can be learnt from your own writing histories in terms of how you want to teach writing now? To keep things fresh, we also recommend that the group occasionally takes part in some paired or collaborative writing.

Conclusion

Key points from this chapter:

- If writing is important in your life, children will think it is important in their lives.
- Take and learn as much from your community of young writers as you give to them.
- Being a writer-teacher involves more than simply doing the occasional shared or model write.
- Writer-teachers write and develop alongside their class and so talk from a position of empathy and experience.
- Writer-teachers model how to make connections between their reading and their writing.
- Consider how you were taught writing and what impact that had on your feelings towards writing now.
- Experiment with notebooks and find a writing process that works for you.
- Join or create a writer-teacher group.
- Attend a teachers' writing retreat.

16 Frequently asked questions and answers to them

When you teach children through the Real-World Writers approach, you may be asked questions by colleagues or senior leadership. This is because writing workshop and its associated practices are often unfamiliar to many educators, despite research consistently telling us that it is the most effective way to teach writing (Young & Ferguson in press). It's also very different to how many teachers were taught to write themselves. With this in mind, we have supplied you with answers to the typical queries we've heard raised in the past.

It's important that people know that the Real-World Writers approach isn't new. It's based on extensive educational research and on what it is the best writing teachers do that makes the difference (Young 2019). It is also based on a contemporary reimagining of *writing workshop*, an approach which is very popular and successful around the world. If you find colleagues are still unsure, invite them to come along and sit in on one of your writing sessions – as long as they bring their writer's notebook with them too!

Meeting potential objections

Handing over writing choices to the children will lead to anarchy in the classroom and a drop in standards

The Real-World Writers approach is a cohesive and carefully conceived pedagogy based on 14 principles of effective practice. These principles are the result of three literature reviews, spanning 50 years of research and involving well over 300 pieces of literature and research on the subject of teaching writing (Young & Ferguson in press) Therefore, Real-World Writers does not advocate for a naturalistic or a 'hippie-free-for-all' approach (Hillocks 1986). Quite the opposite. It requires continual and skilful direct instruction from expert teachers of writing. So let's be clear. Giving children agency over the subjects for their writing and their writing processes does not imply that regular direct instruction from the teacher is not necessary, nor does it mean that maintaining reassuringly consistent classroom routines ceases to be important. Real-World Writers does not advocate for permissive classrooms. Instead, the classroom should be a rich combination of creative writing workshop and the professionalism and attention to detail of a competent publishing house, so as to ensure the highest standard of writing is being produced.

Real-World Writers doesn't care about the quality of children's written products

Whilst we advocate for children discussing and generating their own ideas for class writing projects, it simply doesn't follow that teachers will accept low standards in terms of a final written product. Quite the opposite. Because these projects are serving real audiences, they must be of the highest quality. This means teachers sharing their own and others' writing and identifying what the class will need to do to ensure that their pieces are successful and meaningful. For example, collaboratively discussing and setting product goals is extremely useful. Children are encouraged to write in such a way that they are motivated for their writing to be the best it can be, in terms of both composition and accurate transcription.

I don't have time to give all the children individual attention

To free up time for the teacher to conduct regular pupil conferencing, children need to be able to work independently. This requires high-quality teaching of self-regulation strategies and good classroom organisation. Firstly, resources must be well-organised and understood. Secondly, if children are engaged in writing something meaningful to them, on a subject of their own choosing, they will show a higher degree of focus and will find it easier to get on by themselves, particularly once they have learnt the writing processes and the routines of daily writing. Real-World Writers is based on creating responsible, confident and independent writers.

There isn't enough time for writing every day – We have to teach the basic skills like handwriting and grammar

Authentic and daily application of skills is efficient and effective. When writing makes sense, when it is done for a real purpose, handwriting, spelling, punctuation and grammar are felt by the writer to be relevant and useful. Handwriting practice can be meaningfully absorbed into publishing time. Grammar and punctuation should be taught through daily mini-lessons and can be applied immediately in the subsequent writing time. Spellings can be attended to and discussed during the editing stage.

I'm sure this suits middle-class children but our children won't have anything to write about

There is no lower expectation than believing children have nothing to write about. According to the educationalist John Taylor Gatto, children are already adding value to the world around them by age seven. The author Willa Cather stated that most of the basic material a writer works with is acquired in childhood. Writer-teacher Lucy Calkins tells us that, whilst we can't *give* children rich lives, we can help them see the richness their lives already have. Writing is an important tool for encouraging self-affirmation. If we don't allow this, children quickly learn the life lesson that writing is to be consumed or simply imitated. They will leave school mystified, intimidated and believing that writing and being a writer is immutable – certainly for them. Real-World Writers recognises that children may need help to find their own writing subject, and we suggest many techniques which children can use for idea generation (see Part B). Encourage children to discuss and share their ideas with others, look at other children's published pieces for inspiration, engage in book-talk and draw on their favourite books, family stories, school topics, poetry and the news as ways of finding a topic. Our writing study lessons also introduce planning, dabbling and inclusive ways of developing ideas.

I don't feel happy with the things my children choose to write about

It is important to remember that, at this stage in children's writing lives, not all of their topics will prove to be 'hot' or ground-breaking on *your* terms. However, they will nonetheless be continually practising and honing the craft of writing until a topic that is special to them does come along – just like professional or recreational writers do. Additionally, children don't always write for adults and with their tastes in mind. However, it's surely vital that children are learning that they are *producers* of content and not simply *consumers* of their teachers' writing ideas or desires. The fact is teachers' perceptions of legitimate writing are too often the dominant culture in classrooms and are actually overvalued, while children's cultures are persistently and systematically undervalued. Children don't write about trivial things – if we look closely enough.

Violence is just one example that can be an issue for some teachers. Of course, William Shakespeare wrote violence and he always had very good reason to. A rationale. A metaphor. A comment on something deeper. This is something you shouldn't assume isn't happening in children's compositions, and you can certainly discuss this and any other themes with your class if or when they decide to flirt with challenging subjects. The key is to simply ask the children why they choose the subjects they sometimes do. These can make great PHSE and critical literacy lessons. However, it's important that you do far more listening than telling. It's our opinion that a child can write on a 'controversial' subject, but they must write about it well and learn from the best. Share good examples of how you, other children or indeed other writers have written about contentious subjects and done it successfully, entertainingly and tastefully. Ask children to write challenging stuff – maybe stuff that makes you uncomfortable – but insist that they make it worthwhile and they make it good! Ultimately, though, this comes down to your judgement as a professional. Finally, if you're interested in reading more around the subject of challenging topic choices, we can recommend Ralph Fletcher's *Guy Write* or any of any of Anne Haas Dyson's work.

What about writing exercises?

Many writers use writing exercises to practise their craft or just to have some fun with some low-stakes writing. But to base your writing curriculum on such an approach will not be profitable because it doesn't allow children access to the purposes of writing or what it really means to be a writer. It also adversely affects children's motivation. Therefore, we suggest that any writing exercises or 'drill-skills' be used only very occasionally rather than become the norm.

What about book planning and novel study? Real-World Writers doesn't seem to care about teaching literature

On the contrary. We believe it's right to care deeply about literature and to teach children to care about it too. We know the joy of showing children how they can use the literature they love to inform and inspire their writing. Professional and hobbyist writers talk about how their own volitional reading has led to profitable writing – so we should allow children the same chance too. When we as teachers choose the text, we are actually taking literature out of children's hands. We become the gatekeepers of its meaning. By imposing our own choice and comprehension of a single text, as the centre of a book planning project, and by tethering arbitrary writing assignments to it, we run the very high risk of sapping children's enjoyment of and response to that book. Indeed, Cremin *et al*'s (2014) work has shown children don't like this sort of approach. By teaching this way, many of us end up spending huge amounts of time teaching the 'stimuli' and not how to have genuine response to the book. For more information, see page 91.

What happens if a child writes about a sensitive issue?

The journey you go on from 'assigning' writing to 'teaching' it is an exhilarating one. What is wonderful about Real-World Writers is that it challenges children to write about topics that they believe only *they* can write about with authority. Children delight in having something 'over' adults, and their topics often include subjects such as joyful or bittersweet moments, pretending, rites of passage and looking up to older children. However, there will be some occasions when children decide for sadder moments to enter the classroom too. Because they have felt able to, in the past, we have had children choose to write about things such as the death of pets, illness in the family, parents splitting up, disabilities, nightmares, fears and the death of loved ones. You will need to be sensitive when children make the decision to put these thoughts on paper. You should never pressure or encourage them to pursue such topics, but neither should you actively discourage them. We are sure some teachers have had incidents where children disclose something through writing. Remember that this is sometimes the only way in which children feel they can reach out to you as their teacher about problems they are having. Writing can be a safe space for those who don't always feel comfortable talking. This is a positive thing. You're teaching your class something valuable. You should obviously always follow the appropriate procedures if a child discloses something in writing that is a possible safeguarding issue and trust your professional judgement.

What happens if children don't feel part of the writing community?

What do you do when this happens on the playground? You talk about it. In our experience, when children write about their lives and become a strong, close-knit group of apprentice writers, they are actually far more inclusive, understanding and caring towards their peers. We also found that incidences of bullying went down.

Doesn't the idea of a personal writing notebook going to and from school mean that school is invading children's home writing spaces?

Personal writing should never be treated as a homework task. No one would argue that inviting children to take a reading book home from school invades their home reading space – it supports it. Why should this be different with writing? The Real-World Writers approach doesn't intrude upon children's home writing – it supports it. For example, according to Clark (2017), only 17% of children ever write something that isn't for school. Through Real-World Writers, you will change this. Children can have their eyes opened to the possibility that writing can be something they do at home and at school for pleasure.

There's no one way of teaching writing that suits all children

Chapter 1 of this book explains the inclusion of those enduring and universal elements of good writing teaching which have remained visible for fifty years and in a variety of contexts. And as we show in chapter 12, the Real-World Writers approach is highly responsive to the needs of all the children in your class, whether they are early or advanced writers, writers with specific needs or those who are simply reluctant or tentative. It gives them effective instruction and then offers agency over choice of topic, planning, writing process, style, pace and purpose and provides support at every level for each member of the writing community to become a confident and independent writer. For example:

- Class writing projects invite and help all children to be playful and to manipulate and hybrid different modes of writing.
- Mini-lessons respond directly to the long-term and immediate learning needs of both the whole community and its individual members and can be repeated as many times as necessary.

- Pupil conferencing means that every child can receive high-quality tuition from a writer-teacher in a short space of time.
- Writing goals and targets are jointly agreed on and thus differentiated to suit individual writers.

Since the need for a consistent approach is widely acknowledged, why would you cherry-pick from a variety?

Common misconceptions about teaching writing

Some children just don't like writing

When children claim not to like writing, it's often because they don't know how to do something. Their self-efficacy (the feeling that they can do it!) and self-regulation (I know what to do and how to do it!) is low. For example, *'I don't like writing because I'm not good at it – I don't know how to describe things'*. This child needs a writing study lesson explaining why and how writers go about 'describing things', give the child a resource or technique that will help them out, set them the goal of working on their description and praise them once they've applied it to their writing. This helps builds their sense of self-efficacy and self-regulation; these two things, along with agency, are the kindling that lights the fire in children to want to write and to feel like a writer.

Children need to know in detail what they want to write before they write it

Not necessarily – just ask Peter Elbow (1998). Writing sometimes develops in unexpected ways. A random opening line can be the catalyst. Children may even to decide to switch to another genre during their writing process. For some children, the most successful writing process can be that of an 'Adventurer' (see page 60).

Correct spelling, grammar and punctuation are as important as content in a first draft

As we have described, attention to transcription, editing and writing targets are fundamental in developing writers and creating the highest-quality writing products (see pages 60 and 88). It's important that children know that published writing needs to be made 'reader-ready' so as to ensure it's respected and easily understood by the intended readers. However, children can only cope with so many processes at once. Asking them to attend to transcriptional issues while at the same time trying to compose a first draft is a sure way of ensuring that neither is done particularly well. Instead, teach children to separate these processes by being Vomiters, Paragraph Pilers or Sentence Stackers (see page 60).

Long is better than short

This is not always the case, particularly with young apprentice writers. We recommend at most around 250 to 350 words for a piece. Teach children that a sentence should contain no unnecessary words and a paragraph no unnecessary sentences and that the removal of text is an approved practice. You want quality, not quantity.

Revision and editing are the same thing

Not at all true. **Revision** is literally the process of re-seeing the text, when children should be considering their subject, the focus, the development and their voice within their piece. They may need to expand on something they have said the first time round. This is where you can discuss some of the linguistic or literary features or structures typical of the genre the children are writing in. **Editing** is linked to precision and the conventions of grammar, punctuation and spelling.

To revise a draft, first identify everything that's wrong with it

Children who are good writers seize on what is working well in their piece and develop it further. They do not only confine themselves to correcting the 'problems' in their piece.

17 Terminology

Adventurer: Someone who doesn't plan and is instead adventurous and dives straight in. They will see where their first draft takes them and will often use it as a plan for their second, more cohesive, draft.

Advocacy journalism: A journalistic article that champions a cause, idea, movement or charity (see page 272).

Author's chair: A place where a child can read out and so share their writing with the class (see page 71).

Class sharing: Time that's allocated for children to share their writing with others either in pairs or in groups.

Critical literacy: The practice of reading and writing with a view to considering how texts are socially constructed and represent a certain view of the world. It's also about reflecting on where the power resides within a text read or created. For example, how are money, class, family, sexuality, gender, ethnicity or cultural heritage represented in the texts we create and read?

Dabbling: The process of playing around with drawings, words, phrases, thoughts and ideas on paper to develop an early writing idea.

Diamond moment: The focus for a piece of writing. The vital part that requires the most focus and attention. The heart or spirit of a poem, story or memoir. The area of focus in non-fiction.

Distant goal: Defining what the writing project's ultimate aim is. The final goal. These goals are heavily related to authenticity, purpose and the audience for the writing. Where will the writing end up? How will the writing be 'put to work'? For example, where will it be published? Where will it be performed?

Drafting: Putting down on paper or screen, for the first time, the writer's intentions for their piece.

Editing: Attending to the transcriptional aspects of writing, including error hunting. This process includes checking capitalisation, use of vocabulary, punctuation and spelling, in preparation for formal publication of the writing piece.

Fable: A short story, usually involving animals or children, that conveys a moral message (see page 200).

Field: The subjects or content usually used by writers within a chosen genre.

Flash fiction: Sometimes called 'micro-fiction' or 'sudden fiction', flash fiction isn't just a very short story. It is only a flash moment, often part of a much larger untold story, a story where a great deal is left unexplained. It is typically no longer than 1000 words, but it can be as short as 100 words (known as a 'drabble') or even 50 words (known as a 'dribble'). See page 232.

Functional grammar teaching: An approach to the teaching of grammar that involves sharing and applying the functional purpose and use of certain grammar or linguistic devices. The teaching structure is usually introducing a feature and its functional purpose; sharing real-life authentic examples of the particular feature in use; discussing its effect in a piece of writing; then inviting children to try using it in their own writing (see page 66).

Generating ideas: The process of mining one's own mind for potential ideas/topics for writing, considering the value of each topic or idea and putting these ideas on paper.

Genre: Forms of writing that have particular purposes and intentions and usually follow certain conventions, styles, formats and having grammatical, linguistic or literary features that make them identifiable or effective.

Historical account: An explanation text that aims to account for, or explain why, something has happened in the past, using evidence to support the explanation (see page 289).

Imagism: The technique of not writing explicitly what you think or feel, only describing it.

Lexis: Possible vocabulary that a writer may employ for their writing to be effective and meaningful.

Memoir: The sharing of personal narrative, anecdotes or vignettes that closely resemble the features of story-telling or story writing (see page 187).

Mode: How a genre will typically look and the visual, audio or other devices a writer will employ.

Multimodality: Related to mode, modality is about how a text is to be published and represented. Multi suggests that a number of different techniques and resources can be used to publish or perform a text, for example, through the use of technology like podcasting, vlogging, film making, physical props, illustration or the use of other artefacts.

Painting with words: The artistic use of techniques such as noun phrases, showing not telling, personification, pathetic fallacy, comparison, alliteration, simile, metaphor, symbolism and/or imagism in fiction, poetry or non-fiction.

Paragraph Piler: A writer who plans and then drafts, revises and edits their paragraphs before moving on to draft their next one. Essentially, the writer forms each paragraph perfectly before moving on to the next one.

Pathetic fallacy: The personification of and assigning human emotions to the natural world.

People's history: A genre that brings to light the memoirs, anecdotes and vignettes of everyday people, based within our families or communities.

Personification: Giving objects, animals, abstract qualities, anything non-human, a human persona, personality or quality.

Planners: Writers who need to have a detailed and well-thought-out plan before they begin drafting.

Terminology

Planning: Preparing the structure and content of a piece of writing in preparation for a draft. Alternatively, preparing or rehearsing what you might want to write about next.

Planning grid: A way of approaching the planning process that utilises grids to share the typical cohesive structures that genres are built upon.

Process goals: Deadlines set by writers to finish a certain writing process by a certain time.

Process writing: The theory that writing goes through a recursive, flexible and creative process that can involve generating ideas, dabbling, planning, drafting, revising, editing, publishing and/or performing. It is recursive because writers will move amongst these processes all the time and don't typically go through them in a linear way (see page 47).

Product goals: Goals that, if achieved, will result in a writing product being effective and achieving its intended purpose.

Publishing: The final process of sending writing out into the world for others to read. The writing piece has now become a writing product for others to read (see page 59).

Pupil conferencing: When writers (adult or peer) talk to each other about how their writing is going (see page 80 for more details).

Register: The formality, choice of vocabulary, linguistic features, communicative purpose, social context and relationship with the reader that a genre typically carries, applies or uses.

Revision: Re-reading and improving a completed sentence, paragraph or whole draft. The focus is usually on purpose, audience and the effectiveness of the piece. This is not the same as editing. See page 54.

Roar of the waterfall: Finding the roar of the waterfall is identifying where your writing should start. Often, apprentice writers will write a long, meandering opening to their writing that can be cut right back once they have identified where the 'roar of their waterfall' begins.

Rumbling reading tummy: The phenomenon of having a 'rumbling reading tummy' happens when a reader feels 'hungry' for more detail or information in certain parts of a writing piece. If readers have not been left feeling satisfied then changes may need to be considered.

Self-regulation: Independence from external intervention; the feeling of ownership over your writing craft or product. Self-regulation is closely linked to the concept of writing 'as' and 'for' pleasure.

Semantics: The language or linguistic features that a writer may employ for their writing to be meaningful.

Sentence Stacker: A writer who will make a plan and then draft, revise and edit their sentences before they write their next one. The writer tries to form each sentence perfectly before they move on to the next one.

Show don't tell: The writing technique of removing the moments where the writer simply 'tells' their reader what is happening. This is usually done when *is, was, are* and *were* are used. These sentences can be re-worked by removing these particular verbs and instead showing readers what is occurring rather than simply telling them.

Part A

Slam poetry: The performance, sometimes competitively, of spoken word poetry. The poems are often (but not always) about political or social ideas and topics (see page 181).

Sticky bit: Part of your writing that doesn't run smoothly or sounds strange. This is often due to a change of tense, verb agreement, use of a/an, pronoun and noun use, lack of punctuation, missing words or a lack of explanation.

Teacher-writer: A teacher who writes only when they need to.

Tenor: The formality and closeness of the relationship amongst a writer, the text and the reader(s). Essentially, how the writer interacts with their reader.

Vomiter: A type of writer who likes to draft their writing quickly before attending to revising and editing it.

Writing as pleasure: Enjoying developing and practising your writing craft. Feeling sufficiently confident and empowered to engage with the processes of writing, including talking about them as well as being part of a community of writers.

Writing for pleasure: The satisfaction that comes from sharing a piece of writing to be proud of, as well as the discovery and establishment of your own writing voice.

A *Writing For Pleasure* pedagogy: Devised by Young (2019), it is any research-informed pedagogy which seeks to create the conditions in which writing and being a writer is a pleasurable and satisfying experience. It has as its goal the use of effective writing practices with young apprentice writers and the promotion of the affective aspects of writing and of being a writer (see page 7).

Writing habit: A preferred way of undertaking drafting, for example, being a Vomiter, Paragraph Piler or Sentence Stacker (see page 60).

Writing product: The finished piece. The product to be shared with the world as a published or performed piece.

Writing study: A mini-lesson focusing on teaching a writing technique or strategy that will help children independently tackle a writing process. These are lessons that teach strategies or techniques to make writing more effective for intended readers.

Writer-teacher: A writer who happens to teach, or a teacher who regularly writes. These individuals write for pleasure in their personal lives and will use their writerly knowledge as the basis for planning their writing study lessons. They will share their knowledge, techniques, strategies and ways of navigating the various processes involved in writing with their class. Where possible, they will write alongside the children in the classroom setting and take part in class writing projects. They will also publish their own writing into the class community and beyond.

Writing workshop: An approach to the teaching of writing that involves replicating the conditions of recreational or professional writers. This process involves teachers learning how to create a community of authentic writers within the classroom. It also involves enacting the following lesson structure: writing instruction (through mini-lessons), writing time and class sharing (author's chair).

Yawny bit: Part of the writing piece that labours the point so that it becomes potentially boring for the reader. Unnecessary or pedantic detail that could otherwise be removed.

18 References and further reading

References

Almond, D. (2018) *On Writing* [Accessed 26 May 2019: http://davidalmond.com/on-writing].

Anderson, C. (2000) *How's It Going?* Portsmouth, NH: Heinemann.

Anderson, J. (2005) *Mechanically Inclined*, Portsmouth, NH: Stenhouse Publishers.

Atwell, N. (2014) *In the Middle*, Portsmouth, NH: Heinemann.

Au, W., & Gourd, K. (2013) Asinine Assessment: Why High-Stakes Testing Is Bad for Everyone, Including English Teachers. *The English Journal*, 103(1).

Barrs, M. (2019) Teaching Bad Writing. *English in Education*, 53(1), 18–31.

Benton, M., & Fox, G. (1985) *Teaching Literature: Nine to Fourteen*, Oxford: Oxford University Press.

Calkins, L. (1998) *The Art of Teaching Writing*, Portsmouth, NH: Heinemann.

Calkins, L., & Ehrenworth, M. (2016) Growing Extraordinary Writers: Leadership Decisions to Raise the Level of Writing Across a School and a District. *The Reading Teacher*, 70(1), 7–18.

Chamberlain, L. (2015) *Exploring the Out-of-School Writing Practices of Three Children Aged 9–10 Years Old and How These Practices Travel Across and Within the Domains of Home and School*. EdD thesis, The Open University.

Clark, C. (2016) *Children's and Young People's Writing in 2015*, London: National Literacy Trust.

Clark, C. (2017) *Writing for Enjoyment and Its Link to Wider Writing*, London: National Literacy Trust.

Cremin, T., & Baker, S. (2010) Exploring Teacher-Writer Identities in the Classroom: Conceptualising the Struggle. *English Teaching: Practice and Critique*, 9(3), 8–25.

Cremin, T., Mottram, M., Collins, F., Powell, S., & Safford, K. (2014) *Building Communities of Engaged Readers: Reading for Pleasure*, London: Routledge.

Cunningham, P. M., & Cunningham, J. W. (2010) *What Really Matters in Writing: Research-based Practices Across the Elementary Curriculum*, Boston, MA: Allyn & Bacon.

DfE. (2012) *What Is the Research Evidence on Writing? Education Standards Research Team*, London: Department for Education.

Fearn, L., & Farnan, N. (1998) *Writing Effectively: Helping Students Master the Conventions of Writing*, London: Pearson.

Fisher, R., Jones, S., Larkin, S., & Myhill, D. (2010) *Using Talk to Support Writing*, London: Sage.

Graham, S., Harris, K., & Mason, L. (2011) Self-Regulated Strategy Development for Students with Writing Difficulties. *Theory into Practice*, 50(1), 20–27.

Graham, S., & Sandmel, K. (2011) The Process Writing Approach: A Meta-Analysis. *Journal of Educational Research*, 104, 396–407.

Graham, S., Xinghua, L., Aitken, A., Ng, C., Bartlett, B., Harris, K., & Holzapfel, J. (2018) Effectiveness of Literacy Programs Balancing Reading and Writing Instruction: A Meta-Analysis. *Reading Research Quarterly*, 53(3), 279–304.

Graves, D. (1983) *Writing: Teachers and Children at Work*, Portsmouth, NH: Heinemann.

Hansen, J. (1987) *When Writers Read*, Portsmouth, NH: Heinemann.

Harwayne, S. (2001) *Writing Through Childhood: Rethinking Process and Product*, Portsmouth, NH: Heinemann.

Hoffman, J., Paris, S., Salas, R., Patterson, E., & Assaf, L. (2003) High-Stakes Assessment in the Language Arts: The Piper Plays, the Players Dance, But Who Pays the Price? In J. Flood, D. Lapp, J. R. Squire, & J. M. Jensen (Eds), *Handbook of Research on Teaching the English Language Arts* (2nd Ed, pp. 590–599), Mahwah, NJ: Lawrence Erlbaum Publishers.

Ings, R. (2009) *Writing Is Primary: Final Research Report*. London: Esmee Fairbairn Foundation.

Jean, E., Tree, F., & Clark, B. (2013) Communicative Effectiveness of Written Versus Spoken Feedback. *Discourse Processes*, 50(5), 339–359.

Kaufman, D. (2002) Living a Literate Life: Revisited. *English Journal*, 91(6), 51–57.

Koster, M., Tribushinina, E., De Jong, P. F., & Van de Bergh, B. (2015) Teaching Children to Write: A Meta-Analysis of Writing Intervention Research. *Journal of Writing Research*, 7(2), 249–274.

Kress, G. (1994) *Learning to Write* (2nd Ed), London: Routledge.

McQuitty, V. (2014) Process-Oriented Writing Instruction in Elementary Classrooms: Evidence of Effective Practices from the Research Literature. *Writing & Pedagogy*, 6(3), 467–495.

Myhill, D. (2018) Grammar as a Meaning-Making Resource for Improving Writing. Contribution to a Special Issue Working on Grammar at School in L1-Education: Empirical Research Across Linguistic Regions. L1-Educational Studies. *Language and Literature*, 18, 1–21.

National Writing Project. (2011) *Ten Rights of the Writer* [Accessed 26 May 2019: www.nwp.org.uk/nwp-blog/the-rights-of-the-writer].

Noddings, N. (1984) *Caring*, Berkeley, CA: University of California Press.

Ofsted. (2009) *English at the Crossroads*, London: Ofsted.

Ofsted. (2011) *Excellence in English*, London: Ofsted.

Ofsted. (2019) *Education Inspection Framework: Overview of Research*, London: Ofsted.

Parry, B., & Taylor, L. (2018) Readers in the Round: Children's Holistic Engagements with Texts. *Literacy*, 52(2), 103–110.

Roche, M. (2014) *Developing Children's Critical Thinking Through Picture Books*, London: Routledge.

Rosen, M. (1998) *Did I Hear You Write?* Nottingham, UK: Five Leaves Publications.

Smith, F. (1982) *Writing and the Writer*, New York: HEB.

Smith, F. (1983) Reading and Writing. *Language Arts*, 60(5), 558–567.

Smith, F. (1988) *Joining the Literacy Club*, Oxford: Heinemann.

Tennent, W., Reedy, D., Hobsbaum, A., & Gamble, N. (2016) *Guiding Readers–Layers of Meaning*, London: UCL Press.

Wiliam, D. (2011) *Embedded Formative Assessment*, USA: Solution Tree.

Wrigley, S., & Smith, J. (2015) *Introducing Teachers' Writing Groups*, London: Routledge.

Wyse, D., & Torgerson, C. (2017) Experimental Trials and "What Works?" In Education: The Case of Grammar for Writing. *British Educational Research Journal*, 43(6), 1019–1047.

Young, R. (2019) *What Is It "Writing for Pleasure" Teachers Do That Makes the Difference*, The Goldsmiths' Company, The University of Sussex [Accessed: www.writing4pleasure.com].

Young, R., & Ferguson, F. (in press) *Writing for Pleasure: Theory, Research and Practice*, London: Routledge.

Further recommended reading

Anderson, J. (2007) *Everyday Editing*, Portsmouth, NH: Stenhouse Publishers.

Atwell, N. (2002) *Lessons That Change Writers*, Portsmouth, NH: Heinemann.

Bearne, E., & Reedy, D. (2013) *Teaching Grammar Effectively in Primary Schools*, Leicester: UKLA.

Brownjohn, S. (1980) *Does It Have to Rhyme? Teaching Children to Write Poetry*, UK: Hodder Education.

Chamberlain, L. (2018) *Inspiring Writing in Primary School* (2nd Ed), London: Sage.

Coffin, C., Donohue, J., & North, S. (2009) *Exploring English Grammar*, London: Routledge.

Cremin, T., & Myhill, D. (2012) *Creating Communities of Writers*, London: Routledge.

Crystal, D. (2004) *Making Sense of Grammar*, Harlow: Longman.

DeMile, T. (2008) *Making Believe on Paper: Fiction Writing with Young Children*, Portsmouth, NH: Heinemann.

Dombey, H. (2013) *Teaching Writing: What the Evidence Says UKLA Argues for an Evidence-Informed Approach to Teaching and Testing Young Children's Writing*, Leicester: UKLA.

Dyson, A. H. (1997) *Writing Superheroes: Contemporary Childhood, Popular Culture and Classroom Literacy*, New York: Teachers College Press.

Fisher, R., Myhill, D., Jones, S., & Larkin, S. (2010) *Using Talk to Support Writing*, London: Sage.

Fletcher, R. (1996) *A Writer's Notebook: Unlocking the Writer Within You*, New York: HarperCollins.

Fletcher, R. (2000) *How Writers Work: Finding a Process That Works for You*, New York: HarperCollins.

Fletcher, R. (2001) *Writing Workshop: The Essential Guide*, Portsmouth, NH: Heinemann.

Fletcher, R. (2007) *How to Write Your Life Story*, New York: Collins.

Fletcher, R., & Portalupi, J. (2007) *Craft Lessons* (2nd Ed), Portsmouth, NH: Stenhouse Publishers.

Graham, L., & Johnson, A. (2003) *Children's Writing Journals*, Royston: United Kingdom Literacy Association.

Graves, D. (1989) *Investigate Non-Fiction*, Portsmouth, NH: Heinemann.

Graves, D. (1991) *Build a Literate Classroom*, Portsmouth, NH: Heinemann.

Graves, D. (1992) *Explore Poetry*, Portsmouth, NH: Heinemann.

Hansen, J. (1987) *When Writers Read*, Portsmouth, NH: Heinemann.

Harris, K. R., & Graham, S. (1996) *Making the Writing Process Work: Strategies for Composition and Self-Regulation*, Brookline, MA: Brookline Books.

Harris, K. R., Graham, S., Mason, L., & Friedlander, B. (2008) *Powerful Writing Strategies for All Students*, Baltimore, MD: Brookes Publishing.

Harwayne, S. (1992) *Lasting Impressions: Weaving Literature in the Writing Workshop*, Portsmouth, NH: Heinemann.

Harwayne, S. (2001) *Writing Through Childhood: Rethinking Process & Product*, Portsmouth, NH: Heinemann.

Heard, G. (1998) *Awakening the Heart*, Portsmouth, NH: Heinemann.

Heard, G. (2014) *The Revision Toolbox: Teaching Techniques That Work*, Portsmouth, NH: Heinemann.

Heffernan, L. (2017) *Back and Forth: Using an Editor's Mindset to Improve Student Writing*, Portsmouth, NH: Heinemann.

Heller, M. (1999) *Reading-Writing Connections: From Theory to Practice*, London: Routledge.

Horn, M. (2007) *Talking, Drawing, Writing: Lessons for Our Youngest Writers*, Portsmouth, NH: Stenhouse Publishers.

Jacobson, J. (2010) *No More "I'm Done!"*, Portsmouth, NH: Stenhouse Publishers.

Kaufman, D. (2000) *Conferences and Conversations: Listening to the Literate Classroom*, Portsmouth, NH: Heinemann.

Loane, G. (2016) *Developing Young Writers in the Classroom: I've Got Something to Say*, London: Routledge.

Locke, T. (2015) *Developing Writing Teachers*, London: Routledge.

Martin, J., & Rose, D. (2008) *Genre Relations: Mapping Culture*, Sheffield: Equinox Publishing.

Murray, D. (1993) *Read to Write* (3rd Ed), Fort Worth, TX: Harcourt Brace.

Richmond, J. (2017) *Harold Rosen: Writings on Life, Language and Learning, 1958–2008*, London: UCL Press.

Rosen, M. (2016) *What Is Poetry? The Essential Guide to Reading and Writing Poems*, London: Walker Books.

Rosen, M. (2018) *Writing for Pleasure*, London: Michael Rosen.

Serravallo, J. (2017) *The Writing Strategies Book: Your Everything Guide to Developing Skilled Writers*, Portsmouth, NH: Heinemann.

Shubitz, S., & Dorfman, L. R. (2019) *Welcome to Writing Workshop: Engaging Today's Students with a Model That Works*, Portsmouth, USA: Stenhouse Press.

Tompkins, G. E. (2011) *Teaching Writing: Balancing Process and Product*, Upper Saddle River, NJ: Merrill.

Wray, D., Beard, R., Raban, B., Hall, N., Bloom, W., Robinson, A., Potter, F., Sands, H., & Yates, I. (1988) *Developing Children's Writing*, Leamington Spa: Scholastic.

Young, R., & Ferguson, F. (in press) *Writing for Pleasure: Theory, Research and Practice*, London: Routledge.

Key research

Gadd, M. (2014) *What Is Critical in the Effective Teaching of Writing?* Auckland: The University of Auckland.

Graham, S., McKeown, D., Kiuhara, S., & Harris, K. (2012) A Meta-Analysis of Writing Instruction for Students in the Elementary Grades. *Journal of Educational Psychology*, 104(4), 879–896.

Graham, S., & Perin, D. (2007) *Writing Next: Effective Strategies to Improve Writing of Adolescents in Middle School & High Schools*, USA: Alliance for Excellent Education.

Grossman, P. L., Loeb, S., Cohen, J., & Wyckoff, J. (2013) Measure for Measure: The Relationship Between Measures of Instructional Practice in Middle School English Language Arts and Teachers' Value-added Scores. *American Journal of Education*, 119(3), 445–470.

Hall, K., & Harding, A. (2003) *A Systematic Review of Effective Literacy Teaching in the 4 to 14 Age Range of Mainstream Schooling*, London: Institute of Education.

Higgins, S., Martell, T., Waugh, D., Henderson, P., & Sharples, J. (2017) *Improving Literacy in Key Stage Two*, London: Education Endowment Fund (EEF).

Hillocks, G. (1986) *Research on Written Composition: New Directions for Teaching*, Urbana, IL: National Council of Teachers of English.

Koster, M., Tribushinina, E., De Jong, P. F., & Van de Bergh, B. (2015) Teaching Children to Write: A Mata-Analysis of Writing Intervention Research. *Journal of Writing Research*, 7(2), 249–274.

Langer, J. A. (2001) Beating the Odds: Teaching Middle and High School Students to Read and Write Well. *American Educational Research Journal*, 38(4), 837–880.

Medwell, J., Wray, D., Poulson, L., & Fox, R. (1998) *Effective Teachers of Literacy*. A Report Commissioned by the UK Teacher Training Agency.

Morizawa, G. (2014) *Nesting the Neglected "R" a Design Study: Writing Instruction Within a Prescriptive Literacy Program*, unpublished. Berkeley: University of California Press.

Parr, J. M., & Limbrick, L. (2010) Contextualising Practice: Hallmarks of Effective Teachers of Writing. *Teaching and Teacher Education*, 26(3), 583–590.

Smedt, F., & Van Keer, H. (2013) A Research Synthesis on Effective Writing Instruction in Primary Education. *Social and Behavioral Sciences*, 112, 693–701.

Troia, G. (2014) *Evidence-Based Practices for Writing-Instruction*, USA: CEEDAR Center University of Michigan.

Children's literature references

Aliki. (1998) *How a Book Is Made*, New York: HarperCollins.

Harlon, A. (2012) *Ralph Tells a Story*, New York: Two Lions.

Little, J. (1998) *Hey World, Here I am*, New York: HarperCollins.

Rosen, M. (2015) *Quick! Let's Get Out of Here*, London: Puffin.

Writer-teacher references

Elbow, P. (1998) *Writing Without Teachers*, Oxford: Oxford University Press.

Fletcher, R. (1996) *A Writer's Notebook: Unlocking the Writer Within You*, New York: HarperCollins.

Gardner, J. (1984) *The Art of Fiction: Notes on Craft for Young Writers*, New York: Vintage Books.

Lamott, A. (2007) *Bird by Bird: Instructions on Writing and Life*, Peterborough: Anchor Books.

Provost, G. (1985) *100 Ways to Improve Your Writing*, New York: Penguin Books.

PART
B

19 Introduction to Part B

Welcome to Part B. It's here that you'll find our suggested class writing projects. For convenience, we have separated Part B into six sections: poetry, memoir, narrative, non-fiction, persuading and influencing, and history.

You'll see that each writing project contains the following: a letter explaining why the project is meaningful and worthwhile, advice on how to write your own exemplars, techniques to help you and your class generate ideas, an example planning grid and, finally, suggested reading and mentor texts for you and your class. For information on how to plan a class writing project, go to page 39.

Genre weeks

The genre week which introduces each class writing project teaches children the meaning and purposes behind a genre. The suggested projects contained here make this information explicitly available to you as teachers, but we have also tried to write about them in a child-friendly way. Our projects cover the most popular genres across the curriculum as well as children's favourites. They cover all the reasons we are moved to write. The projects and the supporting materials look to help you and your pupils – without telling you exactly what to do!

Each writing project:

1. Gives a rationale as to why the project is essential in children's development as writers.
2. Explains the social purpose of the genre and why writers are *moved* to write using it.
3. Shares with children what people will usually write about *(the field)*.
4. Explains how the writer can interact with their reader *(the tenor)*.
5. Suggests how to present your writing effectively *(the mode)*.
6. Gives hints about what grammar, linguistic and literary features are going to be useful *(semantics and lexis)*.
7. Provides a planning grid, showing the stages your writing can go through.
8. Gives techniques for generating your own ideas.

It's important to remember that the genre 'norms' that we teach children are not actually fixed but change to reflect the needs and context of our writing. Therefore, we don't believe it is worth obsessing over whether children have included all the so called 'features' of a genre. Instead, consider the success of the piece in relation to the purpose and audience for the writing. If the child has successfully achieved the intentions for their piece, then we believe that constitutes good writing. In fact, children's writing can show far more sophistication when it deliberately contradicts the so called 'norms' of a genre. When children only focus on genre features and not the intentions and audience for the piece, their writing can too often be unnatural and unsuccessful. Once the genre has been taught and discussed as part of genre week, children should be allowed to do three things with their new found knowledge:

- Use it purposefully within the class writing project.
- Experiment with it further in personal projects.
- If they are experienced writers, be given the opportunity to experiment with manipulating, deliberately contradicting and hybridising its structures with others.

A quick note about planning grids

Writing is best learnt through a combination of authentic projects, explicit direct instruction and mastery through repeated practice (Young & Ferguson in press). Explicit teaching and explanation of planning grids can obviously improve the structure of children's writing – particularly for early or moderately fluent writers. However, the criticism of planning grids (if used too rigidly) is that they can become overly prescriptive and place experienced writers in a straitjacket. Teaching genres with a fanatical attention to its 'features' will, over time, block children's writing development. Therefore, planning grids should be used carefully. For more information on teaching children how to plan effectively, go to page 51.

Progression and interconnection

Children develop as writers best when all the teachers in a school work together, adopt a mastery through repeated practice based approach and build on the writing projects and strategies other teachers have taught. Children develop least in schools which take a performance-based and isolated approach. Therefore, here, we offer insights into how projects can and should be repeated and built upon through the school years. We also explain how things learnt in specific projects provide children with transferable knowledge and skills which they and their teachers can put to work in other projects. Finally, we also give you a brief description of what teachers in different year groups should focus on to advance children's writing. In this way, children have an opportunity to master the skills that may have previously been out of reach.

It's important to remember that children will continue to write in previous learned genres as part of their personal project writing.

Progression →				
	Year 3	Year 4	Year 5	Year 6
Memoir	Memoir	Memoir	Memoir	Autobiography
Narrative	Fairy Tales Fables	Character-Driven Short Stories Short Stories Based on Vivid Settings	Developed Short Stories	Flash Fiction
Poetry	The Natural World Animals and Pets	Sensory Poetry Poetry That Hides in Things . . .	Inspired by . . . Poetry	Social and Political Poetry Anthology of Life
Non-Fiction	Information	Information	Explanation	Discussion
Persuasion and Opinion	Instructions	Persuasion for Personal Gain	Advocacy Journalism	Persuasion for Community Activism
History	People's History	People's History	Biography	Historical Account

Progression in memoir

Memoir develops through repeated practice throughout Years 3 to 5. Other class writing projects will begin to influence children's memoir writing. For example, *The Natural World* and *Animals and Pets* poetry projects can have a profound effect on children's topics for memoir during these years and enhance them accordingly. Children begin to use the techniques in the *Short Story* projects, *The Sensory Poetry* and *The Poetry That Hides in Things* projects to influence their 'story-telling' ability and sensory description in memoir. Finally, children use what they have learnt from the *People's History* and *Biography* projects to help them in their *Autobiography* project. This is also complemented by the *Anthology of Life* poetry project.

Year 3

At the beginning of the year, children's memoir writing can seem more like recounting (the 'and then . . . and then' syndrome). It is likely that they won't focus on a specific diamond moment to write about but will include a lot of unnecessary details which don't enhance the memoir. It is likely that their writing ability won't match their oral retellings.

Year 4

By Year 4, memoir can encompass both poetry and *People's History* and maybe even some aspects of non-fiction writing. Young writers in Year 4 should be ready to understand the concept of a diamond moment, meaning a very specific focus on one experience or idea that is central to their writing. This will help children move away from simply recounting events to writing their memoir much more like a story, with a single important theme. They will use poetic description to enhance these stories.

Years 5 and 6

Children are now able to attend to memoir in the same way as story writing. They will consider plot, character development and setting description, just as they do with their fictional pieces. Settings also begin to be written in such a way that they become additional characters. Children are able to understand that story and memoir can blur together and that writers will often use artistic licence, bending the truth or using hyperbole to tell an even more enticing anecdote. They will consciously or subconsciously reveal parts of themselves in their memoirs: their hopes, fears and thoughts about their life so far or the future. Memoirs can therefore become deeply significant pieces of writing.

Progression in narrative

Narrative develops by first setting down how traditional story lines are produced in *Fairy Tales* and *Fables*. Children's personal narrative writing through *Memoir* projects will also have an influence here. The poetry projects of *The Natural World* and *Animals and Pets* are a logical fit for children writing *Fairy Tales* and *Fables*, as animals and the natural world often feature in both genres. By Year 4, children are working on specific types of short stories, focusing on character-driven stories and stories with vivid settings. This is so that they can begin to successfully combine these elements in their story writing in Years 5 and 6. The focus on character development and setting description will also influence their memoir writing. *Sensory Poetry* and *Poetry That Hides in Things* provide children with transferable skills for their narrative projects. They learn to weave aspects of sensory poetry and the ability to bring significance to objects into their story writing. By learning about *Inspired by . . .* poetry, children continue their development in understanding intertextuality, and this too informs their narrative writing. Children begin to see that they can be inspired by, squirrel away or steal aspects they like from poetry and stories to use within their own narratives. Finally, children work on more advanced narrative techniques through the *Flash Fiction* projects in Year 6.

Year 3

Some children may still rely on drawing, and 'telling' the story to an adult as their main 'planning' strategy. Subject choices might be 'close to home', for example events from their own recent past or simple retellings of things they have read, heard or seen in films. There will probably be little character development, and they might need some help with structuring a story, particularly with writing a strong conclusion. Children might also just have the sense of a very immediate and limited audience. At this stage in their narrative development, children feel the focus should be on telling their readers *what* happened as opposed to *how* or *why*. This means many of their narratives will be simply slightly elaborated *'and then . . . '* stories.

Year 4

The emphasis this year will be on encouraging your young writers to think beyond plot and to consider character and setting development as an integral part of story writing. Some children may still need support to create a strong structure for their stories. Using the common story arcs will be advantageous in this case.

Year 5

The emphasis this year will be on encouraging your young apprentice writers to think beyond plot and instead focus their attention on character-driven narratives. Children will move beyond simple physical description and begin to think about how characters behave, why they do the things they do, what and how they think, how they feel and how they talk to others. Children are able, at this stage, to attend to plot, character development and setting description simultaneously as they construct their narratives. They can weave their plot, character descriptions and dialogues together cohesively and their settings begin to be written in such a way that they too become additional characters in their stories. Children pay particular attention to their openings and endings and will revise them until they appear just how they want them to be. Experienced writers can 'paint with words' within their stories, using 'showing' and descriptive detail effectively.

Year 6

Your writers will readily manipulate fantastic sentence constructions, poetic and figurative language, ideas and words from the books they are reading and use them for their own purposes.

There is a real variety in sentence use, structure and type – which is beginning to come quite naturally. They have embedded the concepts of character development and setting description into their writing habits. This includes creating and sustaining empathy with their characters, using internal reflection and making links between their growing understanding of people and their wider knowledge of the world.

These writers will write strong openings and genuinely interesting and unexpected endings to narrative pieces. They choose topics which are honest, have strong feelings and show their personality.

They are now casting a wider net and allowing a range of fictional genres to enter into their writing. You will see more realistic, political and historical fiction. They may write on social issues that matter to them either implicitly or explicitly. You may also find they are more subversive and wish to push the boundaries of what is conventional within literary traditions. Finally, they are able to use flash-backs, tension, atmosphere, deception, character flaws and symbolism, hint at wider meaning, and give clues as to what might happen next. They can also tell more than one related story within a single narrative piece. They are refining their story writing skills through *Flash Fiction*.

Progression in non-fiction

Children develop their ability to share their knowledge and passions in Years 3 and 4. Through the school years, they are able to use what they learn in other projects to create more vibrant and personable non-fiction writing. This happens through the influence of *Memoir* and the poetry projects. It means children include vignettes, anecdotes, personal reflections or poetry into their non-fiction writing. By undertaking instructional writing, *Science Reporting*, *Advocacy Journalism* and *Information* projects, children are well prepared to begin writing *Explanation* in Year 5. Children's experience of persuasive writing coupled with *Explanation and Historical Accounts* makes them well placed to write *Discussion* pieces. By Year 6, children will have moved well beyond simply sharing information and will instead be capable of creatively describing, discussing, sharing their personal response and experiences, analysing and successfully contrasting and comparing the information they share with others.

Year 3

You may need to check that children know a substantial amount about their chosen topic before they begin writing. It is also good to be aware of, as well as point out to children, that they can sometimes assume too much prior knowledge in their reader and end up with a text that doesn't fulfil its purpose of informing or explaining the subject fully. Children may also find 'chunking' their information into specific sections difficult.

Year 4

Writing non-fiction can be a wholly enriching experience for all of us. You should encourage children to be taking advantage of all that it can offer, as well as enjoying it. You may need to check that children are familiar with a substantial amount of information relating to their chosen topic before they begin writing and that they are not making any assumptions about their readers' prior knowledge of the topic. It's at this point that children begin to get a handle on 'teaching' within non-fiction texts as well as looking to entertain or influence.

Year 5

Children are now motivated to ensure that their readers understand the information in their writing clearly and effectively. They will first classify their subject of choice before moving on to discuss its nuances. They are also beginning to include descriptions as well as definitions for technical vocabulary that their readers may not be aware of. They are also able to use a formal and informal voice when describing phenomena, as well as *paint with* words using figurative language and creative comparisons. Children will take part in writing 'faction' and will begin to naturally mix non-fiction genres together through hybridisation. They can maintain their focus on their topic, give weight to significant moments and develop their own and others' thoughts and ideas on a particular subject. Children will also begin to reveal their personal responses to their chosen subject, providing personal anecdotes and feelings that really bring an extra dimension to their writing. Children begin to conclude their pieces in a well-thought-out manner, leaving their reader with a final insight into the subject matter upon which to meditate.

Year 6

Your writers this year will seek the opportunity to play around with non-fiction genres, deliberately turning them on their head in new and creative ways. They can write formally or informally with ease even within the same piece. They will use examples to imply relationships between differing phenomena or to clarify their point. They will also use other sources to back up the points they want to make. They may quote sources and provide a list of references for the reader. They may show signs that they can analyse and pick apart sources. They have complete control over their writing and use subtleties and nuances of language which evoke all the senses and leave their reader genuinely in awe, entertained, thrilled, emotional, persuaded and/or informed – often all within the same non-fiction piece. Their conclusions will ensure that final insight, potential actions, challenges or implications are considered by the reader. They are able to have their own style and voice within non-fiction writing. They can explain with clarity and imply hidden depths of meaning. This can include using figurative language or personal narrative to make their point. They assert their individuality which is valued by the writing community of the classroom. They constructively resist dominant writing values if they are inconsistent with their personal values.

Progression in persuading and influencing

Children start out by writing simple and persuasive *Instructions*. This leads to writing for one's self through *Personal Gain* persuasion in Year 4 and is then built upon and widened to *Advocacy*

Journalism and the concept of writing on behalf of others. This helps prepare children for *The Community Activism* project in Year 6. *The Community Activism* project is supported by the *Social and Political Poetry* project. Children's increasing ability to share information and explanation and to discuss topics through the *Discussion* and *Historical Account* projects will further aid them in these endeavours.

Progression in the history genres

The *People's History* projects help children make the link between *Memoir* writing and writing as a social historian. Both influence each other. This naturally leads into writing *Biography* which in turn helps children write their *Autobiographies* in Year 6. Finally, their ability to write *Historical Accounts* is supported by the *Discussion* writing project.

20 Poetry

How to write your own poem

Use these ideas to help you write your own poem for use in class or to introduce children to the genre.

Why write a poem for yourself or your class?

Poems help you share thoughts, feelings, experiences and dreams and say things in new ways. Poetry is writing that comes from the heart.

Writing free-verse poems gives you a lot of freedom; they don't have to have regular rhythm, line length or rhyme. Best of all, you can play around with words and put them together in any way you like. There are no rules, but here are some tips for writing a strong poem.

What is your poem going to be about?

Poems can be about something ordinary or extraordinary.

- While dabbling with your poem idea, write lists of words and phrases.
- When dabbling, write down the feelings you want to express in your poem.
- Try to compare what you are writing about with something else to help you better understand it.
- **Theme** – make sure you have one clear topic to focus on.
- **Tone** – think about the message and feelings you want to express in your poem, for example loneliness, happiness, comfort, fear, memory.
- **Symbol** – if you like, choose something to be a symbol for something else, for example mountains – wisdom, the wind – loneliness, sword – bravery, fire – starting anew.

What is your role as the writer?

When writing poems, your aim is to describe or show something to readers in a new and interesting way. You can write from your own point of view or imagine things from another point of view – perhaps even the point of view of an object. Your role is to express what you have noticed, felt or imagined and share that feeling with your readers.

What should your poem look like?

You can play around with words and put them together in any way you like. You can also play around with punctuation if you like. You can be multimodal. Combine your poem with a picture, drawing or painting. Accompany it with music or drama in a performance.

How can you make your poem clear and interesting?

- Once you've written your first draft, identify your diamond moment and make sure you have made it the focus of your poem.
- Explore the most passionate part of your poem – where you reveal the most emotion.
- Examine your nouns and verbs, because this is where your poem is really hiding.
- Repeat some of your favourite words or phrases. Maybe repeat the first or last lines.
- Notice your use of metaphors and work on them a little.
- Notice where you are playing around with sounds, rhythm, rhyme and repeated lines.
- Try out sound effects such as alliteration or onomatopoeia.

- Use line breaks or stanzas (groups of lines) to show where you want your reader to pause in your poem. Try out lots of different possibilities.
- Move lines around until you get the best effect.
- Let your last line leave your readers with something to think about.
- Give a lot of thought to the title.

How can your word choices help?

- Use sensory images – hearing, touch, smell, sight and taste.
- If it works, use figurative language, such as simile and metaphor. If you like, choose a subject and make it a symbol for something else: the sun – kindness or danger; the wind – loneliness; a sword – courage; an eagle – power; a mountain – strength.
- Notice where you've personified something not human.

The natural world

Suggested for Years 3 and 4

Why write poems about the natural world?

British poetry has a long tradition of connection with landscape and nature. We cannot separate ourselves from the natural world, and young people are increasingly concerned about it. What we can do is bring into sharper focus for both children and ourselves the joyful, healing, subtle, delicate or terrifying aesthetics of nature. Children can share their experiences of nature with others, and this is the most important aspect of the project. When writing a nature poem, we're aiming to share a particular experience, and we have to resist the temptation to write generally about it. It's about choosing a diamond moment. We are lucky enough to have many experiences with nature, in urban jungles, streets, allotments, gardens, weather, woods, parks, beaches, rivers, seas, peaks, hills and playgrounds. Many of these experiences will be enjoyable; some may not!

This poetry project gives children the opportunity to write an impression, to capture a moment, to use poetry as a symbol and to make something familiar seem unfamiliar. Perhaps the children could even produce a literary magazine showcasing the power and fragility of nature.

Things to bear in mind

- It's important that you approach poetry topics with an understanding that you and your class are discovering poetry together and that you will join them in exploring the theme of the natural world. Poetry is a great way to pick up the habit of being a writer-teacher. It doesn't take much to draft a verse of a poem and you can show children how you are developing your poem over time. So much of poetry is fine-tuning, re-reading and making gradual changes. You will need to model this, as children often have the misconception that once a poem is drafted, it is finished.

- You will need to focus on children's use of general verbs. When conferencing, look out for these and ask children whether they can swap them for something different. Verbs that children typically overuse include *has, was, saw, got, went* and *made*.
- While it's not impossible to plan a poem, you will not be giving children planning grids for poetry. Instead, you will provide them with strategies used by real poets at the 'dabbling' stage. This is where poets play around with lists, words, phrases and lines before slowly building up a first draft.
- Some children may know they have something to say but don't know where to begin. In these cases, simply help them by giving them an opening line. They can always revise it later once they've got going.
- You will notice that children will usually want to focus on any 'action' taking place in a poem. Make it clear to your class that you know this is what they'll do and that your mini-lessons will show them how to take these 'actions' and make them poetic by *painting with words*.
- Children will often find revising their poem easy. However, they may be reluctant to let go of old lines and delete what is no longer required. This is something you will have to encourage and model.

Idea generation techniques

Write lists

- Write an *If I were . . .* poem.
- Write an *I'm the person who . . .* poem.
- Write a list of words that remind you of nature.
- Write a list of natural things you can see, feel and hear right now, and turn one of them into a poem.
- Write about something in nature that is important to you.
- Turn a nature detail or setting from a story that you know (e.g. the forest in *Little Red Riding Hood*) into a poem.
- Turn a nature detail or setting from one of your own stories into a poem.
- Write a poem from the point of view of something in nature, for example a pebble, the wind, an animal.

Poetry from the book you are reading

- Choose a sentence or two from your book and turn it into a poem.

Special object

- Bring in a special natural object from home. Describe what you see – using all the senses. Describe how it makes you feel. Turn it into a poem.

Seeing things differently

- Compare an everyday natural thing to something abstract. For example, a storm and fury.

Important people

- Make a list of the most important people in your life. Then make a list of memories you have with that person that involve something to do with being outside or in nature.

Memories with strong feelings

- Write a list of strong feelings (happy, worried, scared, sad). Then write down a moment when you have felt like that.

Favourite places

- Describe the smells/sights/sounds of your favourite outside place. Jot down what it's like there. Use all the senses, thinking about the emotions it brings up for you and what might be important about the place. Turn that into a poem.

Go outside

- Find something very small that you have never looked at properly before.
- Find something that is growing. How is it doing it?
- Find something that shouldn't really be there or is broken. Why?
- Sit and listen to the sounds around you.
- Feel what the weather is like. First with your eyes open and then with them closed. What does this kind of weather make you wonder about?

Take five ideas

Choose a natural object (e.g. a tree). List five ordinary words to do with the object. Then make each word into a poetic line:

- **Trunk** – serious and silent, sturdy and strong
- **Bark** – crusty and dusty, hugging history to itself
- **Leaves** – whispering secrets to the breeze
- **Branches** – curious fingers exploring the sky
- **Rings** – the life of the tree in layered lines – the story goes full circle.

Part B

Try personification

Write down five things you see when walking outside. Choose one and list five ways it could seem human- or animal-like:

- **Plant pot** – like a cupped hand, taking good care of the flowers.
- **Tree root** – keep a close eye on it – I'm sure I saw it slide through the earth towards us.
- **Leaves** – looking up, I see thousands of little umbrellas doing their best to keep us dry.
- **Seaspray** – Rising up – out of stones – like horses.
- **Seaweed** – It lies across the rocks like forgotten mermaids' hair.

Use drawings and photographs

- With your friends, collect natural things from outside, draw them and write a poem underneath.
- Bring in photographs from home and write a poem about each one.

Use your own memories

- Write down lots of endings to this sentence until a writing idea appears: *Outside, when I was younger . . .*

Suggested books

Poetry Please: The Seasons by various authors

Vacation Time Poems For Children by Nikki Giovanni

I Am The Seed That Grew The Tree by Fiona Waters

All the Wild Wonders: Poems of our Earth by Wendy Cooling

A Year of Nature Poems by Joseph Coelho

Overheard in a Tower Block by Joseph Coelho

Orionmagazine.org: an American-based nature poetry journal and website

Animals and pets

Suggested for Years 3 and 4

Why write poems about animals?

Children love animals. They often ask each other what their favourite animals are and why. Many have pets. Regardless of where we live, we see a variety of animals, and they are important to us for many reasons. Poets write about animals in various ways, and many people enjoy reading or hearing such poems.

Writers sometimes simply focus on an animal in order to be playful and descriptive with language. Others use animals (such as snakes, wolves and foxes) as a metaphor to describe human behaviour, psychology and even philosophy. Some write odes to a particular animal. Poems can be memoir-based (prose poems). Of course, others will write about mythical creatures, as Lewis Carroll did in *Jabberwocky*. Finally, if you read non-fiction texts about animals, you may notice that writers often use figurative language, or what we call *painting with words*, to classify and describe animals. With this writing project you can begin to introduce the idea that poetry and non-fiction can work in harmony.

Things to bear in mind

- What is the focus of a particular child's poem?
- Are they writing a memoir about a particular moment with a particular animal?
- Are they writing about their feelings and describing an animal?
- Is the child writing about a mythical creature?
- Are they personifying an animal to give it human characteristics and feelings?
- Are they simply using an animal to discuss something else entirely?

The important thing to find out from your writers is why they have chosen what they are writing. What are they trying to get across to their readers? How do they want to affect their readers? Are they trying to entertain them, to scare them, to share a memory or even to inform them?

Idea generation techniques

Write lists

- Write a list of all the animals you have seen, heard and encountered today/this week/ever.
- Write a list of your favourite memories of animals.
- Write a list of places where you see animals.
- Write a list of *When I was younger* . . . sentences to do with animals.

Collect your thoughts

- Create a mind map of different animals.

Use your own memories

- Tell your friends a story about an animal or a pet.

Part B

Something from home

- Bring in photographs or pictures from home and write poems about them.

Ideas from an information book

- Choose a sentence from a book about animals and turn it into a poem.

Make comparisons

- Compare two animals. How are they similar? How are they different? How do you react to each of them? What does this make you wonder about?

Suggested books

Cats (and Other Crazy Cuddlies) by Richard and Helen Exley

The Nation's Best Animal Poems by various authors

The Penguin in Lost Property by Jan Dean and Roger Stevens

Sensory poetry

Suggested for Years 4 and 5

Why write poems about the senses?

All poetry is in some way sensory, and much narrative text is sensory too. Writers use the senses to express a feeling that is very personal. The feelings may be quite specific but are often also universal in that others will recognise them and relate to them. Writers might draw on their senses as they reflect on objects that bring back hidden memories. They might use their senses to bring nostalgic moments to mind. The senses can also be used to evoke a mood, to deliberately show things or to explore experiences in different ways.

This poetry project will give children opportunities to practise using sensory description; showing, not telling; observing and expanding on small yet significant details; making comparisons; and painting with words for the pleasure of the artistry.

As this writing project is similar to a writing exercise, it will help children to see the benefits of techniques that writers often practise and use. Children will absorb these techniques as part of their repertoires and will be able to draw on them again in all kinds of future writing.

Things to bear in mind

- The anthology *Sensational*, compiled by Roger McGough, includes many excellent examples of sensory poetry that will inform and inspire children, with sections that focus on each sense.

- It may be best to start with free-verse poems. These don't need to have a regular rhythm, line length or rhyme. Best of all, you can play around with words and put them together in any way you like. You can also play around with punctuation if you like. There are no rules!
- In your mountain of an idea, find that one special diamond moment and focus on it. It's your reason for writing the poem. Treat it with care, think about it a lot and make it shine.
- Remember that the senses can include seeing, noticing, smelling, tasting, hearing, touching, thinking and feeling.
- Show, don't tell. Sometimes cut out words like *is, was, are* and *were* as these are 'telling' verbs, and replace them by showing your readers what is happening instead.
- Give your reader tiny details – little things that only you have noticed.
- Compare a person, place or thing to something else. Pretend that a place or a thing can behave like a person.
- Replace some of your nouns with ones that pack more meaning into a small space, for example people – strangers; light – glare; beach – the water's edge. Sharpen what you actually mean when you use a verb by being utterly precise, for example broke – shattered; hug – clutch; pushed – jostled.
- Give a specific image of something rather than a general one. Picture a cat. Now picture a black cat. Now picture a black cat with shiny silver paws.

Idea generation techniques

'Inspired by . . .' poems
Take a poem you like from the class library and use it to inspire your own poem.

Poetry from the book you're reading
Choose a sentence or two from your book and turn it into a poem.

Special object
Bring in a special object from home. Describe what you see – using your senses. Describe how it makes you feel. Turn it into a poem.

A tour of your home
Guide your reader through a slow tour of your home. Add detail about what you see, hear, smell and feel and what memories each spot brings up for you. Turn it into a poem.

Seeing things differently
Compare an everyday thing to something else. Compare two people who you know.

Where poetry hides
Run around the house and make a list of the things in it you'd like to write a poem about.

Important people
Make a list of the most important people in your life. Then make a list of memories you have about each person. Choose one and write the memory as a poem.

Memories with strong feelings
Write a list of strong feelings (happy, worried, scared, sad and angry). Then write down a moment when you have felt like that. Turn that moment into a poem.

Favourite places
Describe the smells/sights/sounds of your home or favourite place. Jot down what it's like there. Consider all your senses, thinking about the emotions it brings up for you and what might be important about the place. Turn it into a poem.

Peripheral vision
Follow these steps to create a good poem. Write down:

- An observation (As I sit and see . . .)
- Wonder something (I wonder . . .)
- Second observation (I notice . . .)
- Memory (This moment reminds me of . . .)
- Big idea (share what you think this poem might be about with your reader)

Suggested books

Sensational by Roger Mc Gough
    Unexplained Things about My Dad (Ian McMillan, p 25)
    The Puddle (Jean Sprackland, p 29)
    Who Has Seen the Wind? (Christina Rossetti, p 49)
    Paint Box (Phoebe Hesketh, p 58)
    What is . . . the Sun? (Wes Magee, p 65)

Quieter than Snow (Berlie Doherty, p 81)
November Night (Adelaide Crapsey, p 92)
Joy at the Sound (Roger McGough, p 97)
Pleasant Sounds (John Clare, p 102)
Life Is a Bucket (Roger McGough, p 110)
Peach (Rose Rauter, p 115)
The Apple's Song (Edwin Morgan, p 116)
Gregory Gruber (Marian Swinger, p 190)
Vegan (Benjamin Zephaniah, p 200)
Hot Food (Michael Rosen, p 204)

How to Eat a Poem (Eve Merriam in 'You'll Love This Stuff', edited by Morag Styles, p 96)

The Beach (William Hart-Smith, in 'You'll Love This Stuff', edited by Morag Styles, p 85)

Stopping by Woods (Robert Frost, in 'A Shame to Miss', edited by Anne Fine, vol. 1, p 113)

Poetry that hides in things

Suggested for Years 4 and 5

Why write poetry that hides in things?

This project focuses on poetry that hides in things. It provides children with an opportunity to showcase sensory detail as 'things' that can often be touched, smelled, observed, tasted, heard and thought about. The things children own, find interesting, or are disconcerted by will also tell them a lot about themselves. This personal connection makes for a great writing project.

Writing about *things* can lead children to share and suggest something they might have in common with their reader. They might notice the same things or show something in a new light. The familiar can suddenly become unfamiliar.

Children will learn about symbolism. They will understand that the things we hold at a distance or the things we love can be a symbol for something else – once we dig a little deeper for those diamond moments.

Objects often carry within them memories that can be shared through poetry. This project could culminate in an exhibition for families and the local community to visit. The exhibition could be a great opportunity for others to reflect on and reminisce about *things* from their pasts.

The project also has strong connections to memoir. Children will be able to bring what they have learnt about writing effective memoirs into their poems.

Part B

Things to bear in mind

- This writing project should open up a whole new way of writing poetry. Remember that children may want to write multiple poems during the writing week and build up a collection to choose from when it comes to publishing or performing.
- Children will learn that objects can carry revealing things about us and our lives and that these can be shared and perhaps understood by others.
- You may find that you and your class become so immersed and involved in thinking about your objects that you may want to write memoirs to accompany your poems.
- Children will see that objects are used by writers as symbolic of a much larger psychological or philosophical meaning.
- Once children have understood the concept that poetry can hide and be found in anything, they can bring this idea to all their future writing, including narrative writing. They will begin to describe objects of significance in a deeper way. They should also be able to see that the objects they choose to include in their narratives are often symbols to mean something else. They can also be described according to their character's mood.
- You may also see that they begin to understand and use figurative language to describe phenomena within their non-fiction pieces too.

Idea generation techniques

Make a 'where poetry hides' list. Imagine that this is a treasure hunt of your life. Search your house, family and life for places where poems might be hiding!

> *My 'where poetry hides' list:*
> *In the snuggle rugs the whole family get under before a film comes on.*
> *In my little sister's bright green rattle.*
> *In getting parcels through the post.*
> *In my picture book collection.*
> *In my music collection.*
> *In Dad's ukulele playing – and singing!*
> *In the cobwebs in the corners of my ceiling.*
> *In the heart-shaped pebble I found on the beach.*
> *In my first ever teddy – Flat Ted.*
> *In my very first pair of shoes that Mum keeps in a box under the stairs.*

This morning

Write a list of all the 'things' you have used this morning:

> *Your favourite bowl and spoon*
> *Grandad's old piano stool*
> *The worn-out step you sat on while tying your shoe-laces*

Your school bag bursting with books
The door you slammed shut as you left the house in a mood . . .

First things

Close your eyes and write down the first 'things' that come into your head.

Special items

Tell a partner about some things that are really special to you and why.

Hobbies

Make a list of your hobbies and any equipment you use.

Memories

Think about objects you loved when you were younger and simply have not been able to throw away.

Family treasures

Think of an object that might be special to your whole family.

Picture this

Draw a picture of an object that holds special meaning for you.

Lost things

Write a list of things you or your family have lost which were special to you.

Bring them in

You may want to bring in objects from home or a photograph/drawing of them instead if they are really precious.

Suggested books

All My Own Stuff by Adrian Mitchell

'Inspired by . . .' poetry

Suggested for Years 3 through 6

Why write 'inspired by . . .' poetry?

Writer Michael Rosen says the easiest way to write a poem is to read a poem by someone else and then say to yourself 'I could write like that'. This is what this writing project is all about.

Sometimes it can be hard for writers to generate original ideas all the time, and it doesn't represent how they always work. Poets and story writers alike find themselves inspired by things they see, read or hear from other writers, whether consciously or not. This is called 'intertextuality'. You only need to look inside a writer's notebook to see that they are forever collecting, investigating and imitating little diamond moments that they have found lying around in other texts.

The best way to understand poems is to read a lot of them and to read them often. Children begin to think about what writers are writing and why.

Alongside this writing project, you could read *Love That Dog* by Sharon Creech as your class book. It is written in a free-verse diary format, from the perspective of a young boy (Jack) who initially resists poetry assignments set by his teacher. As time moves on, Jack's confidence grows, and he is able to respond to and take inspiration from poems with increasing sophistication. This book makes for an engaging, child-friendly and incredibly valuable demonstration of intertextuality.

Things to bear in mind

- This will be a very lively, sociable and open-ended project. Children should be encouraged to share and perform poems that they like. They should talk about them with one another and ask each other questions about what they take from the poem. You can model this during conferencing.
- If a particular poem attracts them, ask them to read it multiple times. After a few reads, they may start to write notes – little dabblings. They should continue to read the poem again and again until something starts to happen in their mind. Eventually, they will begin to shift away from the poem and concentrate more on their own dabblings. It's at this point that they might want to consider writing a draft.
- Spend some time yourself reading lots of poems and doing the same. Fill a page of your notebook with little snippets, notes, lists and dabbles you've made. Show this to your class so that they can see the sorts of things they can do too.
- You may find that children write a completely new poem, or they may change certain elements, cut things out, switch things around or add things in. All of these processes are legitimate and are used by published or hobbyist writers.
- Tell children that they can do exactly the same thing with the stories they read. They can take parts of a story that they like and turn these into poems.

Idea generation techniques

Poems everywhere!

Read as many poems as you can. Look in your class library and on school noticeboards. Read poems your friends and teachers have written. Can you find any poems at home?

Take inspiration

When reading poems, be inspired by:

- the objects or events in poems.
- the feeling in a poem.
- a word or line in a poem.
- the memories or thoughts a poem reminds you of.
- the rhythm and/or rhyme of the poem.

Use a 'spark line'

- Take a line you like from a book you have read or are reading and turn it into a poem.

Favourite poems

- Use a poem you've remembered from your past.

Suggested books

Love That Dog by Sharon Creech
Poetry for a Change by various
Rhythm and Poetry by Karl Nova
Happy Poems by Roger McGough
Where the Sidewalk Ends by Shel Silverstein
Poetry Jump-Up! by Grace Nichols
You'll Love This Stuff by Morag Styles
Things You Find in a Poet's Beard by A.F. Harold

Social and political poetry

Suggested for Year 6

Why write social and political poetry?

Throughout the history of this country, there have been radical ballads, songs and poems written with the aim of publicising and protesting against certain social and political issues. They have been shared and performed publicly to create a sense of communality and to be an inspiration for radical action and change. They have been about class oppression, race, gender, war, injustice, inequality, freedom, poverty, religion – whatever have been the preoccupations of the age in which they were written, so that a particular piece of history could be passed on from generation to generation and not lost. Spoken word poetry is also becoming increasingly popular amongst young people, and this project can harness that interest.

We all know that today's children are very concerned about many social issues – human, animal and environmental. They learn about social injustice through the media; it may also affect their lives in a personal way. Writing political and protest poetry is important because it gives children a way of expressing their feelings and worries, asking questions about the world and their dreams and hopes for the future. Sharing their fears and concerns, challenging those who have responsibility and influence, and using their voice for social change can feel empowering and maybe even a little reassuring. And of course it's a perfect example of the whole idea of writing personally, persuasively and for a purpose.

Things to bear in mind

- Remember, your children may already be experienced in writing on subjects such as these because, each year, the class will have had a particular cause or charity focus (see page 37).
- You will see that this project has links to other projects you are undertaking this year, including writing persuasively to the editor of a publication or to a local government representative in the *Community Activism* project (see page 275).
- We highly recommend that you link this project with any PSHE work you are doing this year and to Amnesty International's initiatives: *Words That Burn* and *Make a Difference in a Minute*. Any children who choose to write about human rights should be encouraged to submit their poems to Amnesty's website.
- This poetry project has links to children's 'Inspired by . . .' poetry project from Year 5.
- Children could perform their poems and maybe work out a tune to sing them to.
- Poetry of this kind gives children an opportunity to suggest things, express a belief, reflect, borrow voices, make the common uncommon or capture a moment. They can make comparisons, use personification, consider symbolism, show and not tell, and use imagism. This poetry project provides children with the opportunity to use everything they have learnt about poetic techniques over the past four years.
- Children may see a project such as this as an opportunity to disclose certain circumstances in their lives. This is to be seen as a positive thing; however, you may also have to offer the children your support.

Idea generation techniques

What makes you cross?

A good place to start is to think about anything you've seen on the television or read in a newspaper or book that has angered you.

Give a voice

You could think of someone or something that doesn't have a voice, such as a group of people, animals or things that deserve to be heard. You could start writing something on their behalf or from their perspective. This can be particularly effective if the voice is one that people don't expect to hear.

My life would be different if . . .

Try writing a list of sentences that start with *My life would be different if* . . . and see whether any of the things you think of would make a good topic for a social or political poem.

If I were in charge of the world . . .

Think about what things you'd change if you were in charge of the world, and write a list of sentences that start with *If I were in charge of the world* . . . and see whether any of the things you would change are good subjects for a social or political poem.

All powerful

Write a list of people who have power and a list of people who don't – does it seem fair? If not, perhaps it would make a good social or political poem.

That's not fair!

Write a list of people, animals or even things in the natural world which are not treated well. Ask yourself why this is the case and what you could do about it.

Do your research

Find out about the *Universal Declaration of Human Rights* and see what ideas it gives you.

Suggested books

If I Were in Charge of the World and Other Worries by Judith Viorst
Dreams of Freedom: In Words and Pictures by Amnesty International

Reaching for the Stars: Poems about Extraordinary Women and Girls by Liz Brownlee, Jan Dean and Michela Morgan

England: Poems From a School by Kate Clanchy

Funky Chickens by Benjamin Zephaniah

Ranters, Ravers and Rhymers: Poems by Black and Asian Poets by Farrukh Dhondy

Rise Like Lions: Poetry for the Many by Ben Okri

Anthology of life

Suggested for Year 6

Why write an anthology of life?

This project seems somehow fitting for children in Year 6 to mark an important time of transition from primary to secondary school. Children are going to create anthologies of poems about growing up and childhood. We highly recommend that you read *What I'll Remember When I Am a Grown Up* by Gina Willner-Pardo with your class throughout this class writing project.

Poetry is a wonderful medium for looking back on our lives because children's impressions and memories can be captured in a shorter, simpler and more natural way than in prose.

Not only is an 'anthology of life' a means for children to connect with themselves, it can also bring the writing community in your classroom together. This is a purposeful project. It is something that will be cherished and great care will be taken over it.

Children will achieve an anthology of personal poetry based on their memorable experiences. This writing project will give children the time and space to draw on their experiences of the past four years of writing poetry, to look back at poems already written and to write lots of new ones. They will select the best and publish them in any arrangement they choose.

Things to bear in mind

- As with any kind of writing, writers should mine their thoughts for the diamond moment in each piece of writing, hold on to it and polish it up.
- Remember that poems are to be shared with the world. So why not suggest that children make a copy of their anthology and give it as a gift to a friend.
- The best anthologies are those which have a lot of variety. It doesn't all have to be nostalgic in a sad way. Remember anecdotes, significant moments, funny incidents, happy times, surprises and, importantly, the little things. Talk about things the class has experienced together as a group throughout their time at primary school.
- Play around with words and forms. Enjoy the process.
- Children should remember that memoir poetry is about sharing in a poetic way a connection to an experience and their feelings about it. Readers will relate to the writer, connect with their insights and perhaps even feel they know the writer a little better.

- Children don't need to have experienced major 'blockbuster' moments in their lives. It's often better that they write about ordinary, everyday occurrences and consider why these things are significant and important to them as they've grown up.
- Children may feel a desire to write their poems as fully fledged memoirs. This seems wholly acceptable.

Idea generation techniques

Ideas hearts

Create an 'ideas heart' and add to it throughout the year. This is a heart that you fill up with all the things you love and care about.

Photographs from your childhood

Bring in photographs of you when you were little; do you remember when and why the photograph was taken? Does it bring back any special memories? Is there a story behind the photograph that you could tell in the form of a poem?

Artefacts from home

Have you got something special or something that reminds you of someone or some time? What makes it special to you?

Memories

Write down all your treasured memories. What was your first memory? What memories do you have from school? What memories do you have of friends, family and loved ones?

Read other poems to get ideas

Have a go at reading some other poems to get ideas and inspiration.
    Does the poem remind you of any of your own experiences? Could you write a poem like that?

Tell a partner a story about you

Discuss ideas with a partner. They might remind you of something or prompt ideas.

Timeline

Create a timeline of your life so far, recording important events and memories.

Suggested books

What I'll Remember When I Am a Grownup by Gina Willner-Pardo
101 Poems about Childhood edited by Michael Donaghy
Grow Your Own Poems by Peter Dixon
Been to Yesterday: Poems of a Life by Lee Hopkins **(adult only)**
Baseball, Snakes, and Summer Squash: Poems about Growing Up by Donald Graves
The Best of Children's Poetry edited by Jennifer Curry
Heard It in the Playground by Allan Ahlberg
Please Mrs Butler by Allan Ahlberg
A Kid in My Class by Rachel Rooney
Overheard in a Tower Block by Joseph Coelho
Quick, Let's Get Out of Here by Michael Rosen
Neighborhood Odes by Gary Soto
A Fire in My Hands by Gary Soto
A Caribbean Dozen: Poems from 13 Caribbean Poets by Grace Nichols
Swings and Shadows: A Childhood in Poetry by Anne Harvey
The Nation's Favourite Poems of Childhood by Esther Rantzen **(adult only)**

21 Memoir

Suggested for Years 3 through 5

Why write a memoir?

Recounts show us what is remembered but not *why* it is remembered. They are preoccupied with 'information'. This class writing project is different. It shows children that they can share moments from their lives. You and the children will begin to appreciate the things you have in common and the very simple yet heartfelt moments you've already had in life. This is important not only for children's understanding of the power of writing as a reflective tool but also as a social resource. Memoirs are simply little vignettes that occur in everyday life to which we can all relate. They provide a great platform for children to feel they are experts in their topic before they begin writing and give them enough scope as a genre to be playful and try out many of the things they like about writing. Children are also natural memoirists. They love to tell stories of the things that have happened to them but, like all of us, they also enjoy spinning stories which aren't always the whole truth. You can make this a project that brings your whole writing community together.

Things to bear in mind

Year 3

- It's important to encourage children to choose a moment from their lives that has meaning for them. As teachers, we can't give children rich lives, but we can give them the chance to see the richness that is already there. This is what this writing project looks to do. Children's enthusiasm for this project can often result in them writing on too general a theme. They will need you to direct them towards focusing on a single significant 'moment'. This is an important lesson.
- Also bear in mind that memoirs differ from what are commonly referred to as recounts in a number of ways. The major role of a recount is often to ensure that chronological events are described within a conventional time order. However, memoirs are very much about poetry and story-telling. A good memoir will have a topic that has meaning not only for the writer but also for the reader. This means children need to find a subject that rouses emotions in both themselves and their readers. These pieces create the possibility for reflection and empathy in the writing classroom. Memoirs also help young writers to write in a literary way about their personal experiences.
- Children will need to use what they have learnt about story and poetry to tap into their senses and memories for rich description. They need to consider how they can contrast and compare in poetic ways and how sometimes, as memoirists, we bend the truth and use hyperbole to blur memory with effective story-telling.
- More experienced writers will begin to develop a feeling for creating engaging openings and thoughtful endings that make readers reflect.

Year 4

- Children will need to use what they have learnt about story and poetry to tap into their senses and memories for rich description. They need to consider how they can contrast and compare in poetic ways and how, sometimes, as memoirists, we bend the truth and use hyperbole to blur memory with effective story-telling.
- More experienced writers will develop a feeling for creating engaging openings and thoughtful and thought-provoking endings. They will also know how to convey a sense of character in their memoir.

Year 5

- Teaching memoir in Year 5 is a real joy. Children are beginning to get to grips with it as a genre, having been introduced to it in Years 3 and 4. They have also been developing their narrative writing and are really starting to understand the skills required for developing characters and settings. This project will show them how they can bring all these skills together to create possibly some of the best writing you will ever receive.

- Children will have already learnt about how writing poetry can enable them to tap into their senses and memories and create rich description. They should continue to consider how they can contrast and compare in poetic ways and sometimes, as memoirists, bend the truth and use hyperbole to blur memory with telling a good story.
- Children will know from Year 4 that they need to engage their reader with a strong opening and a thoughtful ending to make them reflect.
- In this project, children will focus their memoirs on the people involved. They will move away from plot-driven narrative to look instead at the thoughts and feelings of the people they are writing about. This means you can use many of the lessons and resources that served your children well during their short-story writing.
- The same can be said for setting descriptions. Harness your children's growing expertise in creating vivid settings to transform their memoirs into stunning pieces of writing.
- Finally, you can continue to work on children's ability to 'show' and not 'tell' their narrative.

How to write your own memoir

Use these ideas to help you write your own memoir for use in class or to introduce children to the genre.

Why write a memoir for yourself or your class?

Memoirs are a great tool to help you reflect on and share your experiences. When writing stories about your life you will use many of the same techniques you use when writing fiction. You write a memoir to share an interesting or significant event that has happened to you or that you have observed. Memoirs are also a way of making sure your memories don't disappear. You can share them in the future with family and friends and relive the event(s) yourself. Writing a memoir can also help you to understand the things that have happened and your feelings about them.

What are the basics of a memoir?

When writing memoirs for your class, you will probably want to recall an event that children can relate to. This could be something similar to what they may have experienced themselves. This models the purpose of the writing, and children will be fascinated to hear about your memories, especially if they are about your childhood.

What is your memoir going to be about?

What is great about memoirs is that they can be about anything you have done, seen or experienced in real life! There is a focus in this project on experiences that members of your writing community can relate to. The best memoirs are about something that was really important to you and that you will always remember. These can be happy, sad or funny moments in your life. A good memoir describes an event in an interesting way.

- Your memoir should start by introducing the place and the event to readers.
- Include who, what, where, why and when.
- Explain why this event was significant. Share with readers your reflections on what happened. What was the value of this experience? What did you learn, gain or understand?

What is your role as the writer?

Make sure you choose an event that people will want to read about and that they may relate to.
Readers are often less interested in the event itself than in your thoughts and feelings during it. Set your reader up for the experience in your very first sentence or paragraph, for example *You may not believe it, but this really happened to me.*

What should your memoir look like?

Your memoir will look a lot like a story. Make sure key events are written in paragraphs. You may want to add pictures of important moments to give your reader an image of your event or experience in their mind.

Idea generation techniques

Ask yourself questions

One of the best ways to generate ideas for a memoir is to ask yourself questions like these:

- What are my earliest memories?
- What are the most important things that have happened to me in my life so far?
- What have I seen that I cannot forget?
- What has happened that shows what my family and I are like?
- What has happened that shows what my friends and I are like?
- What has happened that shows what my pet(s) and I are like?
- Is there something that happened to me at home that I'll always remember?
- Is there a time when I had a feeling that surprised me?
- Is there an event that changed how I think or feel about something?
- Is there an event that changed my life?

- Has there been a time/place that I was perfectly happy/very sad?
- Is there a time or place that I laughed a lot?
- Is there a time with a family member/friend that I will never forget?
- What happened when I did something for the first time?
- Who are the most important people in my life?
- What memories do I have about these people?
- What stories have my family told me about their lives?
- What am I most afraid of?
- What hopes and dreams do I have for the future?
- What do I want to change?
- What do I like to daydream about or imagine?
- What makes my friends and me laugh?
- What are the things/people/foods/animals/hobbies that I love?
- Where are my favourite places?
- What hobbies/people/sports/animals do I know a lot about?
- Can I remember a time I learnt to do something or did something for the first time?
- Is there a time when I had a feeling that surprised me?
- Is there an event that changed my life?
- What have I seen that I cannot forget?
- Are there things that particularly frustrate me?
- Is there a time when I have felt ashamed?
- What is my community like?
- How do I feel about my community?
- How do I feel about my school?
- What keeps me awake at night?
- What do I think about when I go for a walk?

Important people

Make a list of the most important people in your life. Now make a list of memories you have with each person.

Memories that generate strong feelings

Write a list of feelings (happy, worried, scared, sad, furious) and moments you've felt each one. Turn one moment into a memoir.

Favourite places

Describe the smells, sights and sounds of your favourite place. Write down what it is like there. Use all of your senses and think about the way those things make you feel. Turn it into a memoir or poem.

Special moments

Make a list of first or last times you have done something. Include times when something changed or when you conquered something. How did these things make you feel? Turn this into a memoir or poem. Try doing an activity to spark your memories.

When I was younger . . .

Write down lots of endings to this sentence until an idea appears.

Scrapbook of your life

Collect items and pictures and ask other people about things you have done so that you can write about them as a memoir.

Something different happened this time

Write down a list of 'always times'. These are things that happen again and again. There are routines you do every day or things you do every year. Think of a time that stands out because it was different to normal.

Illustrate your memories

Bring in photographs from home and write them up as memoirs or poems, describing what you can see and how the picture makes you feel.

Suggested books

The BBC's 'childhood' archive website

The British Library's 'children's playground games' archive website

Michael Rosen's Sad Book by Michael Rosen
Quick, Let's Get Out of Here by Michael Rosen
Hey World! Here I Am by Jean Little
Nothing Ever Happens on 90th Street by Roni Schotter
When I Was Young in the Mountains by Cynthia Rylant
My Rotten Redheaded Older Brother by Patricia Polacco
Gregory Cool by Caroline Binch
Down by the River: Afro-Caribbean Rhymes, Games and Songs for Children by Grace Hallworth
When I Was Nine by James Stevenson
Keeping Clear of Paradise Street by Brian Moses
The Secret Diary of Adrian Mole Aged 13¾ by Sue Townsend
Home by Carson Ellis
Homecoming by Michael Morpurgo
Boy by Roald Dahl
Going Solo by Roald Dahl
War Boy: A Wartime Childhood by Michael Foreman
The Diary of a Young Girl by Anne Frank
What I'll Remember When I'm a Grown Up by Gina Willner-Pard
The Fib, the Swap, the Trick and other stories by George Layton

Part B

Planning grid for a memoir

Introduce the **place** and **your event**. Include: **Who** **What** **Where** **Why** **When**	e.g. You may not believe this, but this really happened to me.
Write, in order, only the most important moments. You might want to use these time connectives. **Last week,** **First,** **When we finally got there,** **After that,** **Finally,**	
To help you plan, write two lists: 1. All **the thoughts that went through your mind.** 2. A list of the **emotions you felt**.	1. Thoughts I had 2. Feelings I had
Why was this event **significant or important** to you? What did you **learn**, gain or understand because of this experience.	

Autobiography

Suggested for Year 6

Why write an autobiography?

People are interesting. Everyone has a story to tell – and an audience eager to read and enjoy it. You might write your autobiography mostly for yourself, perhaps for the pleasure of looking back and being reflective, explaining to yourself how you became who you are, understanding yourself, telling your side of the story. Or you might write it for others to learn new things about you, or for friends to remember you by, or for future readers to learn about the time and the place in which you live. It's a way of making and leaving your mark on the world.

This writing project has a connection to the *Anthology of Life* poetry project, which children will also undertake this year (see page 184). Your young writers will also be drawing on their experiences of writing biography and memoir in other years. Like *Biography*, *People's History* and *Memoir*, children's autobiographies will inform, educate, entertain and give pleasure to themselves and their readers.

Things to bear in mind

- Children's autobiographies can be written as stories, blending facts and feelings to make their text engaging for their readers.
- You might find that children choose to write about too broad a time frame in their lives. Encourage them to try starting small with one memory or part of their life and build the rest of their writing around it, making connections where they can.
- Children can be poetic, paint pictures with words and also be playful. They can stick to a strictly chronological order of events or they can play around with time; for example, begin with the present and then draw on the past to explain it.
- Children should also feel free to use hyperbole when describing any adventures, dramas or tragedies – if there have been any.
- Be careful that you don't try to make this project too formal or serious. These are children's autobiographies and so they should be filled with asides, anecdotes and descriptions of what they see as significant moments in their lives.
- Some children may be concerned that their lives are not worth writing about. Reassure them that what might seem mundane to them will certainly be of interest to their readers. Explain to children that they may well be connecting with their reader through communicating shared experiences.
- If children feel strongly that they do not want to write their own autobiography, they can be invited to write an *autofiction* piece – a fictional piece about themselves or a piece written in the role of a person they have imagined.
- A spin-off from this project is to ask children to write their *future* autobiography. This can show children how writing can enable us to socially dream.

How to write your own autobiography

Use these ideas to help you write your own autobiography for use in class or to introduce children to the genre.

Why write an autobiography for yourself or your class?

To share with others something about yourself and your life.

What are the basics of an autobiography?

You might write your autobiography mostly for yourself, perhaps for the pleasure of looking back and being reflective, explaining to yourself how you became who you are, understanding yourself and telling your side of the story. You might also write it to show young readers how your life was different from life nowadays. In this way, autobiography has much in common with *People's History* (see page 279).

What is your autobiography going to be about?

An autobiography is about yourself, above all. A good autobiography describes what you did, how you did it and the impact it has had on your life so far. It might also put your experiences into the context of the time you live in.

- You will need to introduce who you are, when you were born, where you are from, what you have achieved or experienced in your life so far, and maybe your strongest memory.
- Choose the main event or most significant memory from your life and spend time explaining it. Write something about your early childhood to give more information about you.
- Explain why this moment or event has been significant or important to you and your hopes for the future.

What is your role as the writer?

Make sure you choose something people will like to hear about but might not know about you. You then have to keep it interesting throughout. Remember that this is a historical document that may well be read many years in the future to better understand life at a particular time.

- Only include the most interesting or significant bits of your life. Remember that the everyday can be interesting for people to read about.

- Help readers in the future picture the era and the circumstances in which you lived. You might want to 'paint with words'. For example, you could describe the era or where you live at the beginning of your autobiography.

What should your autobiography look like?

Have a standout title that will intrigue and interest the people reading about you and your life. Autobiographies have a clear beginning and ending. They are paragraphed and usually, though not always, tell events in chronological order. You may want to add pictures or photographs of important things or moments in your life.

Idea generation techniques

A picture speaks a thousand words

Bring in some photographs from home and write them up as autobiography.

Use artefacts

Bring in an object from home which carries with it a story from your life.

Ask yourself . . .

Write down the answers to some of these questions. Think about which memories are important to you and would be interesting for someone to read.

- What are your strongest memories?
- What would you say has been your greatest achievement?
- What stories can you think of from your early childhood?
- What stories can you think of from your school life?
- What stories can you think of from your home life?
- Can you think of a story about a friendship?
- Are there any sad stories from your life that you would be willing to share?
- Can you think of your happiest ever moment?
- Can you think of a cheeky story or a story that will make your readers laugh?
- Can you think of something that changed your life?

Part B

- Can you write a descriptive paragraph, setting the scene and the era you're writing about?
- Can you write a character description about yourself?
- Can you mix your autobiography writing with story-telling?
- Can you write your autobiography as a prose poem?

Suggested books

How to Write Your Life Story by Ralph Fletcher
Looking Back: A Book of Memories by Lois Lowry

Memoir

Planning grid: autobiography

The purpose of my autobiography is to . . .	
Eye-catching title	
Introduce who, when and where. Then briefly mention what you've achieved in your life.	
Talk about your early childhood.	
What led up to the important achievement or memory you have chosen to give detail to? Use dates.	
Your main achievement or memory – Why do you remember it out of all of your achievements and memories?	
Why were these events or memories important and what are your hopes for the future?	

22 | Narrative

Traditional fables

Suggested for Year 3

Why write a traditional fable?

We often tell each other cautionary tales of mishaps, near misses and comeuppances where we have had to learn a lesson the hard way. Perhaps, like me, you learnt that you really should not play with scissors after you accidentally almost cut your friend's finger off! We might also remember our grandparents, parents, teachers and people in authority telling us stern warning stories. Children can't escape fables!

   Historically though, fables have been the main way of socialising children into the norms of society. Some of those stories are new and original, while others have been told and loved

Narrative

by people across the ages. Many tales are still told and retold today because of their universal messages and because they are short, snappy and easy to remember.

Writing fables with children gives them the opportunity to communicate a message or moral in an entertaining way, building narratives from their own experience of being told what to do (and what not to do) and how to behave with and around others. They can then share these fables with their friends, younger children or even foolish parents! Furthermore, children get to express a little bit of themselves in their stories. Writing fables also gives children a strong basis for future story writing.

Things to bear in mind

- Encourage children to think about lessons they have learnt from their own lives or from others.
- Fables are often short and snappy, so children will need to focus closely on their chosen message, plot and main characters.
- Children should understand that not all fables are old stories with animal characters.
- Animals are perhaps traditionally used by fable writers to avoid causing offence to the person the fable is aimed at. Certain animals are often associated with certain human traits, so encourage children to think carefully about which animal will be right for their fable.

Modern fables

Suggested for Years 3 and 4

Why write a modern fable?

In the previous class writing project on fables, children learnt how fables have been told and loved by people of many cultures through the ages. These tales are still told and retold because of their universal messages and because they are short, snappy and memorable.

This class writing project will build on children's existing knowledge of fables. Children can look at how fables are part of their lives. When do they hear fables, and from whom – their grandparents, parents, teachers or friends? Do they tell cautionary tales to the people they know? Allow children to identify the elements that make fables so popular and discuss where they can be found within our lives today.

Things to bear in mind

- Encourage children to consider the moral they are trying to teach through their fable.
- Remind children to think about modern-day settings and perhaps draw on their own experiences of lessons learnt. Be sensitive to the possibility that some children may have had difficult life experiences and do not press them to write from their own lives if they are reluctant to

do so. Focus on familiar mottos that can serve as the moral of a story, and encourage children to work back from there, thinking of real or hypothetical experiences that will illustrate them.

- You may find that children at this stage in their development are still used to 'telling' you what happens in their fable. Their early drafts may read more like a recount than an entertaining retelling. Encourage children to try techniques like 'show don't tell' and to consider other features of narrative writing.
- More experienced writers will certainly begin to play with narrative throughout this project. They will showcase signs of setting description, character development and useful dialogue and perhaps play with pace. They may begin to experiment with what we call 'camera angles' through which they change the focus. They may take a wide-lens view at times or use a close-up.

How to write your own fable

Use these ideas to help you write your own fable for use in class or to introduce children to the genre.

Why write a fable for yourself or your class?

You might enjoy teaching a lesson about life to others in an entertaining way.

What are the basics of a fable?

When writing a fable, ensure you keep it short and snappy and always have a clear moral.

What is your fable going to be about?

Think of fables you were told as a child and focus on what made them memorable or entertaining. Alternatively, think about the cautionary tales you tell the children in your class. Your fable should start by introducing a character(s) to your readers. Give your character a quality, such as greedy, kind, industrious, brave, foolish, lazy or cunning, then describe an event that will either end well or badly. Make the lesson clear, stating it at the end of the story.

What is your role as the writer?

Your role as the writer is to give enjoyment to your readers but also to help them remember the moral of the story. Younger children are always an ideal audience because you can put yourself in the position of an adviser. Make it funny if you like, but it should always have a serious lesson to teach. Keep the story moving quickly.

Narrative

What will your fable look like?

Your text will be a short narrative written in paragraphs. Your readers should be able to identify a clear beginning, middle and end structure to your writing. Pictures in the story will help your readers to form images in their minds and could make the story more amusing.

How can you make your fable clear and interesting?

You can:

- Establish the character and the setting at the very beginning.
- Use adverbials of time: the next day, meanwhile, in the end, once upon a time, soon after, a little later, finally, after that.
- Time openers can make sure your fable has a speedy pace.
- Include dialogue to move the action along and to communicate what the characters are like.

How can your word choices help?

Throughout your information text, you will describe things. You may find the following linguistic devices particularly helpful:

- Use noun phrases to describe the important nouns: characters, places or things.
- Don't always use the first verbs that come into your head – think of alternatives.
- Use adverbs to describe how characters do things.

Idea generation techniques

- Many of the fables we tell today have been told for hundreds of years, but you can still come up with ideas for fables of your own.
- You may have been reading fables recently. You may even have a favourite one. Why not borrow the moral and write your own fable about it?
- You may have a favourite character from a fable you have read. Why not teach that character another lesson?
- Do you tell warning stories to younger children? You could turn one into your own fable.
- You might have had to learn a lesson the hard way! You could turn it into your own fable.

Part B

Read–draw–write!

Read lots of different examples of fables. As you read, make notes of the morals and characters in the stories. Could you explain the same moral with different characters and events? Once you feel you have a clear idea, start writing.

Something I know

You might have learnt a life lesson you'd like to share with others. Could you pass it on as a fable?

Warning stories and proverbs

You might tell warning stories to younger children or know a motto that gives good advice. Why not turn one into your own fable?

I learnt the hard way

Maybe you've had to learn a lesson the hard way! Perhaps you've made a mistake or had to deal with a problem someone else has caused. You could write a fable to pass on what you learnt from this.

Think about how you like to be treated

Why not write a fable that shows how you think people should and should not behave?

Suggested books

Very Short Fables to Read Together by Mary Ann Hoberman
Fables by Arnold Lobel
The Selfish Giant by Oscar Wilde
Fifty Fables for Children by Johann Wilhelm
Cautionary Tales for Children by Hilaire Belloc
Aesop's Fables by Michael Rosen
Aesop's Fables by Michael Morpurgo
Aesop's Funky Fables by Vivian French

Planning grid: fable

The purpose of my fable is to . . .	
Introduce **character(s)** If you have two characters, they could be contrasting, such as • Weak and strong. • Clever and gullible. • Foolish and sensible. • Greedy and unselfish.	
The Event Does one of your characters try to use the other to get what they want? Or is your character acting alone?	
What happens to the character(s)?	
The ending – **revealing the lesson or the moral.**	

Traditional fairy tale

Suggested for Year 3

Why write a traditional fairy tale?

Fairy tales and folk tales have a high status in literature for children. They are a part of cultural heritage; they express and transmit the values and wisdom of a community; they appeal strongly to the imagination and include familiar, much-loved stories that sprang out of an oral story-telling tradition.

There are various interpretations of what fairy tales might mean, why they were composed and how they could be related to a child's psychological development. These interpretations range from psychoanalytical (the subconscious), to historical and material (folk tales: stories for and about peasants), to political (feminism, class, power structures).

Writing a fairy tale is likely to give the children in your class pleasure and enjoyment because they will be confident with the familiar characters, strong narrative shapes, language patterns and structures. They may also enjoy creating the sense of moral justice with which so many fairy tales end. Also, of course, the possibility of subverting the genre or writing from the perspective of another character means that there are many opportunities for a writer to entertain and be humorous, ironic and surprising. Just as Shakespeare is continually reinvented for modern times, the same is true of fairy tales.

Things to bear in mind

- We all tell stories every day. Folk stories are found all around the world and are loved by people of all ages.
- Fables, myths and fairy and folk tales are the earliest forms of stories, told orally but not written down until many years later.
- It is worth discussing how typical fairy tale genre characteristics make stories memorable for oral story-telling, for example:
    - Straightforward familiar characters who do not need a lot of explanation.
    - Simple plots involving opposites (good and evil, rich and poor, child and adult, animal and human) that are familiar to the audience, so they understand what the story is about.
    - The 'power of three' – things happening in threes, for example three wishes, three chances, three Billy Goats Gruff: a memorable oral story-telling structure that children can use in their own writing to create the rhythm and feel of the fairy tale genre.
- Eating and being eaten often feature in fairy tales.
- Animals are common in fairy tales, including personified animals, magical animals and animals used as a possible metaphor for humans.

- Shape-shifting can also feature: frogs and beasts can turn into princes; pumpkins can turn into coaches; mice can turn into footmen.

Playful fairytales

Suggested for Years 3 and 4

Why play around with fairy tales?

Your class should now be confident with the strong shapes, patterns and structures of fairy tales and so giving yourselves the chance to play around with them is likely to bring you all immense pleasure. Children and adults alike enjoy seeing the familiar made unfamiliar, and this is what the writing project is all about. You are providing a space for children to subvert the genre.

Things to bear in mind

- It is worth discussing the idea of 'playing around' with a story or giving a story a 'twist'. What could this mean? For example, if something is 'twisted' like a plait, its ingredients don't change; it's simply mixed up.
- Keep it simple. Choose a fairy tale you know really well and only change one or two parts of the story. You could change:
    - The characters – stereotypes can be subverted.
    - The settings – stereotypes can be subverted.
    - The time – set the story in the present day, in an unexpected period in the past or in a science-fiction future.
    - The problem, the solution or the ending to create a surprising plot.
    - The viewpoint – more experienced writers may want to write the original story from a different character's perspective.

Idea generation techniques

Read–draw–write

Read your favourite fairy tale, and draw what you read as you go along. Finally, use your drawings to help you write your own retelling.

Start with a problem

Think of a problem. What kind of character could solve that problem? Where could this happen (your setting)? How would it end?

Change a bit

Take a fairy tale you really like and change a little bit of it.

Change the characters

Choose a fairy tale character and change their personality – a stroppy prince? An independent princess? An anxious wolf?

Change the setting

Could you set your fairy tale in an unusual place? Snow White in Hawaii? Red Riding Hood in the desert? Hansel and Gretel get lost in space? Maybe you could set it in the real world?

Change the time

Could you set your fairy tale in modern times? Or perhaps in a time in history that you are interested in. How about a Roman Rapunzel or a Tudor Sleeping Beauty?

Change the problem or the solution

Could you change the problem or the solution in the story? Maybe Red Riding Hood makes friends with the wolf.

Change the ending

Could you change the ending so that it surprises readers? Maybe it's not a happy ending for some. . . . Perhaps Cinderella rejects the handsome prince or they don't catch the Gingerbread Man.

Change the viewpoint

Could you tell the story from the point of view of a different character? Red Riding Hood from the point of view of the wolf or Jack and the Beanstalk from the point of view of the giant!

Change the title

Why not start with changing the title and see whether it inspires a story? Play with words or try to make a joke – Cinderfella? The Princess and the Pea-shooter? Little Red Riding Boot?

Suggested books

Collections

Usborne Illustrated Fairy Tales by Rosie Dickins
A First Book of Fairy Tales by Mary Hoffman and Julie Downing
Illustrated Hans Christian Andersen's Fairy Tales by Usborne Publishing
A Year Full of Stories by Angela McAllister & Christopher Corr
English Fairy Tales Collected by Joseph Jacobs
The Illustrated Anansi by Philip M. Sherlock

Individual tales (Picture books)

Hansel and Gretel by Anthony Browne
The Princess and the Pea by Lauren Child
Cendrillon: A Caribbean Cinderella by Robert D. San Souci
The Twelve Dancing Princesses by Errol le Cain
Thorn Rose by Errol le Cain
Molly Whuppie by Walter de la Mare
Anansi and Mr Dry-Bone by Fiona French
The Old Woman and the Red Pumpkin by Betsy Bang
Bimwili and the Zimwi by Verna Aardema
Mufaro's Beautiful Daughters by John Steptoe
What Made Tiddalik Laugh by Joanna Troughton
Tortoise's Dream by Joanna Troughton

Subversive fairy and folk tales

Fairy Tales: The Villain's Version by Kaye Umansky
Mixed Up Fairy Tales by Hilary Robinson

The Cat, the Dog, Little Red, the Exploding Eggs, the Wolf and Grandma's Wardrobe by Christyan Fox

Snow White in New York by Fiona French

Revolting Rhymes by Roald Dahl

Once Upon a Wood by Chris Riddell

After the Fall by Dan Santat

The True Story of the Three Little Pigs by Jon Scieszka

Inside the Villains by Clotilde Perrin

The Gingerbread Man 2: What Happened Later? by Stephen Dixon

Beware of the Bears by Alan MacDonald

The Three Little Wolves and the Big Bad Pig by Eugene Trivizas

The Wolf's Story: What Really Happened to Little Red Riding Hood by Toby Forward

Little Red Reading Hood by Lucy Rowland

Goldilocks and the Three Dinosaurs by Mo Willems

The Stinky Cheese Man and Other Fairly Stupid Tales by Jon Scieszka

Prince Cinders by Babette Cole

The Paper Bag Princess by Robert Munsch

Jim and the Beanstalk by Raymond Briggs

Seriously Silly Stories by Lawrence Anholt

Not All Princesses Dress in Pink by Jane Yolen

The Knight Who Wouldn't Fight by Helen Docherty

Planning grid: fairy tale

The purpose of my fairy tale is to . . .	
Introduce **your place** and **character**.	
The **problem**	
The **solution**	
The ending – the resolution Write a list of potential endings and then pick your favourite one. 1. A short, sharp emotional line 2. A poetic line	

Setting and character-driven short stories

Suggested for Year 4

Why write a short story?

We tell stories all the time and so it is natural for apprentice writers to want to write them. Children at this age can, however, have the misconception that engaging stories are simply based on action and plot alone. These writing projects will show children how writers think carefully and deeply about their characters – and also about their settings. In Year 4, we suggest that you focus on two narrative writing projects. One should develop children's ability to write stories which focus on **creating a vivid setting**. The other should focus on **character-driven** stories. They will then be able to combine what they have learnt in their short story projects in Year 5.

Idea generation techniques

What is on your mind?

- What do you think about when you go for a walk?
- What keeps you awake at night?
- What really gets on your nerves?
- What do you try not to think about?

What if . . . ?

Write a list of 'What if . . . ' questions. Roald Dahl famously came up with the idea for *Charlie and the Chocolate Factory* by writing this question:

What if a crazy man ran a chocolate factory?

When I was younger . . .

Write a list of 'When I was younger . . . ' sentences.

Imagine a day when . . .

Write down some 'Imagine a day when . . . ' sentences.

Start with a problem

Think of a problem. What kind of character could solve it? Where would this happen (the setting)? How would it end?

Use a 'spark line'

Take a line you like from a book you have read or are reading. Turn it into a short story.

Write three – choose one

As a whole class, in a group, with your partner or even on your own, write down three story ideas that come into your head. Choose one you would like to turn into a short story.

Read–draw–write

Read examples of short stories. As you read, make notes about and draw the events and characters in the stories. Once you feel you have a clear idea, start writing.

Setting-focused short stories

Things to bear in mind

- Children will have a good understanding of plot through their narrative projects in Year 3. This writing project should therefore focus on writing intriguing openings which might suggest a character or a setting – read some short stories and you'll see. They can also write a variety of endings. In a short story the main event is normally, but not always, resolved at the end.
- Limit the children's stories to no more than two pages in length. You might want to limit less experienced writers to just a page. The reason for this is so that children begin to use their revision pages more effectively.
- Settings can be treated as additional 'characters' and take on human traits and emotions – this is known in writing circles as 'pathetic fallacy'. Seeing settings as characters influences how they are described and how they behave.
- Additionally, you should teach your children that setting descriptions can be based on how the setting is observed through a character's eyes at the time. For example, two

people may well describe the same place in very different ways depending on their mood, morality or intentions.
- This writing project builds on what the children have learnt in Year 3 and prepares them for what they will tackle in Years 5 and 6. You will also see these techniques influencing their other writing, including memoir and poetry.

Character-driven short stories

Things to bear in mind

- Characters can be developed through sensory description and dialogue, but there is much more to it than this. For example, children will also learn that writers associate their character with a specific emotion or quality. It is here that children will use what they have learnt about comparison, simile, metaphor and symbolism in poetry projects to develop their characters further.

How to write your own short story with a vivid setting

If you are writing about a place your reader is unlikely to have seen or know anything about, you need to provide an effective setting paragraph to make them feel at home. It is also an opportunity to 'paint with words' and bring some poetry to your story.

Some stories barely talk about the setting. Many fairy tales, for example, don't write about the setting very much at all. Instead they often use 'Once upon a time, in a far-away land' to set the stage.

If you're writing about a specific place, it can be important to ensure your reader understands the historical period or the geographical location your story is set in.

What is your text going to be about?

Setting doesn't just mean location, though this is one important part of setting. You need:

- Location
- Weather
- Time of day
- Historical time
- Character's feelings
- Setting as a character

What is your role as the writer?

- Everyday settings don't often need to be described because your reader will know about them, unless of course you are writing about an ordinary day when something unusual happens. It is the extraordinary places, where your reader may never have been, that need to be described well.
- If the weather is a part of your story, you need to describe early what the weather is like, particularly if it is something your reader may never have witnessed for themselves.
- The time of day can have a real impact on your reader, particularly if you are writing ghost or scary stories.
- If your story is set in the past or future you need to let your reader know. They may become confused if you include things that would not have been possible in a past era or if they aren't told that the location is set in the future.
- How you describe your setting can tell your reader a lot about how your character is feeling at the time.
- Finally, through personification, you can use your setting as an additional character in your story.

What does your setting look like?

Sometimes a paragraph at the start of your story is where you describe your story's setting. Otherwise, it's often when a new setting or scene is first introduced to your readers, and this can be at any point in the story.

How do you keep your reader on track?

Using powerful nouns and verbs is an effective way to describe setting. You could use verbs to describe the sights, sounds and smells of a busy street. You do not have to rely on adjectives to write a vivid setting.

How to write your own character-driven short story

Use these ideas to help you develop a powerful and realistic character in your story.

Why develop a character?

Your character is what your story is centred around. Readers can only choose a favourite character if they know a lot about them, so writers work hard to share information about their characters.

Characters might be people, robots, magical creatures or personified animals. Writers such as Roald Dahl would use either the best or worst characteristics of themselves or others as inspiration for their characters.

How will you develop a character?

Writers typically develop characters in six ways:

- **Appearance:** When introducing a character for the first time, writers will describe how their character looks: facial features, body shape, dress and mannerisms.
- **Action:** What a character does and how they do it (verbs and adverbs) will tell you a lot about them. Why do they do the things they do? What do they believe in? What do they believe is right and wrong?
- **Speech:** A writer will think about what their character says and how they say it.
- **Emotions:** A writer thinks about the way their character will be feeling and what their emotions will be throughout the story. Their emotions will often be based on what the character cares about the most.
- **Monologue:** A great way to let your audience know about your characters is to let the characters themselves tell readers their thoughts and feelings.
- **Poetic metaphor:** Some writers will create a character to be a metaphor or a symbol for something else. The character is there to represent an idea, a way of living your life, a way of thinking or behaving. You can use a character or even a setting to disguise the idea. Writers sometimes make their characters represent themes such as friendship, responsibility, courage and kindness to others.

When will the character's personality be revealed?

You will often write about a character's qualities when:

- you introduce a new character to your story
- a character is doing something
- a character speaks
- a character thinks

How can you maintain your character?

Writers will often 'dabble' (think and make notes) before they start a plan or a draft for a story. A lot of their dabbling centres on their character(s). They will at least consider and often make notes on some of the following:

Narrative

- What are you disguising your character as?
- What would you compare them to?
- Sight: What do they look like?
- Smell: What might they smell like?
- Touch: What is their mood like? What do they feel like to touch?
- Sound: What do they sound like? What might they say?
- Action: What might they do and how they might do it?
- Motives: Why do they do the things they do?
- Taste: If your character had a taste, what would it be?
- Monologue: What do they spend their time thinking about?
- What do other people think of them? How do they live their life?

How can your word choices help?

Use the best verbs, adverbs, adjectives, noun phrases and poetic devices to:

- Describe characters.
- Show how a character says something.
- Write about your character's thoughts.
- Describe what your character does and how they do it.

The 'best' means the ones which will really express what you want to communicate about your character.

Dabbling for a vivid setting

Dabbling is like doodling with words. You can draw or write down ideas, thoughts, words, sentences, phrases – anything you like really! It is good to dabble for a bit, thinking about your setting and how you might want to describe it. Think about these things.

- What might be going on? What action might you see?
- How might your character be feeling?
- If the setting were a person, what might they be feeling?
- What might your character notice?
- What might they touch?

Part B

- What might you hear there?
- What might it smell like?
- What's the weather like? What could you compare it to?
- What time of day is it? Will the time of day affect how your character sees the setting?
- What historical period are you writing in? Is it the present day, the past or the future?
- What could you compare your setting to?
- If your setting were a person, what would they be like?

Dabbling for a character-driven short story

Dabbling is like doodling with words. You can draw or write down ideas, thoughts, words, sentences, phrases – anything you like really! It's good to dabble for a bit, thinking about your setting and how you might want to describe it. Try to think about these things:

- How might your character be feeling?
- If your setting were a person, what might it be feeling?
- What might your character notice?
- What might they touch, hear or smell? What might they compare these things to?
- What time of day is it? Will the time of day affect how your character sees the setting?
- What historical period are you writing in?
- What could you compare your setting to?

Planning grid: short stories with a vivid setting

You can fill out this grid in any order.

I want my reader to think these things about my setting.	
Introduce **place** and maybe **your character**	
Location	
Weather	
Time of day	
Historical time	
Character's mood	

Planning grid for a character-driven short story

Name: What's their name and how old are they?	
Sight: What do they look like?	
Smell: What do they smell like?	
Touch: What is their mood like? What do they feel like to touch?	
Sound: What do they sound like? What might they say?	
Action: What might they do? How they might do it?	
Motives: Why do they do the things they do?	
Taste: If your character had a taste, what would it be?	
Monologue: What do they spend their time thinking about?	
Reputation: What do other people think of them? How do they live their life?	
Comparison: What would you compare them to?	
Disguise: What are you disguising your character as?	

Developed short stories

Suggested for Year 5

Writing a developed short story

In Year 3, children will have experimented with fairy tales, fables and the typical story arcs that writers employ. Last year, they will have written stories with a greater focus on character development and creating effective settings. The role of this writing project is to build on those experiences and give children an opportunity to bring together and develop all they have learnt so far.

- Children will have a good understanding of plot through their writing projects in Year 4. This writing project should encourage them to write intriguing openings that might suggest or establish a character or a setting. Read some short stories, and you'll see. Children can also write a variety of endings. Their short stories don't necessarily have to be resolved at the end.
- We suggest that you still limit the children's stories to no more than two pages in length; you might want to limit less experienced writers to just a page. The reason for this is so children continue to use their revision pages more purposefully.
- Children should now be developing their characters through sensory description and dialogue. They will also be aware that, when writers dabble and write, they associate their character with a specific emotion or quality. Children will use what they have learnt about comparison, simile, metaphor and symbolism from other projects to develop their characters even further.
- Children will be further aided by their experience of writing memoir, in which focus on character occurs quite naturally.
- Remind children that settings can be treated as additional 'characters' and take on human traits and emotions – this is known as 'pathetic fallacy'. Seeing settings as characters influences how they are described and how they behave.
- Additionally, you should teach children that setting descriptions can be based on how the setting is observed through a character's eyes at the time. For example, two people may well describe the same place in very different ways depending on their mood, morality or intentions.
- This writing project builds on what the children have learnt in Year 4 and prepares them for what they will tackle in Year 6. You will continue to see these techniques influencing their other writing, including memoir and poetry.

How to write your own short story

Use these ideas to help you write your own short story for use in class or to introduce the genre to the children.

Why write a short story for yourself or your class?

To share an experience, entertain, explain a mystery of the world or teach a lesson about life to other people.

What are the basics of a short story?

Stories are all around us; we tell them every day when we recount events to others. Storytelling is the same all around the world in every culture and language and amongst people of different ages. An effective story has the power to grip your readers' imagination whether they are adults or children.

What is your short story going to be about?

In a story something always happens: an event! This event needs to be interesting or exciting for your reader and smaller events lead up to it. At the end of the story the main event is usually resolved or partly resolved. All may end happily (or not!). Begin by introducing a place and your character(s) to your audience. Writer Ralph Fletcher uses the metaphor of a waterfall when starting a story. He says that you shouldn't start your story 'too far up stream' away from the roar of the waterfall. Always start at the roar of the waterfall.

You then need to think of a 'problem' or 'main event'. The problem/event could be:

- Between your character and nature.
- Between a character and a powerful person or group of people.
- Within the character themselves.
- Something that the character(s) have to prepare for, for example a contest.

Your character should explain how they feel about the problem. They must find a way to solve this problem and any other problems that may present themselves throughout the events. Your story will end when most of the problems have been solved. You could choose to write a familiar story but from a different character's point of view.

What is your role as the writer?

Your role as the writer is to entertain and give enjoyment to your audience. Your story can:

- Be funny or serious.
- Be fast paced (although remember not to tell your audience everything). Use 'big sweeps of time' or fronted adverbials, for example as time went by . . ., the months and years came and went . . ., all that time we . . .

Narrative

- Teach your reader a life lesson or try to explain something magical that happens in the world.

Remember that your story shouldn't be too long – don't write unnecessary words! Try to write no more than 350 words.

What should your short story look like?

Your short story will be written in paragraphs. Add illustrations to help your reader understand events further.

Idea generation techniques

Write about what you are most afraid of

What keeps you awake at night? What really gets on your nerves? What do you try to avoid thinking about? Writer Donald Barthelme said 'write about what you're most afraid of'.

What if . . .? Imagine if . . .?

Write a list of 'What if . . .' questions. Roald Dahl famously came up with the idea for *Charlie and the Chocolate Factory* by writing this question: 'What if a crazy man ran a chocolate factory?'

When I was younger . . .

Write a list of 'When I was younger . . .' sentences.

Use your ideas heart

Create an 'ideas heart' and allow children to add to it throughout the year. This is a heart that you fill up with all the things you love and care about.

Use a 'spark line'

Take a line you like from a book you have read or are reading. Turn it into a short story.

Part B

Write three – choose one

As a whole class, in a group, with your partner or even on your own, write down three story ideas that come into your head. Choose one you would like to turn into a short story.

Read–draw–write

Read examples of short stories. As you read, make notes of the events and characters in the stories. Once you feel you have a clear idea, start writing.

Real-life events

Flick through some newspapers or magazines to see whether any headlines grab you.

Start with a character

Think of a really interesting character – perhaps based on someone you know, or made up entirely, and then think of something they might do.

Start with a place

Choose the setting and decide what it is like, who lives there, and what sort of things happen there.

Suggested books

A Sackful of Stories for Eight-Year-Olds by Pat Thomson
Story Shop: Stories for Literacy by Nikki Gamble
Stories for Eight-Year-Olds by Wendy Cooling
Summertime Stories by Enid Blyton
Scary Stories by Val Bierman
Topsy Turvy Tales by Leila Berg
Granny's Wonderful Chair by Frances Brown (collection)
Shakespeare Stories and Greek Myths by Orchard Publishing
Tales from the Caribbean by Trish Cooke
Short Christmas Stories by Maggie Pearson

Planning grid: short story

The purpose of my story is to . . .	
Introduce **place** and **your character**. Try out opening your story with the following and pick your favourite one: 1. **a question** 2. **a description** 3. **an action** 4. **dialogue** 5. **shock/surprise**	
The **problem** 1. The problem could be between your character and nature. 2. It could be between a character and powerful people (parents, police or teachers). 3. It could be a problem within the character themselves.	
How the character **feels** about the problem	
The ending – the **resolution** Write a list of potential endings and then pick your favourite one 1. An ending that matches your opening sentence in some way. 2. A short, sharp emotional line. 3. A poetic line.	

Part B

Graphic novel

Suggested for Year 5

Why write a graphic novel?

Traditionally, graphic novels have been politically charged and have now become a vital part of contemporary culture. Many of the books children love have taken on the multimodal nature of graphic novels. Children are reading them and also watching them come alive on the big screen.

This project is all about narrative writing. Historically, the narrative themes that tend to inspire graphic novels have included good versus evil, strengths and weaknesses, revenge, betrayal, haunting back-stories, understanding one's self and saving the people and the things we love. They are universal themes which have been sources of great writing for centuries.

What will be new and interesting for you and your class is the concept of using pictures to do some of the story-telling for you. You will begin to appreciate how much readers enjoy learning about characters through the images that graphic novelists create. Graphic novelists consider their characters with real care and attention, just as more traditional narrative writers do. The hope is that, as a result of undertaking this writing project, children will consider their characters in more detail in their future narrative writing too.

Things to bear in mind

- Children will first draft their graphic novels in a traditional way. They will write a short narrative, considering their settings, characters and plots just as they are used to doing. Children will therefore find the guidance on 'How to write a vivid setting' (see page 212) and 'How to develop a character' (see page 215) useful.
- Once they have written, children will consider how they are going to translate their characters' actions, feelings and thoughts in a visual way. This process is called 'storyboarding'. When their storyboards are complete, they can then publish their story as a graphic novel.
- Children must think about how they will convert their figurative language and sensory detail into an image on the page. They should understand that their drawings will have to show the necessary detail that is usually in their writing. It is important to note that this project is not designed to assess children's artistic ability.
- Children will have to make decisions about what is going to be put into their graphic novel and what will be left out. They must also think about how they will clearly show transitions between place and time.
- When they use captions and speech in their graphic novels, children will need to think hard about what they are going to write. They will need to ask themselves what is essential and what can be left out.
- Children will also have to think about how their story is going to affect their drawing style. Their illustrations should match the tone and theme of the story.

How to write your own graphic novel

Use these ideas to help you write your own graphic novel text for use in class or to introduce the genre to the children.

Why write a graphic novel for yourself or your class?

Many people have a passion for bringing words and pictures together. Good graphic novelists use their illustrations to show drama and emotion in characters that they may not be able to show in writing.

What are the basics of a graphic novel?

It tells a story using a mix of pictures and text, with no rules for artwork style or amount of text used.

What is your graphic novel going to be about?

These are some of the typical plots used in graphic novels:

- A supervillain has to steal a number of things to take over the world and needs to be stopped.
- A supervillain is trying to kill a number of people who have something in common and needs to be stopped.
- A supervillain plays on a superhero's weaknesses (e.g. they are trusting of people and loved ones).
- Something or someone from a superhero's past comes back to haunt them.
- A superhero was born with superpowers they don't understand and cannot control.
- Someone who a superhero cares about is in trouble and needs to be saved.
- Someone has been mind-controlled or impersonated by a shape-shifter.
- Revenge.
- A victim comes to a superhero for help.
- A superhero has to work with someone they detest to save the world.
- A superhero is betrayed by a friend.

What is your role as the writer/illustrator?

You need to take care that your story is simple enough to be followed using only a small amount of text and detailed illustrations. Also consider the following:

- Graphic novels usually show how good defeats evil.
- There is a lack of female heroines in graphic novels, and this needs addressing.
- There is a lack of ethnic diversity in the heroes in graphic novels, and this needs addressing.

What should your graphic novel look like?

Before you begin creating a storyboard for your graphic novel, you will first need to write your story. This will look the same as any other short story or flash fiction. Once you have written your story, you'll turn it into a storyboard. A storyboard is where you write the story as small captions and make quick, rough drawings that will show the descriptions and characters you have created in your story. Once you have created your storyboard, you can begin publishing your graphic novel for real.

How can your word choices help?

- They can tell your reader where the characters are.
- Fronted adverbials signal when and where events happen and move the story on.
- They can tell us about sound effects.
- Dialogue tells your reader what your character is like and shows how your character says something.

How should your graphic novel be illustrated?

The importance of the illustrations can make writing effective graphic novels difficult. You will need to decide on an illustration style. This style should match the theme and tone of your story. Your illustrations provide your reader with information that is not written anywhere on its pages (a raised eyebrow from a character, a tear running down a cheek, etc.) Graphic novels often don't need long descriptions because the detailed illustrations will show **feelings, noticing, imagining, hearing, touching, action, asking, tasting** and **smelling**.

Your illustrations must make an impact on your reader and be memorable. They need to show the detail that you would usually include through writing. How can you show your characters' feelings and create a certain mood with the use of colour and shading?

Idea generation techniques

Draw it!

You could start by drawing your ideas. You could draw the following:

- Lots of different superheroines and superheroes.
- A supervillain who has to steal a number of things to take over the world and needs to be stopped.
- A supervillain who plays on a superhero's weakness (e.g. a superhero who trusts people too easily).
- Something or someone from your hero's past who comes back to haunt them.
- Someone your superhero cares about and who is in trouble and needs saving.

- A person who can be a shape-shifter.
- Someone who might need to come to your hero for help.
- A person who your superhero detests and who they might have to team up with and trust to save the world.

What are you afraid of?

Try writing about something you are afraid of. What keeps you awake at night? What do you try to avoid thinking about? How about a world taken over by a gang of giant, villainous spiders or child-eating sprouts!

Questions and phrases

Write down some questions or phrases and see if they spark any ideas.
You could try:

- *What if* . . . questions. Did you know that Roald Dahl came up with the idea for *Charlie and the Chocolate Factory* by simply writing the what if . . . question 'What if a crazy man ran a chocolate factory?'
- *When I was younger* . . . sentences.
- *Imagine a day when* . . . sentences.

Use a 'spark line'

Take a line you like from a book you have read or are reading and turn it into a short story.

Write three – choose one

Write down three story ideas that come into your head and choose one you would like to turn into a short story.

Read–draw–write

Read examples of short stories. As you read, make notes of the events and characters in the stories. Once you feel you have a clear idea, start writing.

Dabbling for a graphic novel

Dabbling is like doodling with words. You can draw or write down ideas, thoughts, words, sentences or phrases – in fact, anything you like! It is good to dabble for a bit, thinking about your setting and character and how you might want to describe them.

Think about these things:

- What might be going on?
- How might your character be feeling?
- What might they touch or hear?
- What is the weather like?
- What time of day is it?
- What historical period are you writing in?
- What action might you see?
- If the setting was a person, what would they be like?
- What might your character notice?
- What might it smell like?
- What could you compare it to?
- Will this affect how your character sees the setting?
- What could you compare your setting to?

Suggested books

The Arrival by Shaun Tan

Northern Lights: The Graphic Novel by Philip Pullman

The Golden Compass by Philip Pullman

The Adventures of John Blake by Philip Pullman

Bravo Mr William Shakespeare by Marcia Williams

The Iliad and the Odyssey by Marcia Williams

Chaucer's Canterbury Tales by Marcia Williams

Oliver Twist by Marcia Williams

Some Swell Pup or Are You Sure You Want a Dog by Maurice Sendak

Mr Wolf's Class (series) by Aron Nels Steinke

Glitch by Sarah Graley

Narwhal: Unicorn of the Sea!; Super Narwhal and Jelly Jolt; Peanut Butter and Jelly by Ben Clanton

The Cardboard Kingdom by Chad Sell

Hilda (series) by Luke Pearson

Kai and the Monkey King; Arthur and the Golden Rope; Marcy and the Riddle of the Sphinx by Joe Todd Stanton

Amulet (series) by Kazu Kibuishi

New Kid by Jerry Craft

El Deafo by Cece Bell

Akissi by Mathieu Sapin

Mega Robo Bros by Neill Cameron

Bunny vs. Monkey by Jamie Smart

Planning grid: graphic novel

The purpose of my story is to . . .	
Introduce **place** and **your character**. Try out opening your story with the following and pick your favourite one: 1. **a question** 2. **a description** 3. **an action** 4. **dialogue** 5. **shock/surprise**	
The **problem** 1. The problem could be between your character and nature. 2. It could be between a character and powerful people (parents, police or teachers) 3. it could be a problem within the character themselves.	
How the character **feels** about the problem	
The ending – the **resolution** Write a list of potential endings and then pick your favourite one 1. An ending that matches your opening sentence in some way. 2. A short, sharp emotional line. 3. A poetic line.	

Flash fiction

Suggested for Year 6

Why write flash fiction?

Sometimes called 'micro-fiction' or 'sudden fiction', flash fiction isn't just a very short story, it's a flash moment – part of a much larger untold story, where much is left unexplained. It is typically no longer than 1000 words, but can be as short as 100 words (when it's called a 'drabble') or even 20–50 words (a 'dribble'). Flash fiction challenges children to move forward in their narrative writing from Year 3 and 4, where they are asked to write short stories, to become more discerning with words and to infuse their pieces with aspects of poetry. Indeed, flash fiction can be seen as an extension of free-verse poetry.

Children tend to enjoy writing flash fiction, as it encourages them to come away from the habit of writing at length and to think more carefully about how they can say the things they wish to say. Flash fiction shows children that their narrative writing in the past may have sometimes 'lost its way' by becoming rambling and disorganised. The hope with this writing project is that it has a lasting positive effect on their future story writing. Writers have to be disciplined at the revision stage, deleting rather than adding, and being honest with themselves as to whether that particular adjective or adverb is really vital to the piece. Flash fiction will become a genre enjoyed by the children in your class and is a pleasure to hear read aloud.

Things to bear in mind

- An interesting observation is that, when writing short stories, children often opt for a spooky, mysterious or unexplained ending, typically indicated by ellipsis . . . Alternatively they attempt to reveal or tie everything up in the final sentence. So it's worth encouraging children to consider their last line carefully. An interesting strategy is to get children to actually write their ending in the middle of their piece and have the narrator conclude with a passage reflecting on the significance of what has happened in the story.
- A successful piece of flash fiction does not tell readers the whole story but leaves them to fill in the gaps, what it could have been about or what will happen next. Reading one is often like walking in halfway through a film or leaving before the end. Looking at a narrative painting or photograph is another useful analogy here.
- Discourage children from introducing too many characters. One is often enough. They don't even need to explain who the character is or where they came from and can choose one physical feature of their character (eyes, mouth, voice) through which to convey their personality.
- Ultimately, children should be encouraged to choose between developing a setting or a character within their flash fiction. It's also a good idea to think of a good hard-working title, which children should do after their piece has been drafted.

How to write your own flash fiction

Use these ideas to help you write your own flash fiction for use in class or to introduce children to the genre.

Why write flash fiction for yourself or your class?

It allows you to write and publish stories very quickly. It's similar to writing poetry. Flash fiction means you won't lose your way as you might do if you're writing a long story.

What are the basics of flash fiction?

Limit yourself to only 250 to 300 words. It's a good idea to keep the first draft to one page, which you can then revise and rework to two pages if you want to.

What is your text going to be about?

Luckily, in flash fiction you only need one interesting or exciting event to write about!

- Writer Ralph Fletcher uses the metaphor of a waterfall when starting flash fiction. He says that you shouldn't start your story 'too far up stream'; always start at the roar of the waterfall – at the heart of the action.
- Because words are limited, focus either on character development or description of place or things.

What is your role as the writer?

Your role as the writer is to give enjoyment to your readers and also to make them think.

- Make it funny or serious.
- Keep the story moving quickly – you shouldn't tell your reader absolutely everything! Use 'big sweeps of time' or time connectives such as the following: As time went by, the months and years came and went, all that time we, 10 days later, nothing changed until one day . . .
- Don't write more than around 1000 words – it can be as short as 20 words.

Idea generation techniques

- Start by looking at a picture, photograph, painting or postcard. What is left to the imagination? Focus on that and try to develop it.

Part B

- Visualise a particular scene in your mind, from a book or a film, and put yourself in that scene. 'Picturing' like this is an effective strategy for triggering a flash fiction idea.
- A single word such as darkness, hunger, locked, hide, golden, door, rainforest, or silence can sometimes spark an idea.
- Use a single phrase or sentence (maybe taken from a song or a book) and turn it into a flash fiction: It came from nowhere; rushing towards disaster; blowing in the wind; just in time for tea.
- Bring in a photo or an object from home to spin a story around.
- Think about what you're most afraid of and write about that. What keeps you awake at night? What do you try to avoid thinking about?
- Write a list of 'What if . . .' questions. Roald Dahl came up with the idea for *Charlie and The Chocolate Factory* by simply asking: 'What if a crazy man ran a chocolate factory?'
- Write a list of *'Imagine a day when . . .'* sentences and see whether any of them could be made into flash fiction.
- Re-read a text you have loved this year and look for a moment you would like to have a go at writing as flash fiction.
- Start by thinking of the style of your favourite writer, one of your favourite characters or a favourite setting you've read and build a piece of flash fiction from there.

An ideas map

When drawing an ideas map, take two characters from a book you've read, two settings and two problems and see whether you can connect them to make a flash fiction idea.

Read a moment

Re-read a moment from a text you have loved this year and look for a moment in it you would like to have a go at writing for yourself as flash fiction.

Fan fiction

Write flash fiction in the style of your favourite writer. Write flash fiction using one of your favourite characters. Write flash fiction using a favourite setting you've read about.

Narrative

Stories about people

Stories often involve a person struggling against themselves, a person versus another person, a person versus nature or a person against society. Write down a list of ideas that could work under these categories.

Twenty words

Write a story using only 20 words then turn it into flash fiction.

Create a character

Draw a character. Write about their:

- wants
- needs
- likes
- dislikes
- problems

Describe them and finally place them in a flash fiction moment.

That's me! I wish that was me! That's the worst of me!

Find and use characters from the books you've read and loved. In your own story, use a character that reminds you of yourself, even if it's the darkest and worst part of yourself! Or create a character who you wish you could be more like. This is exactly what real writers do when developing and writing characters.

Parallel stories

Think of two main characters. Plan one character's experience of the story. Beside it, plan what will happen to the second character. Draft it.

Suggested books

Rules of Summer by Shaun Tan
Short! A Book of Very Short Stories by Kevin Crossley-Holland
Short Too! by Kevin Crossley-Holland
A Pocketful of Stories by Stuart Purcell

Part B

Planning grid: flash fiction

The purpose of my story is to . . .	
Introduce **place** and **your character**. Try out opening your story with the following and pick your favourite one: 1. **a question** 2. **a description** 3. **an action** 4. **dialogue** 5. **shock/surprise**	
The **problem** 1. The problem could be between your character and nature. 2. It could be between a character and powerful people (parents, police or teachers) 3. It could be a problem within the character themselves.	
How the character **feels** about the problem	
The ending – the **resolution** Write a list of potential endings and then pick your favourite one 1. An ending that matches your opening sentence in some way. 2. A short, sharp emotional line. 3. ssA poetic line.	
Final line. Write what your final line to your story *could* be before you begin writing.	You can always change this line later.

23 Non-fiction

Information

Suggested for Years 3 through 5

Why write information texts?

Children accumulate lots of information every single day. It is vital to their development as writers that they are given the opportunity to share their knowledge and expertise with others and to experiment with the language and organisation of non-fiction genres.

This class writing project will show children that they can be knowledgeable about a subject and that sharing this knowledge is an enjoyable, social and satisfying thing to do. You and your class will begin to appreciate the pockets of 'communities' that make up a writing classroom – with children talking and sharing with each other their passions, interests and aspects of their lives. It is important for children to understand the power of writing as information-giving but also to experience it as a social resource.

Part B

Things to bear in mind

YEARS 3 AND 4

- Non-fiction can and should give a sense of personal presence. Children should be able to show their personality and use their voice. It is important to encourage children to choose a topic which they are interested in or passionate about, but which they also know enough about to share with the 'community'.
- Non-fiction texts should be kept short throughout primary school – a page to a page and a half is adequate. Children should not be trawling around for information. It's better if they have too much and are required to use their judgment about what to include and what to leave out.
- Children's enthusiasm for writing information texts can often result in their chosen theme being too general. Directing them towards a more focused approach is an important writing lesson. Children often struggle with the generality and sheer size of their initial topic ideas. For example, 'animals' is often a popular topic choice. However, you will find that children initially choose to write about all types of animals. Encourage them to narrow down their topic to, for example, 'dogs', and then maybe to a particular breed of dog. They can enhance the text by referring to their own dog!
- Often at this stage in their writing development, children will assume that others share the same knowledge of the subject. This results in children often failing to give enough basic information to orientate their reader.
- More experienced writers should not only share information but also reveal something of themselves in their writing. One way of doing this is for children to infuse their information text with aspects of memoir writing. For example, they might add a personal note about why their chosen topic interests them.
- Finally, you may find that children slide into writing which is more in keeping with explanation texts. This is thoroughly acceptable as it demonstrates the beginnings of 'genre-hybridising'. You could make this an interesting teaching point.

YEAR 5

- Children last encountered information as a class writing project in Year 4. It is likely they will have continued writing information texts in their personal writing projects. Now that children know the basics, this project will show them how rich and varied this genre can actually be.
- There are three likely avenues that children's chosen topics will go down throughout this project:
    - **Poetic information text:** This is where children may write a traditional information text in an entertaining and poetic way. Using figurative language and comparison in their descriptions can really bring an extra dimension to their non-fiction writing.

- **Memoir-infused information text:** This is where children exploit their personal connection with a topic and bring personal anecdotes, feelings, thoughts and information together in their writing.
- **'Faction' information text:** This is where children explore the opportunity of mixing factual and fictional writing. Teaching and entertaining at the same time. For example: 'How to look after your pet ghost'. Alternatively, they may do what Terry Deary has been so successful at in his *Horrible Histories* series: mixing his knowledge and passion for history with his ability to tell amusing stories.

- Break the misconception that information texts must be overly formal. Show children how personable and entertaining information writing can be. It can in fact evoke all the senses and leave readers genuinely in awe, entertained, thrilled, emotional, persuaded and informed – often all within the same piece.
- Children's conclusions to their pieces could provide final insight, potential actions, reflection, discussion points, challenges or implications to be considered by their reader.

How to write your own information text

Use these ideas to help you write your own information texts in class or to introduce children to the genre.

Why write an information text for yourself or your class?

If you are an expert on a topic, you can tell people about it.

What are the basics of an information text?

When writing an information text, you should focus on the 'whats' and 'hows' of your topic. Avoid writing too much about why things happen, because this is the purpose of an explanation text.

What is your information text going to be about?

Are you an expert on cats, the Vikings, or gymnastics? Tell your audience about it and inspire them too. It is best to write an information text about something you really love or know a lot about and that you would like to share with your readers. Information texts do not have to be factual; they can also be about things that are not real, for example mythical creatures.

You should focus on three things: **classifying** what your topic is, **describing** your topic and the **effect** your topic has on the world.

What is your role as the writer?

If you are writing information texts for children, make the facts sound as exciting and as interesting as possible. Often, your role as the writer of an information text is to deliver the facts clearly so that people can learn from them. It is helpful to use a question as a subheading and then write a paragraph answering the question. Remember that readers may need some words (technical vocabulary) explained to them.

What should your information text look like?

Your information text should be multimodal. This means that you will use lots of different ways (or modes) to demonstrate what you know. For example, you could use:

- Diagrams, photos, pictures, fact-boxes, lists, bullet points or a key.
- Different font sizes and colours.
- Headings are extremely important too. Write down a few possible headings when you are planning your information text and use them in your writing.

How can you make your information text clear and interesting?

You can:

- Use generalisers, for example *all, many, most, few*.
- Compare things, for example *biggest, smallest, longer, shorter*.
- Use colons – these tell your reader that an example is about to be given.

Idea generation techniques

I'm an expert in . . .

Write an 'I'm an expert in . . . ' list and turn your passion into an information text.

Write about your class topic lessons

Use what you are learning about this term to write an information text.

Read–sketch–write

Read to learn some more information about a topic you are interested in. As you read, sketch and label what you are learning about. Once you feel you have enough information, start writing.

Have you ever wondered about . . .?

End this sentence and talk to a friend about it. Write some notes and then turn them into an information text.

Think fiction!

Write a list of fictional things you could write an information text about. Why not start with fairy tales, folk tales and myths, or your favourite books or films?

Have you ever wondered about . . .?

End this sentence and talk to a friend about it. Write some notes and then turn them into an information text.

What information is important to share?

Think about something that is really important for people to know.

What have I always wanted to find out about?

Have you ever really wanted to find out about something but never had the time? Has something you have never known much about caught your attention? Do you long to learn about the mythology of pixies or have you always been curious about what snail snot is? Do some research and challenge yourself to write an information text about it.

Ask your audience . . .

Ask the same question of your classmates. Is there something they have always wanted to learn more about? Could you write your information text to help them learn? Score each suggestion to show how interested you are in the topic and whether you already have any knowledge of it.

Suggestions	My interest level Score 0–10	My knowledge level Score 0–10

Suggested books

The Earth Book by Jonathan Litton

Dragonology: The Complete Book of Dragons by Dugald Steer, Helen Ward and Douglas Carrel

True or False by Andrea Mills

Until I Met Dudley by Roger McGough

Wallace & Gromit: The Complete Cracking Contraptions Manual by Derek Smith and Graham Bleathman

Flanimals by Ricky Gervais

The Emperor's Egg by Martin Jenkins

The Way Things Work by David Macaulay and Neil Ardley

Corpse Talk (series) by Adam Murphy and Lisa Murphy

A Viking Adventure; A Roman Adventure; An Egyptian Adventure by The Histronauts

Chop, Sizzle, Wow by The Silver Spoon

What's The Difference? by Strack Plantevin and Guillaume Plantevin

Creaturepedia; Plantopedia by Adrienne Barman

The World of the Unknown (series): Ghosts, Monsters, Mysteries of the Unknown, UFOs by Usborne

Planning grid: information text

My plan The purpose of my information text is to . . .	
Classification Introduce what your topic is.	
Description Describe, give details and facts about your topic and be **multimodal**.	Write down some **headings**, e.g. **Food Homes Behaviour Appearance Health**
Effect Finish by writing about why this topic is important to you or the world.	

Instructions

Suggested for Years 3 and 4

Why write instructions?

Instructional writing – the recounting of processes – is an important genre that is vital to science, business, and art and design. It is also, perhaps surprisingly, a remarkably rich genre, offering children many possibilities for innovative writing and for creating hybrids with, for example, information, explanation, memoir, poetry, 'faction' and persuasion. A good book that showcases exactly this is *How To* by Julie Morstad. Children can write instructions for a number of reasons: to share their expertise with the community; to enable others to take part in pleasurable, useful or necessary activities; and sometimes simply to help themselves remember how to do something they have just learnt. It is a genre of writing that they can stretch, expand and take in different directions. Why not be enthusiastic, entertaining, ironic, poetic, sarcastic and experimental and let your own voice come through?

Things to bear in mind

- Non-fiction can and should give a sense of personal presence. Children should be able to show their personality and use their voice. It is important to encourage children to choose a topic which they are interested in or passionate about, but which they also know enough about to share with the 'community'.
- Non-fiction texts should be kept short throughout primary school – a page to a page and a half is adequate. Children should not be trawling around for information. It's better to have too much and be required to make judgments about what to include and what to leave out.
- More experienced writers should also reveal something of themselves in their writing. One way children can do this is by infusing their instructions with aspects of memoir writing. For example, they might add a personal note about why their chosen topic interests them.
- Often at this stage in their writing development, children will forget that their audience is not actually present to watch the process. This can result in a failure to give enough information. Therefore, it is often best for children, at home or at school, to write down the stages of the process as they are actually carrying it out. Including brief personal tips for the audience makes the instructions more reader-friendly. For example: 'Be careful not to go away and let it boil dry!' Or 'I was silly enough to . . . so don't make the same mistake I did . . . '.
- Finally, you may find that children slide into writing that is more in keeping with explanation texts. This is thoroughly acceptable, as it demonstrates the beginnings of 'genre-hybridising' and indeed could make for an interesting teaching point.

How to write your own instructional text

Use these ideas to help you write your own instructions for use in class or to introduce children to the genre.

Why write instructions for yourself or your class?

To pass on to others your knowledge about a particular activity and to instruct them on how to carry it out.

What are the basics of instructions?

When writing instructions, you should focus on specific imperative actions.

What is your text going to be about?

- Choose a subject and a good title.
- Say what the purpose of your instructions is.
- List what materials, ingredients or equipment are needed.
- Write instructions in the correct order.

What is your role as the writer?

- In the introduction, hook your readers by explaining just how good your instructions are and what can be achieved if they follow them.
- Talk directly to your readers.
- Be friendly, and make your reader feel the task is possible for them to do.
- You can use 'you' sometimes. (If you prefer . . ., you simply have to . . .)
- Wish your reader well at the end. (Enjoy it! You will be an expert in no time!)

What should your instructions look like?

You could present your text in two ways:
- As a numbered list.
- As a series of instructions written in paragraphs.

Use diagrams, a flow-chart or pictures to help make your instructions clear.

Idea generation techniques

I'm an expert in . . . I'm interested in . . . I'm excited about . . .

Write a list of things that you're an expert in or that interest or excite you. Turn one of your passions into an instructional text.

Write about your class topic lessons

Use what you are learning about this term to write an instructional text.

Read–draw–write

Read to learn how to do something you are interested in. As you read, sketch and label what you are learning to do. Once you feel you know how to do this thing, start writing.

Have you ever wondered how to . . .?

End this sentence and talk to your friend about it. Write some notes and then turn them into some instructions. These can be real or 'faction'.

Think faction!

Write a list of things you could write instructions for from the land of fiction. Give your reader instructions for something fictional.

Suggested books

How To by Julie Morstad
This Is How We Do It by Matt Lamothe
Everything You Need to Build a Treehouse by Carter Higgins
How to Look After Your Cat by Colin Hawkins

Planning grid: instructions

My plan The purpose of my instructions is to teach people how to . . .	
Title	
Encouraging hook and boast.	
What they will need	
How to do it: **Numbered list** **or** **paragraphs**	
Final piece of **encouragement.**	

Non-fiction

247

Part B

Explanation

Suggested for Years 5 and 6

Why write explanation texts?

Explanation texts are a gift. All of us 'own' knowledge capital. Indeed, many people make great sums of money from disseminating this capital. Others, though, choose to share their knowledge freely because of the joy and the benefits it can bring to other people. It teaches your reader something and this is the wonderful thing that children will learn during the project.

This introduction itself is an explanation text. You can tell this because it does three things:

1. It says **what** an explanation text is.
2. It says **why** it is a useful genre for children to write.
3. It says **how** it is best taught.

By Year 5, children will be very familiar with reading and writing information texts. Explanation texts are very similar, but where an information text simply tells you what something is like, an explanation text goes on to explain how and why things happen. Explanation texts are probably the type of non-fiction that children will read most as they go through school.

Children know how to do many things that their peers or adults around them know nothing about. It can be very rewarding and self-affirming to share this knowledge through writing. Children will become aware that they have valuable expertise to pass on to others.

This class writing project will show children that sharing knowledge is often an enjoyable, social and satisfying thing to do. You and your class will begin to appreciate the pockets of 'communities' that make up a writing classroom, with children talking and sharing with others their passions, interests and parts of their lives. It is important that children understand the power of writing to inform but also experience it as a social resource.

Every day, children explain things so that others can understand them. They often have to explain things to adults. There may be many topics from the lives and cultures of your pupils that you don't know much about, so this writing project is an opportunity for your pupils to teach you a thing or two!

Explanations can be about something physical in the world (such as geography), things people do or even abstract ideas. It is best to write an explanation text on a topic you know a lot about. Think: do I know exactly why something happens? Or exactly how something works? Could this be useful to somebody else?

Things to bear in mind

YEAR 5

- Non-fiction can and should give a sense of personal presence. Children should be able to show their personality and use their 'voice'. It's important to encourage children to choose a topic they are not only interested in but also about which they have some knowledge to share.

- Non-fiction texts should be kept short. Keep them to a page or a page and a half.
- Children's enthusiasm for this writing project can often result in their wanting to write on too general a theme. Direct them to focus on something specific. They will often struggle with the generality and sheer size of their initial topic ideas. For example, if they choose computer games, children will often try to explain how all types of computer games work. Instead, encourage them to focus on their favourite computer game – or better still, a particular aspect of it.
- Often children will assume that others hold the same knowledge that they have about their subject. This can result in a failure to give enough basic information to orientate their reader at the start of their text. They will also often fail to describe technical or subject-specific vocabulary.
- More experienced writers can also reveal something of themselves. One way of doing this is for children to infuse their explanation text with aspects of memoir writing, such as beginning the text with a personal note about why the topic interests them.
- Don't be surprised to see instruction, information, memoir and poetry coming together in a single piece during this project.

YEAR 6

- The easiest way for children to orientate their reader and ensure a cohesive explanation is to give a lot of attention to what their title will be: *Why do . . ., How to . . ., Why does . . ., How does . . .*
- They should be mindful that they don't assume too much knowledge on the part of their reader. They should also explain any technical or subject-specific vocabulary.
- Their explanation text is unlikely to be effective if it doesn't also try to entertain readers. It must aim to make them feel involved.
- They should try to get across their interest and passion for the topic they are sharing.

How to write your own explanation text

Use these ideas to help you write your own explanation texts for use in class or to introduce the genre to the children.

Why write an explanation text for yourself or your class?

Every day we explain things so that other people can understand them. This can be something physical in the world (such as geography), things people do, or even an idea.

Part B

What are the basics of an explanation text?

An information text tells you what something is like, whereas an explanation text goes on to explain how and **why** things happen.

What is your explanation text going to be about?

It is best to write an explanation text on a topic you know a lot about. Think: do I know exactly why something happens? Or exactly how something works?
Your text will do two things. It will:

- Tell your reader what the topic is that you'll be explaining.
- Explain step-by-step how or why something happens.

What is your role as the writer?

You might need to think about these things:

- Your readers may know nothing about your topic.
- You will probably have to explain the meaning of some special words (technical vocabulary).
- You can talk to your reader directly by using the word 'you'.

What should your explanation text look like?

Your text will be multimodal. This means you will use lots of different modes to show off what you know. Some examples of modes are as follows:

- Pictures, photos, diagrams, fact-boxes and headings.
- Different text sizes and colours.

You may want to use A3 paper and spread your different modes across the page.
Headings might be extremely useful to you. You might want to write down a few possible headings on your plan.

How can your word choices help?

Because you will be describing and explaining things, you will find these coordinating and subordinating conjunctions particularly helpful. They will make it easy to explain things to your reader.

- Cause – because, so, therefore, even though, but, however
- Condition – if, then, provided that, as long as, may even, even then
- Means – by

Idea generation techniques

Be an expert

Write an 'I'm an expert in . . .' list and turn your passion into an explanation text.

Questions

Write lots of the following types of questions:

- How does . . .
- How to . . .
- Why do . . .
- Why does . . .
- Where does . . .
- Where do . . .

Use your topic

Write about your class topic. Use what you are learning about this term to write an explanation text.

Read–sketch–write

Read to learn some information on a topic you are interested in. As you read, sketch and label what you are learning about. Once you feel you have enough information to be able to explain the subject, start writing.

Have you ever wondered about . . .?

End this sentence and talk to a partner about it. Write some notes and turn it into an explanation text.

Thinking 'faction'

Write a list of things you could write an explanation text about from the land of fiction. Why not start with fairy tales, folk tales and myths, or your favourite books or films?

Solve a problem

Is your pet dog always hungry? Is your bedroom always messy? Do you hate helping with the housework? No problem! Simply invent a machine that will help solve the problem and explain how it works. Or, if you can't think of a problem, why not write an explanation text about a game you've invented?

Suggested books

How to Handle Grownups by Jim Eldridge
Why? Encyclopedia: Brilliant Answers to Baffling Questions by DK
How Dogs Really Work by Alan Snow
How Things Work by Tamara J. Resler
How Things Work Encyclopedia by DK
The Way Things Work by David Macaulay and Neil Ardley
How to Wash a Woolly Mammoth by Michelle Robinson
What on Earth Happened?: The Complete Story of the Planet, Life and People from the Big Bang to the Present Day by Christopher Lloyd
Before And After by Matthias Arégui and Anne-Margot Ramstein

Planning grid: explanation text

My plan The purpose of my explanation text is to . . .	
Title:	Why do . . . How to . . . Why does . . . How does . . .
Introduce what your topic is.	This is an explanation of . . . (why, how) You're about to read an explanation of . . .
Use **a question to hook** your reader into reading more.	Do you . . . ? Have you thought about why . . . ? Ever wondered why . . . ? Need to know more about how . . . ? Need help with understanding how . . . ?
Step-by-step explanation Explain **how** the action or the process is achieved or **how** an idea develops.	The first thing to understand . . . This is done by . . .
Explain **why** it happens/should happen.	This occurs because . . .
What you think. Tell your reader why this was an important topic for you to write about.	

Part B

Discussion text

Suggested for Year 6

Why write a discussion text?

Discussion builds on what children have learnt about non-fiction projects in previous years. For example, they have learnt how to recount. They've learnt how to tell stories and write memoirs of their past. They've learnt how to give information to others and how to explain themselves. They've learnt how to account for and explain why things happen in both history and science and, finally, they've learnt how to hold a position on something they care about through persuasion. However, there are subtle differences between this project and all of the others. Discussion isn't just explanation. It's not about simply giving facts or writing about the consequences of something, nor is it just a persuasive piece. It's not there simply to promote and champion your position, nor is it there simply to challenge or destroy another's. Instead, discussion brings all of these skills together. Children will learn to consider more than one point of view and use recounts, evidence, explanation and persuasion to better understand both sides. Writing discussion pieces is about being both thoughtful and penetrative.

We discuss things all the time. We weigh things up and discuss things in our heads. We hear people out – we might challenge their thinking from time to time and we will probably try to justify our thoughts with some kind of explanation. We might also challenge what we've heard but still be open to changing our own opinion. In the world of social media, globalisation and political polarisation, discussion is an important life and academic skill that children should be exposed to, and they should know how to use it for themselves.

Things to bear in mind

- Give children plenty of time to consider what their discussion text might be about. Encourage them to look out for current and contentious topics.
- Depending on their area of interest or expertise, writers like to discuss current or historical events; scientific ideas; geographical problems; local, social and political issues; art (in all its forms); sporting events; and philosophical ideas. Children will therefore have a wealth of thoughts and feelings within these topics.
- Children may fall into groups with a shared interest. They will need to decide what they want to bring to people's attention and, most importantly, what they want to try to understand better for themselves.
- This is a new and complex genre of writing. Let children experiment with it. You might see them using personal anecdotes or other people's stories or information they know on the subject they have chosen. You may see them explaining certain things for their readers – who might not know as much about their topic of choice.

- Don't be too concerned about whether children are getting the conventions of the genre absolutely right. Instead, encourage them to get into the spirit of what discussion texts can do for them and for readers.
- Children might hold complex and perhaps even contradictory positions on complex situations. You should ensure children know this is acceptable and that life often isn't black and white.

How to write your own discussion text

Use these ideas to help you write your own discussion text for use in class or to introduce children to the genre.

Why write a discussion text for yourself or your class?

It could be for yourself, to express and organise your own thoughts or ideas about a subject, and to help you make up your mind about something. Sometimes things become clearer in your mind when you write them down. It could be to present two sides of a question for others to think about. Maybe your text could be used as the basis for a class debate, published in a school magazine, or sent to a local newspaper with a view to getting something done. Teachers often ask pupils to write discussion texts about things they learn in other subjects, for example in history, geography and PSHE. This is to encourage you to see something from different angles and to give evidence both for and against a point of view before you come to your conclusion.

What are the basics of a discussion text?

When writing a discussion text, you should explore different aspects of an issue, present the evidence that supports each point of view, and then reach your own personal stance on the issue.

What is your discussion text going to be about?

Choose something you feel strongly about. It could be an issue that affects the whole world, your country, your town, your school or your personal home life.

What is your role as the writer?

Make sure that you choose a topic that people are interested in and will have different views about.

- Say clearly what the discussion is about and why it is important. Hook in your reader.
- Give reasons for and against what you are discussing. There should be a balance (not 10 reasons for and 3 against).

- State your conclusion and why you have decided this. You will be giving your reader the chance to think about whether or not they agree with you. You may want to add a little persuasion. You may find that you need to add some information or explanation in the main part of the writing.

What should your discussion text look like?

Your text can be multimodal if you wish. This means that you can include lots of different forms of evidence to support the two viewpoints in your text, for example charts, tables, quotations and photographs.

How can you make your discussion text clear and interesting?

You can:

- Present all the arguments for, followed by all the reasons against (counterarguments).
- State an argument for and against each point before moving on to the next. Write in paragraphs.

How can your word choices help?

Throughout your discussion text, you will need to present arguments for and against an issue. You may find the following linguistic devices particularly helpful:

- Use conjunctions (furthermore, however) to show where you are about to give an argument for or against the topic.
- Signal your conclusion (I would like to finish by . . .; After considering . . .).
- You may need to use generalisers to refer to groups of people (e.g. some, most, a few, the majority [believe, think]).
- Use an attention-grabbing title to bring people in.

Idea generation techniques

Think about anything you have discussed recently that people have different opinions about.
 Write down what you think about some of these issues. Add any more topics you can think of. Which issues are important to you? Are there any you are undecided about?
 Have a look at the lists here and see whether you can think of any more. Discuss with your friends and draw your own table of ideas.

Personal issues	Community issues	National issues	Global issues
Should our family get a dog? Should a child choose their own bedtime?	Should children be forced to pick up litter as community service? Should there always be some safe green space on housing estates?	Should the government implement a sugar tax? Should everyone have to have at least some army training?	Should people be allowed to move around the world freely? Should people only be allowed to earn a maximum amount of money?

Suggested books

Real-Life Mysteries by Susan Martineau

Thinkers' Games by Jason Buckley

Politics for Beginners by Louie Stowell

The If Machine: Philosophical Enquiry in the Classroom by Peter Worley

History's Mysteries by Kitson Jazynka and National Geographic Kids

What Is Right and Wrong? Who Decides? Where Do Values Come From? And Other Big Questions by Michael Rosen and Annemarie Young

First News

Planning grid: discussion text

My plan The purpose of my discussion text is to . . .	
Thought-provoking title. Usually a question direct to the reader.	
Tell your reader what your issue is.	**Today I am discussing whether or not . . .**
Give good **reasons for both arguments.**	Many people believe . . . Their main argument in favour . . . Those who are against . . . You also have to consider . . . Finally . . .
Conclude with what you think	e.g. I have come to the conclusion that . . .

Science report

Suggested for Years 3 through 6

Why write science reports?

Reporting a science experiment clearly and accurately is important because every experiment can, in effect, offer new knowledge. In writing a description of the aims and methodology, writers are able to share this new knowledge with their community and perhaps inspire others to repeat the experiment or take it a step further. We suggest children devise their own experiments, which can be linked to the current class science topic or be an investigation into something of personal interest. We say this because the science reporting should be genuine and shared with others in the class. There is little point, and little to be learnt, by asking 30 children to write up the same science experiment.

Things to bear in mind

- In choosing what experiment to carry out, children should formulate their prediction clearly but not know the outcome in advance. Remind children that they must be very explicit when writing the method and be aware that their readers were not present when the experiment was carried out.
- In recording the stages of the process, children are describing a personal experience and will be using the pronouns 'I' or 'we'. We are not advocating the traditional impersonal approach to the writing up, but children should know how to organise their report conventionally, using numbers or bullet points for the sequence of steps.
- You may need to help children formulate a grammatically clear and precise expression of their aim and final conclusion. Some less experienced writers will also find using subordination difficult, particularly when justifying their prediction or explaining why something occurred.
- You might find that some children would like to express their passion for science in a different way, for example as a poem or a story – fiction or faction. They might also like to write a letter of appreciation to a scientist whose work they admire. You should encourage these responses.
- Finally, in our 'idea generation techniques' section, you will find some tips on how children can write about science in a variety of ways. You may want to use some of these ideas in your traditional science lessons. For example, why not let children showcase their scientific knowledge through drawings, presentations, plays, poetry, story, memoir, explanation or information text?

How to write your own science report

Use these ideas to help you write your own science report for use in class or to introduce the genre to the children.

Part B

Why write a science report for yourself or your class?

Science reports are interesting because they tell a very special kind of story, the story of an event you took part in, which could be described to others and then may be repeated by them.

What are the basics of a science report?

It's important that a science report should tell readers what was being investigated, how the experiment was done and what happened. It should explain what interesting new thing was discovered or inspire the readers to investigate for themselves.

What is your science report going to be about?

- First, you will inform your reader what your experiment was about, using one or two sentences as a short introduction.
- Next, share your prediction with your reader. What did you expect to see?
- Then tell your reader what equipment was needed.
- Describe each step of the experiment.
- Show the results. You can use writing, tables, graphs or photographs.
- Explain how your prediction was correct or incorrect.
- Comment on what worked or didn't work about your experiment.
- Maybe share what you plan to investigate next because of what you found out in this experiment.

What is your role as the writer?

- Inform your reader of your experiment and prediction.
- Give your reader a very clear description of each stage of the experiment.
- Describe your results.
- Interpret what your results mean – draw your conclusion.
- Suggest possible next steps to take the investigation further.
- You can write up the experiment as a set of instructions if your aim is to encourage readers to try it out for themselves. Be very clear.

What should your science report look like?

Your report is likely to include diagrams, pictures, photos, tables and graphs. You will probably write your list of equipment inside a box and number the steps of your experiment.

How can you make your science report clear and interesting?

You can:

- Write in the first person, for example *I, we, my, our*.
- Write about what you did in the past tense, for example *did, were, went, saw, -ed*.
- Write your conclusions in the present tense, for example *I think, we conclude*.
- Use adverbs, for example *gently, calmly, carefully, with some pressure*.
- Use numbered points and time connectives, for example *1. First, 2. Next, 3. Finally*.

How can your word choices help?

Throughout your science report, you will describe and explain things. You may find the following linguistic devices particularly helpful:

- Conjunctions showing cause, for example *because, so, therefore, even though, but, however*.
- Conjunctions showing means, for example *by, through*.

Idea generation techniques

Read–draw–write

Read to learn some information about a topic you are interested in. As you read, sketch and label what you are learning about. Once you have an idea about how you could investigate this topic further, start writing a plan for your experiment.

Have you ever wondered about . . . ?

End this sentence and talk to a friend about it. Write some notes, turn them into an experiment plan and then write a science report.

What about your other school topics?

What things are you learning about in science at school? Write a list of things you could do an experiment about.

Adapt someone else's ideas

Try taking inspiration from someone else's experiment idea, or adapt an idea from a book.

Investigating things around you

Look around you for ideas at home and at school. What everyday things could you investigate? Here are some ideas to start you off.

- What type of biscuit is the best for dunking in tea?
- What strength of bubble mixture makes the best bubbles? Use different amounts of water to dilute washing-up liquid and test the results. Do different-shaped hoops make different-shaped soap bubbles? Make simple wire hoops in different shapes and investigate what sort of bubbles you get.
- Plant mustard or cress seeds in pots. Give them different environments by controlling heat, light and water. How do you think the different growing conditions will affect them?
- Build a bridge using two blocks and a sheet of card. Try arranging the card in different ways, for example doubled over, folded into a concertina, arched. Which design supports the most coins without collapsing?

Suggested books

How to Be a Scientist by Steve Mould
101 Great Science Experiments by DK
101 Brilliant Things for Kids to Do in Science by Dawn Isaac

Planning grid: science report

My plan The purpose of my experiment write up is to . . .	
Title	Testing whether . . . An investigation:
Abstract: Explain your experiment in one or two introductory sentences.	
Prediction: What did you think was going to happen, and why? It's a good idea to write your prediction before you start the experiment.	I predicted that . . ., and this is because . . .
Equipment: List the equipment that will be needed to conduct the experiment.	
Method: Step-by-step, explain how the experiment is [1] done so others can follow it.	Firstly . . . Next . . . After . . . When that's done . . . Simply . . . Then . . . Finally . . . Or use numbers: 1. 2. 3.
Result: Display your results. You may use a table, graph, photographs or write to show your results.	The results show the following . . .
Conclusion: Explain whether your results match your prediction. If not, explain why not.	In conclusion, the experiment showed that . . .
Discussion: **What went wrong?** Tell your reader about anything that might have caused the experiment to go wrong and things they should avoid if they try to copy your experiment. **Future experiments:** Finally, share things ideas you might want to investigate in the future because of what you found out in this experiment.	If you plan to do this experiment you may want to think about . . . The conclusion to this experiment might not be trustworthy and it may need to be done again because . . . This experiment has made me think about . . . As a result of this experiment, I plan to . . .

Part B

Match report

Suggested for Years 4 through 6

Why write a match report?

I once played a very important squash match when I was 11. It was the Under 12's East Sussex County Championship, Division Three, Group F, Section B relegation playoff. As I say, very important. I was concentrating so hard on the game that I decided to forget about breathing – it was obviously too much of a distraction. I ended up making myself unconscious as the result. My point is that sport is really important to many people's lives – particularly children's. For example, it was Liverpool manager Bill Shankley who famously declared that *'some people think football is a matter of life and death. I assure you, it's much more serious than that'*. Football, and in fact all sport, is full of drama and stories. A match reporter's job is to try and share that story.

Things to bear in mind

- Note taking. It's impossible to write a match report if you're watching the event live. Instead you're going to want to take notes. One method reporters use is to take a notepad and draw a line down the middle. Write the home team's name on one side and the away team on the other. Start jotting down anything significant that happens. You might want to note down any opinions you may have on the game too.
- Sports writing is more than simply regurgitating facts and scores. It's about 'painting with words' the drama of the game for people who weren't there. It's story-telling. It needs to be entertaining and informative in equal measure. This sometimes needs to be pointed out to children.
- A headline should attract a reader's attention immediately. Make sure it is short and sharp – ideally no longer than six words.
- Write the story of the match in the order of important events, rather than chronologically.
- We've found that sometimes children's non-fiction match reports can turn into fictional stories. We feel this is fine, but it's worth pointing out the differences. Let them read examples from the BBC sport website and ask them what the differences are.
- You're allowed to give your own opinion on the match. You can share what you think needs work and give your opinion on key decisions or vital errors.
- This guide is written with football in mind, but we've found children are able to apply most of the basic principles to all kinds of sports.

How to write your own match report

Why write a match report?

To share with others a match that you attended, watched, played in or imagined.

What your text is going to be about

- The introduction should only be about 30 words long and should sum up the entire match. At this point, only mention the most important event in the game.
- Next, you'll explain why the game was important and what the result means for each side.
- Then, in order, describe the goals.
- Finally, choose one team to focus on. Tell your reader their next fixture and what they might achieve this season.

Your role as the writer

You have to make sure you choose a match that people will want to read about. Readers don't want to get bored.

- You have to be clear about what happened.
- Only include the most interesting bits.
- Use only the best descriptions for goals; don't be afraid to use words like *thunderbolt*, *hammer* or *pile driver*.

What it looks like

- Match reports are paragraphed.
- You may want to add pictures of important moments.
- Make sure you have the final score at the top of the page along with a list of the scores and the time of the goal in brackets. If you're not sure what this looks like, look at examples.

Keeping your reader on track

- Match reports are written in the third person (he, she, they, them).
- Match reports are written in the past tense (was, were, had, been, -ed).

- A goal should be described in just one sentence.
- Make sure you mention a player by their full name the first time you introduce them. Afterwards you can use the pronouns (he, she, they) or try and find other ways of describing players such as *teenager, Spanish winger, England international*.
- Mention the time any goal was scored, the scorer (by name) and who assisted the goal.

Idea generation techniques

School or club matches

Schools are always on the lookout for a match report for school sporting events. Why not report on one and put it in the school newsletter? You might play for a club outside of school. Have you ever thought about reporting on any of the matches you see or take part in?

Live events

You might attend sporting events with your family. These are a great place to try out your match reporting skills. You can then share your report with friends or family who weren't able to attend. Many clubs also have online forums. This is another place your writing could be published.

Sofa fan!

Maybe you prefer to watch sport from the comfort of your own home. This is the perfect environment in which to hone your match reporting craft.

Dreaming

Sometimes being a fan can be tough; our teams often don't win – so why not write a fantasy match report? Maybe you're really passionate about a sport. Maybe one day you'd like to play it as your profession. Well, why not write a match report imagining what your future could be like?

Planning grid: match report

My plan	
Describe the match and tell the reader the **result** in **one sentence**. Explain why the result was important (around 30 words).	
Give more detail about the **one major event** you have chosen from the match.	
Describe, in an interesting way, the major events of the match **in order** (including goals, who set the goal up, near misses and sending offs).	
Pick one team and tell the reader what their fixture is and what that team's chances might be. Finally, what might the team achieve this season?	

24 Persuading and influencing

Persuasive letters (for personal gain)

Suggested for Years 3 and 4

Why write persuasive letters?

Sometimes we get the things we want and sometimes we get the things we don't want. When children make requests, whether at home or school, they are often denied. It usually happens like this: their point of view is briefly acknowledged, then a list of rational reasons as to why they cannot have what they want follows, and so the status quo is maintained. Being given the opportunity to put forward a point of view and make a successful request through persuasive writing should capture children's interest. At last they will learn a way of possibly getting what they want!

This project is about learning to write a persuasive letter for personal gain. Children will be writing to someone in a position of power or influence such as family members, celebrities, organisations, or to you, their teacher! Children are likely to focus on the following opportunities:

- Purchase something or have something purchased for them.
- Get a response from a celebrity or organisation.
- Do something or go somewhere.
- Change their circumstances, responsibilities or level of independence.

Things to bear in mind

- In Year 3 or 4 you are introducing the idea of persuasion for individual and personal benefit. Next year children will progress further and consider persuasion for a collective benefit by raising money for a local charity. Finally, in Year 6, they will write persuasively in the collective interest to bring attention and change to a local or national issue.
- Teach children not to get too involved in the subject matter as they could become overly subjective and emotional in their writing. They should also ensure that it does not simply become a 'begging letter'. While part of writing persuasively is appealing to their reader's emotions, it is important that children keep focused on making an objective, logical argument. They should write polite and well-reasoned letters.
- Children should be mindful of making any requests which involve money needing to be spent. They are better off requesting things which cost little or nothing. After all, the best things in life are free!

Idea generation techniques

Lists!

Try writing lists of the following:

- *It really frustrates me . . . . I think this is unfair . . . . or I would really like it if this changed.*
- Things you'd like the opportunity to acquire or to have secured for you. Remember, though, that it is best to make a request for something that costs little or nothing.
- People you'd like to get a response from, such as a celebrity or organisation. You could ask them for something. This might be an autograph, a visit, or an answer to a question.
- Things you would like to do or places you would like to go.
- Things you would like the opportunity to change at home or at school.

Part B

- You might like to be given more responsibilities or more independence or to change your routines.

Have you ever wondered about . . .?

- End the sentence *Have you ever wondered about* . . . and talk to your partner about it. Write some notes and turn it into a persuasive letter.

Before you start writing, try these planning tricks

On a planning page, try answering these questions:

What do I think about the issue?	Why do I think it?	How can I suggest what I think is right or important?
How does the issue make me **feel**?	What do you want <u>them</u> to do?	Notes:

Planning grid: persuasive letter text

The purpose of my persuasive text is to . . .	
Hook Tell the reader what your issue is and what you would like to happen.	
Give your reasons Present several good reasons that the issue is important both for you and others. **Firstly,** **In addition to this,** **Also,** **Even more importantly,** **Another good reason for . . .** **I'm sure that . . .** **Finally,** Name someone who could support your idea.	
Saying thank you Repeat what you would like to happen. Finish by saying how you and others will feel if action is taken. Thank your reader for their attention.	

Advocacy journalism

Suggested for Year 5

Why write advocacy journalism?

Advocacy journalism, as the title suggests, is when you advocate for something. It means you champion it, support it and try to stand up for it. This project will give children first-hand experience of undertaking and writing up original research. It will also provide the opportunity for them to learn about local causes and the power of community action. It is a legitimate way for them to learn how news/magazine articles are used to inform, entertain and persuade people.

This can be a truly collaborative project that brings home and school together. Parents and carers can be involved and children will see their writing 'get to work' by informing others in the local community about their chosen charity. They see what writing an article in a journalistic style can do.

You will be struck by the sheer variety of local charities and the children's personal commitment to them. You may want to compile a list of charities yourself which the children could potentially use. A great many children will, however, be able to choose charities that they, or someone close to them, have been directly involved with or received help from. This will make the project feel even more important to them personally.

Things to bear in mind

To make the writing truly purposeful, your school could set up a small charity grant fund and invite the community to top this up. This fund could then be used as a 'prize' for the best three articles. The prize money could be sent along with the articles to the 'winning' charities. Depending on the focus, each article could be placed into one of three groups, for example:

- Helping people
- Helping animals
- Helping the environment

- The articles could be presented to a group of Year 6 pupils who are then asked to determine which are the most effective in informing, persuading and providing a personal touch.
- It is a good idea to introduce this project just before a school holiday. This gives children plenty of time to talk with their families and choose a local charity, organisation or cause that is worthwhile or important to them. They then have the holiday to research the charity and bring their information into school. They may be able to visit the charity in person or could possibly phone to get a quote summing up the role of the charity. Alternatively, they could try getting in touch using email.

- What will become clear to you over the course of this project is what a multifaceted genre this can be. It requires children to investigate aspects of informing and persuading as well as recounting a small anecdote relating to the charity.

Idea generation techniques

Keep it personal

Think about charities that you or your family care about or have been personally affected by. You may already know some charities that fall into each of these three categories:

- Helping people
- Helping animals
- Helping the environment

Make a change!

Write about something you want to see happen or something you want to change. Then decide who has the power to change it and write to them.

What do you believe in? What is important?

Tell someone about a belief or conviction you have. Convince them it is important.

Be a reporter

Ask someone you know if you can help them solve something – can they think of something they wish was different? Is there something they would like to change? Go out there and change it for them!

Suggested books

Amnesty International's website (www.amnesty.org.uk)
First News
The Week
Charity magazines

Part B

Planning grid: advocacy journalism report

The purpose of my advocacy journalism report is to . . .	
Headline:	
In one or two sentences – introduce the **name, place** and **purpose** of the charity.	
Tell the reader **why the charity has to exist.**	
What does the organisation do to help?	
Explain who **the staff** are, what they are like and **how they are funded**.	
Give a **personal story** about something the charity has done for <u>you</u> or someone else.	
Use your **quote** from an expert.	
Persuade your reader to start supporting the charity.	
Give contact details. How do people get in touch?	
If you haven't already, tell your reader why you decided to write about this charity.	

Persuasive letter (community activism)

Suggested for Year 6

Why write a persuasive letter?

This writing project sits comfortably amongst the other projects you might do this year, such as *Discussion* pieces and *Social and Political Poetry*. The project will move children on from the *Advocacy Journalism* project they undertook in Year 5 and will give them a final opportunity to see that writing, if they use it carefully and intelligently, can be a powerful tool for good. The children will have chosen a cause or charity as their class focus in each year and so are well acquainted with the idea that their writing can make a difference (see page 37). This time, it's about your class coming together and using their writing voices to try to influence decision makers, such as local government representatives, or raise awareness of the need for a positive change to occur in their local community.

Things to bear in mind

- It will be really great if you could all get together, as a class, and consider the most important social and political problems in your local community. Once this is decided, children write persuasive letters detailing what they think should be done and why. Send these as a packet to your local government representative. Children can then learn that a collective voice is often the strongest one.
- Alternatively, children can also write independent letters to government or charity representatives.
- You may wish to introduce your class to the idea of 'letters to the editor'. This is when people share their views by writing to their local or a national newspaper. You should collect examples of these pieces and consider giving it a go yourself. You can of course include examples of writing taken from 'comment sections' on local and national news websites. Children should then write a 'letter to the editor' on an issue of their own choosing.
- Just as we suggested for *Discussion* texts and *Social and Political Poetry*, please try to make *Usborne's Politics for Beginners* available in your class library.
- Amnesty has a poster called *Right Up Your Street* depicting a local community scene, which can be found on the website. This is a useful resource for the project and could help children to generate ideas for their letters. We highly recommend checking the education section of Amnesty's website too as there are many opportunities offered to children to write something purposeful.

Idea generation techniques

There are lots of ways you can get ideas for your persuasive letter. Try some of these:

This is unfair!

Try writing a list of sentences that start with either *'I think this is unfair . . .'* or *'I feel strongly about . . .'* and turn your frustration into a persuasive letter.

Your class topic

Perhaps you've discussed or studied an issue in class that you feel strongly about or that you want to change people's minds about? Use what you are learning about this term to write a persuasive letter.

Read all about it

Are there any interesting, topical news items at the moment? Try looking in the national or local papers or community magazines to find issues that affect your community or class or young people as a whole.

Follow your heart

What are you passionate about? Why not try to persuade your whole class to write letters on this topic?

Right up your street

Look at this street activity from Amnesty International: **amnesty.org.uk/resources/right-your-street-activity**. Perhaps there are things happening on it that happen on your street or near where you live. What do you wish you could change about where you live?

Suggested books

This Book Is Not Rubbish by Isabel Thomas
Politics for Beginners by Usborne
All About Politics: How Governments Make the World Go Round by DK Publishing
Rise Up: Ordinary Kids with Extraordinary Stories by Amanda Li
First News

Planning grid: persuasive letter text

The purpose of my persuasive text is to . . .	
State your purpose. Start by outlining the purpose of your letter.	
Hook Tell the reader what your issue is and what you would like to happen.	
Give your reasons Present several good reasons that the issue is important both for you and others. **Firstly,** **In addition to this,** **Also,** **Even more importantly,** **Another good reason for . . .** **I'm sure that . . .** **Finally,** Name someone who could support your idea.	
Saying thank you Repeat what you would like to happen. Finish by saying how you and others will feel if action is taken. Thank your reader for their attention.	

25 History

People's history

Suggested for Years 3 and 4

Why write people's history?

Many interesting things have happened to ordinary people which are almost forgotten. By writing them down for others to read, we make sure they are remembered. Even though these events or experiences are not well-known or previously recorded in detail, they are still an important part of human history. Everyday events can be incredibly interesting, and it is important to write about them so that they are not hidden. Everyone in our society has a story to tell. By sharing these stories publicly, children learn that they can give a voice to those people who would never otherwise have had an audience.

People's history writing has strong elements of memoir, although the writer will not be writing about their own experiences. Instead they will be writing about other people they know personally or have heard of through family members, friends or the community. This project encourages a great sense of community. By bringing in and celebrating stories from outside your school, you can strengthen and enhance the sense of community and connection inside the classroom. There may well be gains, too, for the person being interviewed.

Things to bear in mind

- It is important to encourage children to choose someone they have easy access to for interviewing. In your homework letter about interviewing, you may like to make it clear that the interviewee is encouraged to share a single anecdote with the child. Writing someone's whole life comes under *Biography* and is undertaken later as a Year 5 project.
- It is also important to bear in mind that people's history differs in a number of profound ways from what is commonly referred to as historical recount. Historical recounts usually record events chronologically, within a conventional time order. However, people's history is very much about story-telling and sharing the significance of a moment. A good people's history piece will have a subject that creates the possibility for reflection, empathy or a shared understanding of an individual and their experience.
- People's history also provides young writers with the opportunity to find out more about their family or friends or significant members of their communities in or outside of school. They will begin to understand the role historians have in documenting and preserving the past. They should also start to understand that memories are not always accurate and can twist and turn with time.
- You can expect that writers will develop a sense of story-telling when writing their people's history pieces.
- Interestingly, you may find children sliding into writing from the point of view of their interviewee, in the first person, or writing in the present tense. This is fine.

How to write your own people's history

Use these ideas to help you write your own people's history text for use in class or to introduce children to the genre.

Why write a people's history text for yourself or your class?

To share with others an interesting event that has happened to someone.

Why is a people's history text important?

Historians like to retell events that have happened to other people in the past. People's history is a particularly important genre to them because it can lead to the writing of full biographies, stories and legends. It can describe the 'feeling' of a particular time but also how people maybe viewed the same event differently.

History

What is your people's history text going to be about?

The great thing about people's history is that it can be about anything from the past. The best people's histories are written by people who are interested in an event or person. They will have spoken to someone involved in the event, asked lots of questions and learnt a great deal about that person and the event. It is a wonderful thing to ask someone you know whether you can interview them about an event they remember.

- Your text should start by introducing the person, place and event to your readers.
- Make sure you include information on who, what, where and when.
- Tease your readers with a hook to tempt them to read on!
- Explain why this event was significant or important for the person involved.

What is your role as the writer?

Make sure you choose an event in someone's life that really interests you. You then have to share this enthusiasm with your readers to ensure that they are interested too.

- Be clear about what happened.
- Let the event speak for itself. Try not to give a judgement until your last paragraph.
- If you are interviewing someone, it is vitally important that you let your readers know how the interviewee feels about the event.
- Include only the most interesting bits!
- Write about someone or something that you feel comfortable with.

What should your people's history text look like?

- Give it a standout title.
- You may want to add pictures or use photographs to illustrate the text.

How can you make your people's history text clear and interesting?

You should write in the third person: Use *he, him, his, she, her, hers, they, them, their*. People's history is usually written in the past tense.

How can your word choices help?

You may need to use fronted adverbials. They allow time to pass and ensure your text has a speedy pace.

Use phrases like *last week, first, next, after that, finally, the next day, meanwhile, in the end, soon after, a little later, looking forward, looking back*.

Idea generation techniques

Use a picture

Bring in an old photo from home and write about someone in it.

Use artefacts

Bring in an object from home which carries with it a story from history.

Interview someone

Make sure you know where they were and how old they were when their story happened. You could ask questions like these:

- Can you tell me one story from your childhood?
- Do you have an interesting story from your school days?
- Can you tell me a story from when you were at work?
- If you would like to, can you tell me a sad story from your life?
- What was your happiest moment?
- Do you have a cheeky story or one that will make me laugh?
- Can you tell me about something that changed your life?

It might be useful to video or record them telling their story to help you remember it. Make sure they don't mind!

Suggested books

Visit your library or local history centre where you will find many examples of people's history, often self-published, by local historians.

Reader's Digest Local History Detective by Reader's Digest

QueenSpark Books is an interesting website which showcases local history publishing **(adult only)**

Planning grid: people's history

The purpose of my people's history is to . . .	
Introduce your place and event. Include: • Who • What • Where • When	
Write in order and in more detail on what happened.	
Why did you write about this topic? What did you learn from it?	

Biography

Suggested for Year 5

Why write biography?

This writing project will show children how they can document the lives of people in their communities. They will discover how the lives of ordinary people they know can be sources of great historical, social and personal interest – not only to themselves as the writer but to others too. All people's lives are interesting, but we don't always realise it ourselves. Everyone in our society has a story to tell, and by asking the right questions and sharing these stories publicly, children learn that they can give a voice to those people who would never otherwise have had an audience.

Biography writing has strong elements of memoir, although it will be about other people that the writer knows personally or has heard of through family members, friends or the community. At their very best, biographies can carry within them great opportunities for poetic description and rich anecdote. One of the great benefits of this writing project is that the writer can bring in and celebrate stories that can strengthen and enhance the sense of community and connection inside the classroom. There may well be gains, too, for the person being interviewed and written about.

A good biography topic creates the possibility for reflection, empathy or a shared understanding of a person or an experience. Children will come to understand the role biographers have in documenting and preserving people's past.

Things to bear in mind

- Encourage children to choose someone they have easy access to for interviewing. In your homework letter about interviewing, you are going to want to make it clear that the interviewee is encouraged to share background information about their early life, their main achievement or strongest memory and what happened after this memorable event or moment occurred.
- Children might want to write about someone they know of who is no longer alive. They can interview someone who knew them well.
- You may want to encourage more experienced writers to dig a little deeper into the era about which they are writing. They can start their biography with a descriptive setting of the scene.
- Additionally, as this is a historical genre, you should encourage children to seek out a historical source that could enhance their biography. The source could be used to directly support the subject of the biography or instead be used to give a greater flavour of the era in general. Sources include photographs, videos, audio, objects, letters, newspaper articles, emails, postcards or direct quotations.
- On 'publishing day', you could invite the community into the classroom to view the artefacts and biographies that the children have written. You may also want to get in touch with your local museum or history centre about showcasing the writing.

How to write your biography

Use these ideas to help you write your own biography for use in class or to introduce the genre to the children.

Why write a biography for yourself or your class?

To share with others the life-story of someone from the present or past who has captured your interest.

What's the basis of a biography?

Historians and biographers like to tell others about remarkable people: what they did and how and why they did it. They talk about the impact that person has had on their community or the world.

What is your biography going to be about?

You can write about world-famous people, though we often already know about them. It is more interesting to choose extraordinary people from your own life or community, whether they are dead or still alive. A good historical biography describes what someone did, how they did it and the impact this has had on the world, their country, their community or their friends and family. You should seriously consider writing about a woman because, unfairly, there is less written about women in history compared to men.

- You will need to introduce who your biography is about, when they were born and when they died (if they have yet!), where they are from, and what they achieved in their life.
- Choose the main event of their life and spend time explaining it. Write something about their childhood or later life to give more information about them.
- Explain why this person is significant or important to you and others.

What is your role as the writer?

Make sure that you choose someone people will like to hear about but might not have heard of. You then have to keep the biography interesting throughout:

- Be clear about who they are and why they are worth reading about.
- Only include the most interesting bits of their life.

Part B

- Focus on the achievements or memories that make them remarkable to you as the writer.
- Choose someone you know a lot about, even though you may not be able to interview them.
- You might want to 'paint with words', for example you could describe the person or the era at the beginning of your biography.

What should your biography look like?

Your biography should have a standout title and a clear beginning and ending and be organised into paragraphs.

You may want to add pictures of important moments. You could also make your biography multimodal by using photographs, maps, letters and newspaper cuttings.

How can you make your biography clear and interesting?

- Write about your subject in the third person because the piece isn't about you, for example *he, him, his, she, her, hers, they, them, their*.
- Biographies are written in the past tense, for example *was, were, had, been, -ed*.
- Biographies can be tricky if you have to cover long periods of time. Use dates and places to help your reader.
- Contrast and compare is another good technique to talk about the tough and the good parts of their life.

How can your word choices help?

You will need time connectives. These will allow time to pass in your biography. Time connectives make sure your writing has a speedy pace: *In the 1960s . . . At that time . . . Until the age of. . . . During those years. . . . Later on. . . . After that. . . .*

You will often talk about the cause and effect of an event. Using the conjunctions *so* or *because* will be very useful.

Idea generation techniques

Use a picture

Bring in photographs from home and write them up as a biography.

History

Use artefacts

Bring in an artefact from home which carries with it a story about someone. This could be:

- A letter.
- A newspaper article.
- An email.
- An audio recording or video.
- A postcard.
- An object.

Interview someone

It is a good idea to ask different kinds of questions, and probably all of them.

- What are your strongest memories?
- What would you say has been your greatest achievement?
- Can you tell me a story from your school days?
- Can you tell me a story from when you were at work?
- If you would like, can you tell me a sad/happy story from your life?
- Can you tell me about something that changed your life?

Also make sure you know where they were and how old they were when their story happened.

Suggested books

Goodnight Stories for Rebel Girls by Elena Favilli and Francesca Cavallo
Stories for Boys Who Dare to Be Different by Ben Brooks
Women in Science: 50 Fearless Pioneers Who Changed the World by Rachel Ignotofsky
Little People, Big Dreams (series) by Frances Lincoln Children's Books

Part B

Planning grid: biography

The purpose of my biography is to . . .	
Title	Have an eye-catching title which includes the person's name.
Introduce **who, when, where.** Then briefly mention **what** they achieved in their life.	*When finding out about your subject's greatest achievement, encourage your interviewee to think about 'one diamond moment'. Encourage them to be specific.*
Early life–Childhood	
What led up to the important event you have chosen to give detail to. (Use dates.)	
Their main achievement (use dates) and why they remember it out of all the memories that they could choose from.	*Try to include an anecdote or a quote from the person you are writing about or someone else who knew them.*
What they did after their main achievement (use dates).	
Why they are important to **you** and should be seen as **important** by others.	

History

Historical account

Suggested for Years 5 and 6

Why write historical accounts?

In other writing projects, children will have described past events and turned them into personal narratives, or memoirs. They will have also written histories of those close to them or those who are part of their community. They will have written the biographies of those who inspire them too. Throughout this time, children will have begun to understand that story-telling, hyperbole and memory can result in history being more subjective than it can sometimes appear in the non-fiction texts they read. Couple this with social media, 'fake news' and the ever-growing dismissal of the 'expert', and children learning how to explain phenomena using evidence is more important than ever.

In this project, you will discuss how historians try to explain and give an opinion on the past by using evidence (such as primary sources) to *account* for it. Don't forget that the children should be well prepared for this type of writing since they have written *Information* and *Explanation* texts for several years now. However, the move from retelling to accounting is still a profound one in the development of apprentice historians.

This project is different because the texts may not be organised in any kind of chronological order, nor are they a simple retelling of events. Instead, writers will have to explain what they think the factors were that produced a certain outcome and the consequences of it. Ultimately, it is about cause and effect – after all, everything happens for a reason and has repercussions.

Things to bear in mind

- A historical account can focus on the *factors* that resulted in something happening.
- A historical account can also focus on the *consequences* of something happening.
- Explaining why something happened in the past is opinion giving. However, historians use evidence (primary sources) to support their ideas.
- You will want to discuss what primary and secondary sources are.
- You might want to discuss how objective or subjective the work of historians can be.
- You may wish to invite more experienced writers to write their piece as *debating* the past because, as they will know, historians can interpret primary sources in very different ways. Therefore, they can debate the past in order to champion their own particular view of a past event (even if the conclusion is inconclusive). Ask the children to choose something they feel strongly about. It could be a past issue that has affected the whole world, their country, their town, their school or their personal life.
- As part of the project, children could be encouraged to contact an expert and share their historical account with them to seek out their opinion on their explanation.

Part B

How to write your own historical account

Use these ideas to help you write your own historical account for use in class or to introduce children to the genre.

Why write a historical account for yourself or your class?

Alongside retelling the past, historians try to account for it – to explain why something happened. They don't always agree with each other about the cause of an event or the effects of it.

What is your historical account going to be about?

A historical recount often just describes one event after the other. A historical account adds to this by explaining why these things might have happened.

- Your account should start by introducing the place and the event to your reader.
- Include who, what, where and when.
- Explain why you think the event happened. Give three reasons and try to use one piece of evidence from a primary source. A primary source is an artefact, painting, photograph, interview or writing from the time of an event. A secondary source is anything created later by someone who did not experience it first-hand or participate in an event.
- Explain what you think the impact of the event was and why you thought it was important to write about it.

What is your role as the writer?

It's important to choose an event that people will want to read about. You then have to keep it interesting throughout.

- Be clear about what happened.
- Choose a historical event you have an opinion on.
- Choose a historical event you have evidence for.

What should your historical account look like?

- Accounts have a title which usually begins with *Why* . . .
- They are written in paragraphs.
- They can include pictures, photographs, paintings or text as important evidence.

History

How can you make your historical account clear and interesting?

- Write your account in the past tense.
- You will help your reader follow what you are saying if you can give them some clear signals about what is coming next. These are some examples, but you can also think of other ways of doing it.
    - *The decision to . . .*
    - *The consequence was . . .*
    - *This meant that . . .*
    - *This shows evidence of . . .*
    - *The effect of this was . . .*

How can your word choices help?

You will need time connectives. These will allow time to pass in your account. Time connectives make sure your writing has a speedy pace.

In the 1800s. . . . At that time. . . . Until the age of. . . . During those years. . . . Later on. . . . After that. . . .

You will often talk about the cause and effect of an event. Using the conjunctions *so, or, because* will be very useful.

Idea generation techniques

There are many ways you can get ideas for your own historical account:

School topics

Think about the history topics you have explored at school over the years. Did anything really interest you? Why not read more about that topic to come up with an idea for your historical account?

Museums

You may have recently been to a museum or other historical site. Did you learn anything there that you could find out more about?

Television programmes

Do you watch programmes about history on television or online? Think about whether an event mentioned in one of these programmes interests you. Could you write your historical account about this?

Books you are reading

Have you read about an event or time in history that you have strong feelings or opinions about? Why not find out more and write your historical account about this?

Primary sources

Maybe you've come across an interesting primary source from history. You could find out more about this and use it to come up with a question to explore for your historical account.

Suggested books

History's Mysteries by Kitson Jazynka and National Geographic Kids
Our Island Story by H.E. Marshall
What on Earth Happened? by Christopher Lloyd
What Happened When in the World by DK Publishing
100 Things to Know About History by various authors

Planning grid: historical account

The purpose of this explanation of history is to . . .	
Introduce **place** and **your event**. Include **Who** **What** **Where** **When**	
Explain why you think this event happened. Try to **give three strong reasons** as evidence. If possible, **use at least one primary source** of evidence from someone/something other than you to back up your reasons.	
What were **the consequences** of the event after it happened. What do **you** think of this event, and why did **you** write about it?	

Professional development opportunities from The Writing For Pleasure Centre

The Writing For Pleasure Centre
- Promoting research informed writing teaching

The mission of The Writing For Pleasure Centre is to help all young people become passionate and successful writers.

We look to accomplish this goal by investigating what world-class writing teaching might be. We do this through:

- Our school residencies and teacher training workshops.
- Curriculum development and creating resources.
- Conducting, disseminating and publishing research.
- Working with children, teachers, school leaders, teacher-educators and charities.

We have developed a research-rich website which shares the most effective writing teaching practices. It's our hope that teachers regard The Writing For Pleasure Centre as a place where they can access a specialist network and continued professional development, and read action research and examples of practice written by other teachers.

The centre enables us to provide research-informed CPD through our school residencies, specialist teacher institutes and our single or multi-day school-based teacher workshops. We also provide teacher and pupil writing retreats as well as creative school-based writing days.

School residencies

Our school residencies involve visiting for several days to work with senior-leadership, teachers and children. Over the course of the week, we provide after-school teacher workshops, observe and mentor teachers in their classrooms and provide each teacher with their own summary report. Once the residency is over, schools are encouraged to engage in action-research and to work on their own examples of practice. We maintain contact with our school affiliates over the long-term and continue to make ourselves available to staff who need us. We see this as embedded PD based on what research tells us is the most effective type of teacher development.

Institutes

We have created our out-of-term-time institutes so that teachers can come together and enjoy a 'working holiday' learning about different aspects of teaching writing and can network and enjoy the company of like-minded colleagues. We have found that these 'working holidays' can be particularly attractive to schools that are committed to improving children's writing experiences and outcomes but may have limited budgets.

Writing retreats

We run affordable retreats, throughout the year, for writer-teachers who want to develop their own writing craft and enjoy some time talking, writing and networking with sympathetic fellow writers and teachers. Our retreats take place in sites of natural beauty where everyone can throw themselves into days of expressive and immersive writing.

Our retreats for schools provide an opportunity for children to enjoy the great outdoors. Children explore a huge range of poetic forms whilst learning to think poetically and mould feelings into words. Generally, a few schools join together, with each one sending a small number of children and a teacher. We begin the project as strangers, but by the end we are friends, united through our shared experience as writers.

For more information, please visit **www.writing4pleasure.com** or by follow us on Twitter at **@WritingRocks_17.**

About the authors

Ross Young was a primary school teacher for 10 years and holds an MA in applied linguistics in education. He now works around the UK and abroad helping teachers and schools develop young writers. He is also a visiting lecturer at a number of UK universities and a passionate writer-teacher. Ross was the lead researcher on *What is it Writing For Pleasure teachers do that makes the difference?* His work continues to focus on the learning and teaching of young writers and is informed by his ongoing work with classroom teachers and early years educators.

Felicity Ferguson was a primary school teacher for 40 years, working as an EAL specialist, SENCO, deputy and head teacher. She has MA degrees in applied linguistics and children's literature and has been involved in a number of literacy-based projects, including children's reading development. An avid writer herself, Felicity, along with Ross, was the series creator of the *Power English: Writing* approach written for Pearson Education. Her current interest is in how classroom talk affects the development of children as writers.

Copyright credits

- Excerpt from *Lessons That Change Writers* by Nancie Atwell. Copyright © 2017 by Nancie Atwell. Published by Heinemann, Portsmouth, NH.
- Excerpts from *Writing Through Childhood: Rethinking Process and Product* by Shelley Harwayne. Copyright © 2001 by Shelley Harwayne. Published by Heinemann, Portsmouth, NH.
- Excerpts from *The Writing Teacher's Companion* by Ralph Fletcher. Copyright © 2017 by Ralph Fletcher. Published by Scholastic Inc.

Index

abandoning projects 77
abstract 263
action 216, 220, 225, 228, 231
adapt 262
add 55
advanced writers 114–115, 117, 118–119; how to support 126–128
Adventurer 52, 60, 61, 147
advocacy journalism 147, 272–273
agency 11
'always times' 192
animals 172–173
appearance 216
approach *see* reassuringly consistent approach
affective domains 9–15
anthology of life 184–185
argument 258
artefacts 185, 197, 282, 287
asking 228
assessment 68, 111–120
attainment 131
attention 141
audience 44, 241–243
authentic 18
authors: author's chair 71–72, 147; mentor author 102
author's chair 71–72, 147
autobiography 195–199; the basics of 196; how to write your own 196–197; idea generation techniques 197–198; planning grid 199; suggested books 197

balance 21–22
biography 284–288; the basis of 285; how to write your own 285–286; idea generation techniques 286; planning grid 288; suggested books 287
boast 247
book planning 143
books: advocacy journalism 272; autobiography 199; biography 287; discussion text 257; explanation text 252; fables 204; fairy tales 209–211; flash fiction 235; graphic novels 229–230; historical account 292, 292; information text 243; instructional text 246; memoir 194; people's history text 282; persuasive letter text 277; poetry 170, 172, 174–177, 179, 181, 183–184, 186; science report 263; short stories 224; about writing 102–103; for writing projects 37–38

caring: sharing is caring 101–102
cause 37, 250
celebration 88–89
challenge 84
change 55, 208–209, 272
character-driven short stories *see* setting- and character-driven short stories
characters: character-driven short stories 214–220; developed short stories 224, 225; flash fiction 235; graphic novel 231; how to develop 215; maintenance 216–217; personality 216; playful fairytales 208, 211
charity 37, 273–274
checklists: for editing 57–58; for revision 55–57
classification 243
classifying 240
class library 33

Index

class publishing house 35–36, 108–109
classroom: organising your classroom 32–33
class sharing 63, 71–72, 147
class topic lessons 246
class writing projects 29–30, 39–46, 63; creating your own projects 40; final goal for 40–42; subject-specific 107–108
club matches 266; *see also* match report
collecting 126
comments 83
community issues 257
community of writers 16, 32–38; and advanced writers 126; reading–writing community 92–93
comparisons 174, 220
composition 21–22
conclusion 256, 258, 263
condition 250
conferences: mini-conferencing 125; pupil conferences 23–24
conference table 33
confidence 128
conjunctions 256
consequences 293
consistent *see* reassuringly consistent
contact details 274
content 44, 145–146
critical literacy 147
curriculum 104–110

dabbling 52, 90, 147; for a character-driven short story 218; for a graphic novel 229–230; learning to dabble 98–99; for a vivid setting 217–218
description 225, 231, 240, 243, 267
developed short stories 221–225; the basics of 222; how to write your own 221–223
dialogue 225, 231
diamond moment 50–51, 147
discussion 263
discussion time 138
discussion text 254–258; the basics of 255; how to write your own 255–257
disguise 220
distant goal 147
drafting 53–54, 90, 124, 147; and conferences 85–86; paragraph piling and sentence stacking 124; spelling 124

drawing 123, 179, 228–229; *see also* illustrating
drawings 172
dreaming 266
dribbling 99

EAL 121; supporting writers with 128–129
early writers 112–113, 115, 117–118; how to support 121; writing workshop for 122
editing 57–58, 90, 125, 146, 147; checklists 57–58; and conferences 86; top tips 59
effect 240, 243
emotions *see* feelings
encouragement 247
ending 208, 211, 225, 231
entertain 5, 105
equipment 263
event 194, 267, 283, 293; live events 266; real-life 224
examples 42–45, 65, 68; intertextuality in action 92; writing target list 88–89
exercises 143
experienced writers 113–114, 116–117, 118; and confidence 128
experiments 263
expert 251; genre experts 126
explain 293
explanation text 248–253; the basics of 250; how to write your own 249–251

faction 239, 246, 252
fable 147; the basics of 202; how to write your own 202–203; modern 201–205; traditional 200–205
fairy tale 83, 92: playful 207–211; traditional 206–210
family treasures 179
fan fiction 233
fear 223, 229
features 44
feedback routine 89–90
feelings: memoir 191, 194; narrative 216, 225, 228, 231; poetry 171, 176
Ferguson, Felicity 297
fiction: and explanation text 252; and information text 239, 241; and instructional text 246; *see also* fable; fairy tale; flash fiction; graphic novel; short stories

Index

field 147
film director 126
flash fiction 148, 232–236; the basics of 232; how to write your own 233
flexibility 71
fluent writers 113, 116, 118
free-verse poems 167
functional grammar lessons 28, 66–67; functional grammar teaching 148

gaps 101
generalisers 240, 256
generating ideas 45–46, 49–50, 90, 148; advocacy journalism 272; autobiography 196–197; biography 286; discussion text 256; explanation text 251–252; fables 203–204; fairy tales 207–208; flash fiction 232–235; graphic novel 228–229; historical account 291–292; information text 240–243; instructional text 246; match report 266; memoir 190–193; people's history text 282; personal writing project books 123; persuasive letter text 269–271, 276–277; poetry 170–172, 173–174, 175–176, 178–179, 180–181, 182–183, 185–186; science report 261–262; short stories 212–213, 223–224; telling stories 122; top tips for 50; treasures from home 123
genre 148
genre experts 126
genre-hybrids 106–107
genre-study week 28
genre weeks 159–160; how to teach 42–45
global issues 257
goals: for class writing projects 40–42; goal-setting conferences 84; setting product goals 42–45; see also process goals; writing goals
grammar 141, 145–146; see also functional grammar lessons
graphic novel 226–231; the basics of 227; how to write your own 227–228

handwriting 60, 141
headings 243
headline 274
hearing 228; see also sounds

historical account 148, 289–292; how to write your own 290–291
historical time 219
history: biography 284–288; historical account 289–292; people's history 279–283
history genres: progression in 166
hobbies 179
home 174, 175, 179, 185
hook 247, 253, 271, 278
hot topics 76
hybrids see genre-hybrids

ideas: and conferences 85; ideas hearts 185, 223; ideas map 233; and poetry 171; see also generating ideas
illustrating 228
illustrator: role as 227
images see pictures
imagining 228
imagism 148
important people 171, 176, 191
improve 56–57
individual attention 141
influencing see persuading and influencing
information 68; see also information text
information book see information text
information text 174, 237–243; the basics of 239; 'faction' 239; how to write your own 239–240; memoir-infused 239; poetic 238
inspiration 181
'inspired by...' poetry 179–181
institutes 294
instructional text 244–247; the basics of 245; how to write your own 245–246
interconnection 160
interest 37
intertextuality 92
interview 282, 287
introductions 42, 68, 253
investigate 262
invitation 68; invitation questions 83

journalism see advocacy journalism

K-W-L 108

leadership 132
length 146

300

Index

lexis 148
library *see* class library
linear model 47
lists 170, 173, 178–179, 194, 240, 247, 269–270
literacy: critical literacy 147; for pleasure 24
literature 91–92, 103, 143; books about writing 102–103; dabbling 98–99; and gaps 101; mentor author 102; personal response 94–95; pictures 101; reading aloud 92–93; search and store 99–100; seeing is believing 101; sharing is caring 101–102; stories within stories 100; unearthing writing topics together 97–98
LKS2: setting process goals in 70
location 219; *see also* place

make a record 6, 106
management: benefits to 132–133
marking 88–90
match report 264–267; how to write 265–266
materials 33
mature writers: and confidence 128; *see also* advanced writers
means 250
meeting area 32
memoir 96, 148, 187–193; the basics of 189; how to write your own 189–190; progression in 115–117; *see also* autobiography
memories 171–173, 176, 179, 185, 191, 193
mentor author 102
metaphor 216
method 263
mind map 173
mini-conferencing 125
mini-lessons 22, 63, 64–68; planning 67–68
mode 148
modern fables 201–205
momentum 78
monologue 216, 220
mood 219
move 55
motivation 13
motives 220
multimodality 148, 243
museums 291

name 220, 274
narrative 126–127; developed short stories 221–225; fables 200–205; fairy tales 206–211; flash fiction 232–236; graphic novels 226–231; progression in 162–164; setting- and character-driven short stories 212–220
national issues 257
natural world 169–172
non-fiction 108, 127–128; discussion text 254–257; explanation text 248–253; information text 237–243; instructional text 244–247; match report 264–267; progression in 117–119, 164–165; science report 259–263
notebooks *see* personal writing notebook; writer's notebooks
noticing 228
novel study 143

objections, potential 140–145
objects 171, 175; family treasures 179; *see also* things
open-ended questions 83

painting with words 5, 105, 148
paragraph 247
Paragraph Piler 35, 59, 148
paragraph piling 35, 59, 124, 148
parallel stories 235
pathetic fallacy 148
peer conferencing 84
people: stories about 235; *see also* important people; people's history
people's history 148, 279–283; how to write your own 280–282
peripheral vision 176
personal issues 257
personality 216
personal project weeks 75–76; expectations for 76; routines for 77–79
personal response 94–95; and non-fiction writing 108; and writing 95–96
personal story 274
personal writing notebook 114, 144
personal writing projects 21, 29, 71, 75–79; project books 30, 35, 123
personal writing time 93–96

301

personification 148, 172
persuading and influencing 5, 105, 268–278; progression in 165–166
persuasive letter text: community activism 275–278; for personal gain 268–271
pets 172–174
photographs 172, 185, 193, 197
phrases 229
pictures 101, 172, 179, 185, 192, 197, 282; see also drawing; illustrating
place: poetry 171, 176; advocacy journalism 274; fairy tale 211; graphic novel 231; historical account 293; memoir 192, 194; people's history 283; short stories 220, 224, 225
Planners 60, 148
planning 51–52, 90, 149; and conferences 85; drawing 123; mini-lessons 67–68; talking 123–124
planning grids 51–52, 149, 160; for advocacy journalism report 274; for autobiography 198; for biography 288; for discussion text 258; for explanation text 253; for fables 205; for fairy tales 211; for flash fiction 236; for graphic novels 231; for historical account 293; for information text 243; for instructional text 247; for match report 267; for memoir 194; for people's history 283; for persuasive letter text 271, 278; for science report 263; short stories 220, 225
planning tricks 270
play 29–30, 51–52, 118–119, 122–123, 167–168
pleasure: literacy for pleasure 24; reading for pleasure 126; writing as pleasure 8; writing for pleasure 7–9, 131, 150, 294–295, 297–298
poetic information text 238
poetic metaphor 216
poetry 30; animals and pets 172–174; anthology of life 184–186; how to write your own 167–169; 'inspired by. . . ' poetry 179–181; the natural world 169–172; poetic information text 238; poetic metaphor 216; poetry that hides in things 177–179; sensory poetry 174–177; social and political poetry 181–184
political poetry see social and political poetry

portfolios see writing portfolios
posters: product goal poster 43–44
practicalities: for pupil conferences 82–83
prediction 263
primary sources 292
principles 25
problem 207, 208, 211, 213, 225, 231, 252
process goals 49, 69–71, 149
process questions 83
process writing 149
product goals 42–45, 149; product goal poster 43–45
professional development 132–133, 294–295
progress: reporting on 119–120
progression 160–161; in the history genres 166; in memoir 161–162; in narrative 162–164; in non-fiction 164–165; in persuading and influencing 165–166
progression scales see writing progression scales
project books, personal writing 123
proverbs 204
publishing 59, 90, 125, 149; publishing personal writing 78
publishing house see class publishing house
publishing menu 41–42
punctuation 145–146
pupil conferences 23–24, 80–86, 149; how to conduct a conference 81–82; purposes of 80
purpose 43, 68, 274, 278, 283
purposeful 18

quality 141
questions 133–134, 225, 229, 231; frequently asked 140–146; generating ideas for autobiography 198; generating ideas for explanation text 251, 253; generating ideas for memoir 190–191; 'What if. . . ' 223
quote 274

read–draw–write 204, 207, 213, 224, 229, 246, 261
reading 17; connecting reading with writing 126; for generating ideas 185; literacy for pleasure 24; and personal writing time 93–96; for pleasure 126; read–draw–write 204, 207, 213, 224, 229, 261; reading

Index

aloud 92–93; Read–Sketch–Write 106, 241, 252; re-reading 54; with rigour 126; *see also* books; reading–writing connections
reading–writing community 92–93
reading–writing connections 91–92; and books about writing 100–102; and dabbling 98–99; and gaps 101; and mentor authors 102; and personal writing time 93–96; and picture books 101; and reading aloud 92–93; search and store 99–100; seeing is believing 101; sharing is caring 101–102; stories within stories 100; unearthing writing topics together 97–98
Read–Sketch–Write 106, 241, 252
real-life events 224
Real-World Writers 3; and the affective domains 9–15; and common approaches 25–26; how Real-World Writers works 29–31; the most effective practice 16–25; and quality 141; and a reassuringly consistent approach 4; why children are moved to write 4–7; *Writing for Pleasure* 7–9
reasons 271, 278, 293
reassuringly consistent 20; reassuringly consistent approach 4
reflect 6, 105–106
register 149
remove 55
repetition 30
reporting: on children's progress 119–120
reputation 220
re-reading 54, 233
research 183; research questions 83
residencies 294
resolution 211, 225, 231
response *see* personal response
responsibilities *see* rights and responsibilities
result 263
retreats 294–295
revision 55–57, 90, 124–125, 146, 149; and conferences 86; mini-conferencing 125; revision checklists 55–57
rhythm 67
rights and responsibilities 33–34
rigour: reading with 126
roar of the waterfall 149

role as illustrator 227
rumbling reading tummy 149

school matches 266; *see also* match report
school residencies 294
science report 259–261; the basics of 260; how to write your own 259–261
scrapbook 192
secretary 60–61
seeing: peripheral vision 176; seeing is believing 101; seeing things differently 171, 175
self-efficacy 10
self-regulation 12, 149
semantics 149
semi-colon 66–67
senior leadership 132
senior management: benefits to 132–133
senses 174, 220, 228
sensitive topic choices 78, 143–144
sensory poetry 174–175
Sentence Stacker 35, 59, 149
sentence stacking 35, 48, 59, 124, 149
setting 207, 215; vivid 214–215, 217
setting- and character-driven short stories 212–220; dabbling for 218; how to write your own 214–217
sharing 17; sharing is caring 101–102; sharing time 138; *see also* class sharing
shock 225, 231
short stories: developed 221–225; setting- and character-driven 212–220
show don't tell 149
sight 220; *see also* seeing
sketch: Read–Sketch–Write 106, 241, 252
slam poetry 150
smell 220, 228
social and political poetry 181–182
solution 208, 211
sound 220
'spark line' 181, 213, 223, 229
special moments 192
speech 216
spelling 124, 145–146
squirrel away 38, 66, 74, 83, 99–100, 108
staff 274
step-by-step explanation 253
sticky bit 150

Index

stories 100; developed short stories 221–225; and generating ideas 122, 185; about people 235; personal story 274; setting- and character-driven stories 212–220; warning stories 204
story writing: progression in 112–115
style 44
subject lessons 109
subject-specific class writing projects 107–108
sugar rush projects 45–46
surprise 225, 231
symbol 168

talking 17, 53, 123–124
target setting 88–89
taste 220, 228
teacher-writer 150
teaching 4, 104; benefits to teachers 132–133; class sharing and author's chair 71–72; common misconceptions about teaching writing 145–146; the diamond moment 50–51; drafting 53–54; editing 57–58; explicitly teach the writing process 18; favourite writing habits 60–62; generating ideas 49–50; genre week 42–44; mini-lessons 22, 64–68; objections to Real-World writers 140–145; planning 51–52; publishing 59; revising 54–55; teaching decisions 83; teaching something writers do 83; writer-teacher 23; writing lessons 63–73; writing processes 47–62; writing time 69–71
television programmes 291
tenor 150
theme 168
things 177–178
thinking 17, 195; and dabbling 99; and poetry 173; through writing 104–110
time 208; historical time 220; time of day 220
timeline 186
title 209, 247, 253, 256, 258, 263, 288
tone 81, 168
topics 44, 68, 140–144; autobiography 196–197; biography 285–286; class topic lessons 246; dealing with children's sensitive topic choices 78; discussion text 255; explanation text 249, 252; fables 202; flash fiction 232; graphic novel 227;
historical account 290, 291; hot topics 76; information text 239–240; instructional text 245; match report 265; memoir 190; natural world 169–170; people's history text 281; persuasive letter text 275; poetry 168, 172–173, 174–175; science report 260, 261; short stories 215, 222; unearthing writing topics together 97–98
touch 220, 228
traditional fables 200–201
traditional fairy tale 206–207
transcription 21–22
treasures form home 123
tricks *see* planning tricks
twenty words 235

UKS2: setting process goals in 69–70

viewpoint 208
voice 183
volition 14
Vomiter 60, 61, 150

warning stories 204
weather 220
webbing 52
Welcome Project 29–30, 32–38
word choices: history 281, 286, 291; narrative 203, 217, 228; non-fiction 250, 256, 261; poetry 169
working wall 37
workshop *see* writing workshop
writer 60–61; writer-identity 15; *see also* writer-teacher; writing habits
writer-identity 15
writer's notebooks 74–79
writer's workshop *see* writing workshop
writer-teacher 23, 135–139, 150; creating a writer-teacher's group 138–139; how to share your writing with your class 137–138; how to be a writer-teacher 136–137; why be a writer-teacher 135–136
writing: books about 102–103; common approaches 25–26; connecting reading with writing 126; great writing 65; most effective practice 16–25; as pleasure 8; for pleasure 7–9; and reading 24, 92–93; Read–Sketch–Write 106; unearthing writing topics

Index

together 97–98; why children are moved to write 4–7; *see also* reading–writing connections; Real-World Writers
writing as pleasure 8, 12, 150
writing choices 140–142; *see also* topics
writing community *see* community of writers
writing coordinators 130–134
writing exercises 143
writing for pleasure 24, 80, 91, 131, 133, 136, 150
Writing For Pleasure Centre, The 294–295, 297–298
Writing For Pleasure pedagogy 3, 7–9, 16, 150
writing goals 19
writing habits 60, 150
writing lessons 63–64; class sharing and author's chair 71–72; mini-lessons 64–68; writing time 69–71
writing portfolios 111
writing process: teaching 18, 47–48
writing product 150
writing progression scales 111–119
writing projects 18; books for 37–38; personal writing projects 21, 29; sugar rush projects 45–46; *see also* class writing projects
writing register 77
writing retreats 294–295
writing spot 33
writing study 64–65, 150; lessons 28
writing time 63, 69–71, 138, 141
writing tricks 68
writing workshop 16, 28–29, 63–73, 150; class sharing and author's chair 71–72; for early writers 122; first three weeks 34–35; mini-lessons 64–68; rights and responsibilities in 33–34; writing time 69–71
written marking 89–90

yawny bit 150
Young, Ross 297